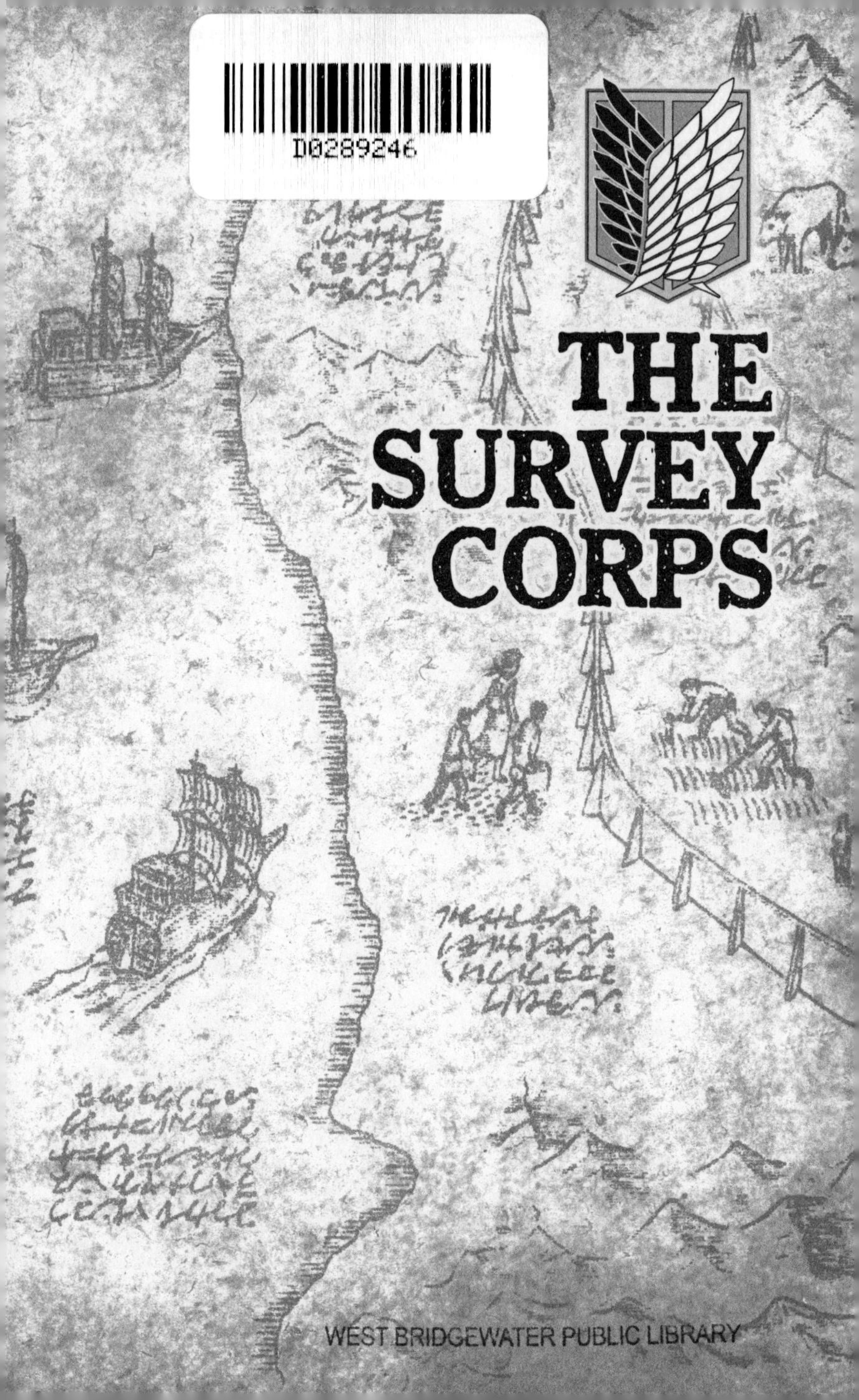

THE SURVEY CORPS

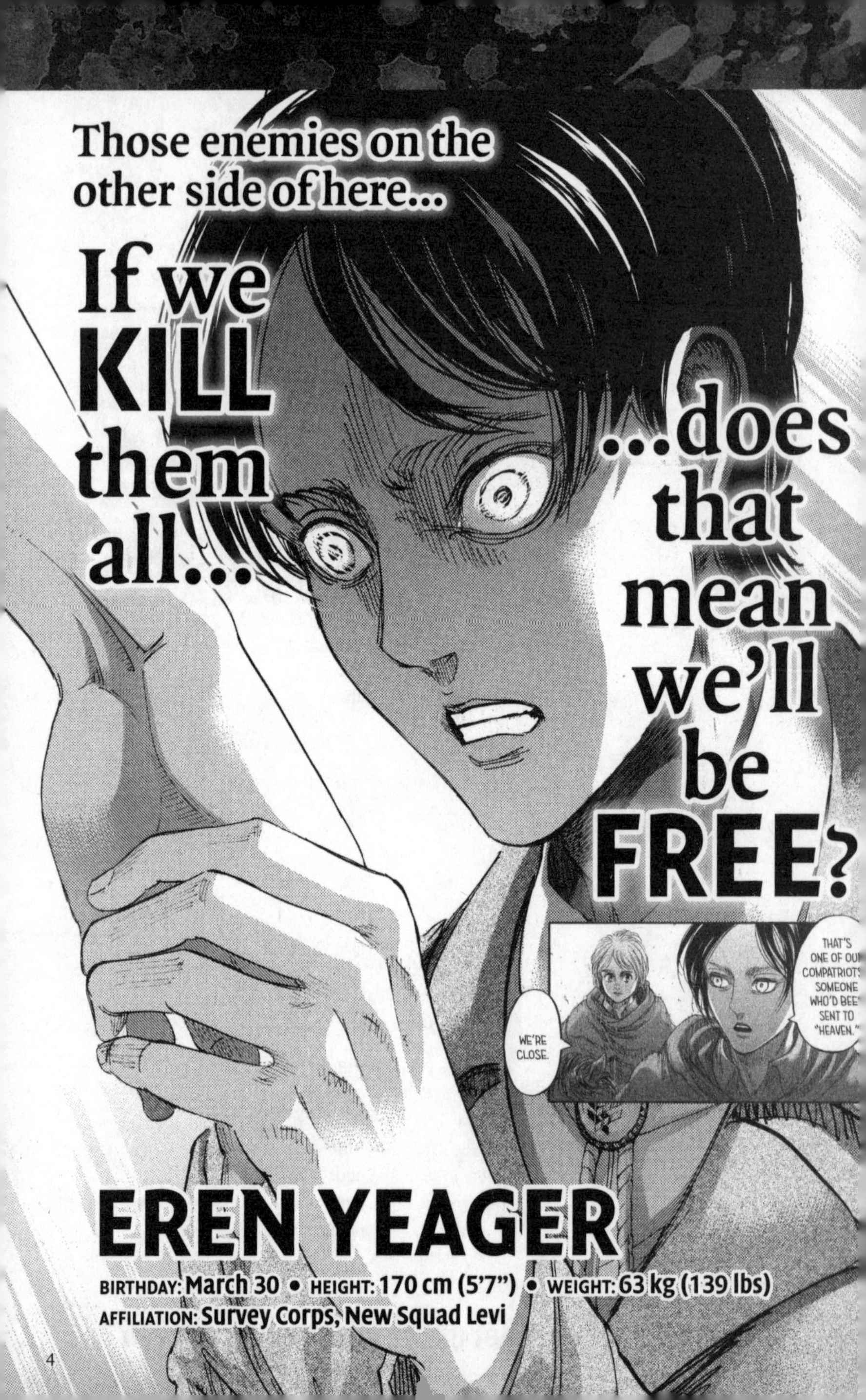
Those enemies on the other side of here...
If we KILL them all...
...does that mean we'll be FREE?
THAT'S ONE OF OU COMPATRIOT SOMEONE WHO'D BEE SENT TO "HEAVEN."
WE'RE CLOSE.

EREN YEAGER

BIRTHDAY: March 30 • HEIGHT: 170 cm (5'7") • WEIGHT: 63 kg (139 lbs)
AFFILIATION: Survey Corps, New Squad Levi

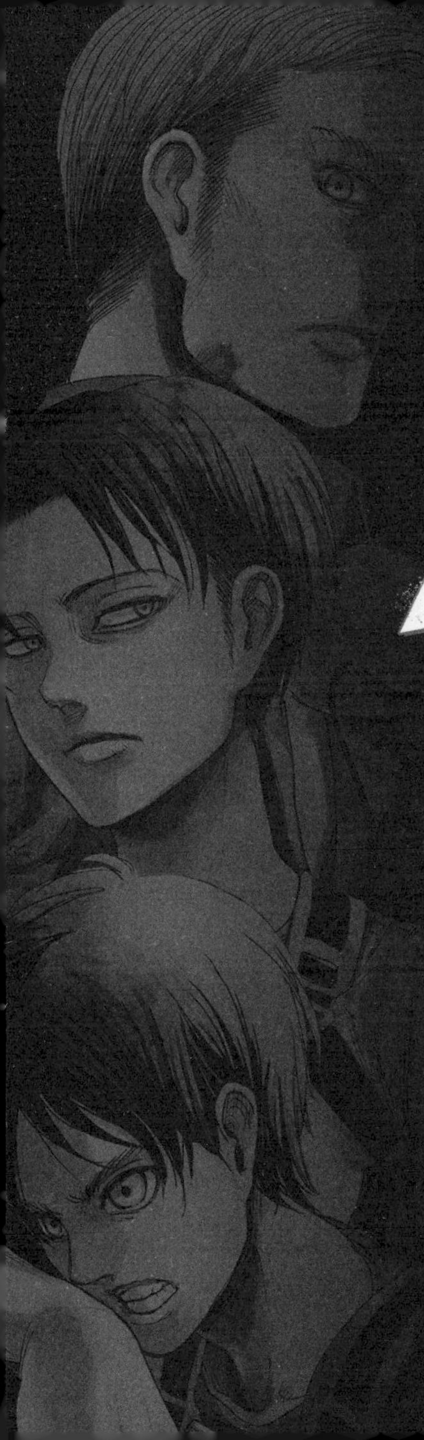

ATTACK on TITAN
CHARACTER ENCYCLOPEDIA

HAJIME ISAYAMA

ATTACK on TITAN CHARACTER ENCYCLOPEDIA

*This volume is based on the events of the *Attack on Titan* manga through Volume 23.

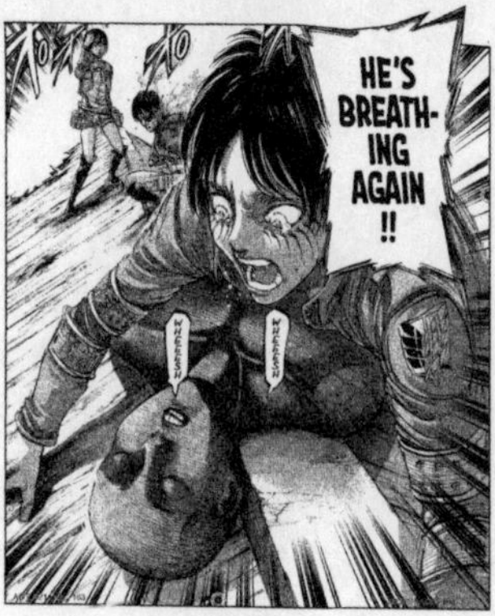
HE'S BREATH- ING AGAIN !!

A young man who grows as he witnesses countless deaths

Eren's rage toward the Titans is what first causes him to throw himself into battle, but he begins to change over the course of many tragedies. He witnesses the death of close allies; has Hannes, a man he has known since childhood, taken from him (Volume 12, Episode 50); he even nearly loses Armin (Volume 21, Episode 83). It seems that he has learned how to hold back his anger, but there may be more beyond the surface…

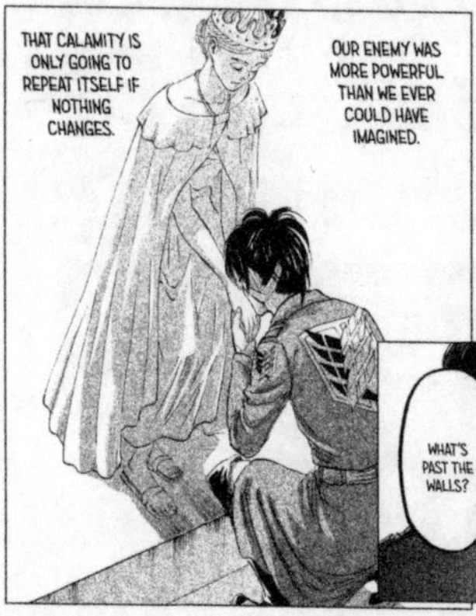
OUR ENEMY WAS MORE POWERFUL THAN WE EVER COULD HAVE IMAGINED.
THAT CALAMITY IS ONLY GOING TO REPEAT ITSELF IF NOTHING CHANGES.

Something must change... Eren finds a new reason to fight

Eren learns the true identity of his enemies when he sees his father's records and memories… Which is to say that he learns of the existence of the great nation of Marley. From there, he begins to think about what he must do in order to regain his freedom from the hands of this mighty foe (Volume 22, Episode 90).

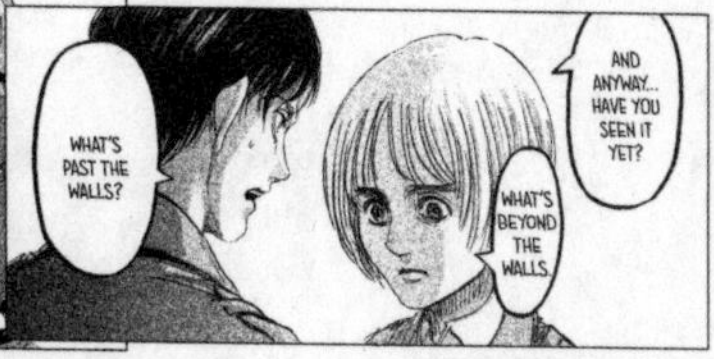
AND ANYWAY... HAVE YOU SEEN IT YET?
WHAT'S BEYOND THE WALLS
WHAT'S PAST THE WALLS?

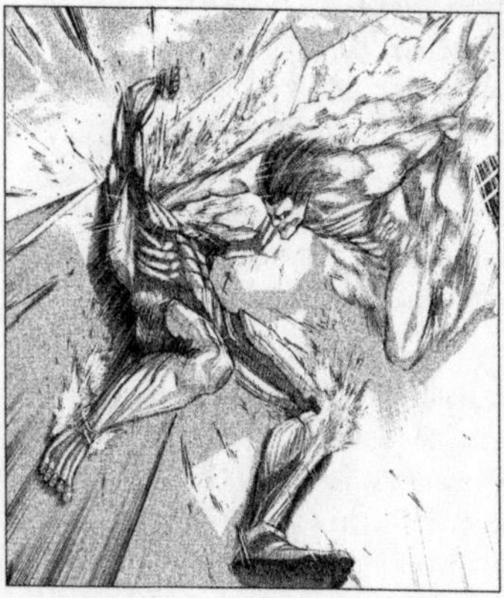

Within his body dwells the Founding Titan and the Attack Titan

Eren's power to transform into a Titan comes from the Attack Titan, a member of what Marley calls the Nine Titans. Eren can also transform into the Founding Titan, which has the ability to control all Titans (Volume 22, Episode 88 and more). The very reason that Reiner and Annie—who are both Eldians—snuck inside the Walls was to capture the power of this Founding Titan.

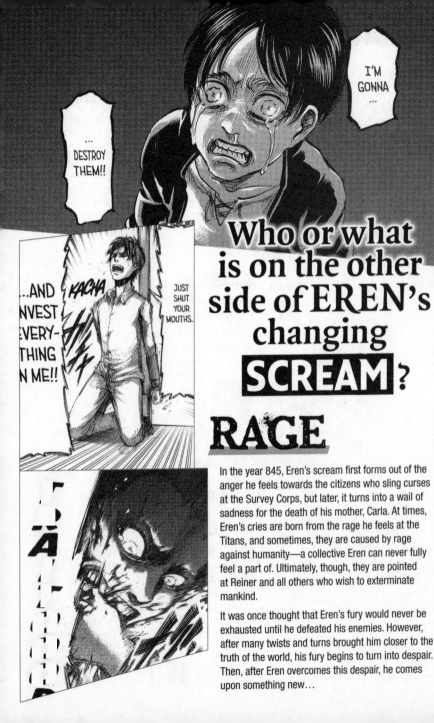

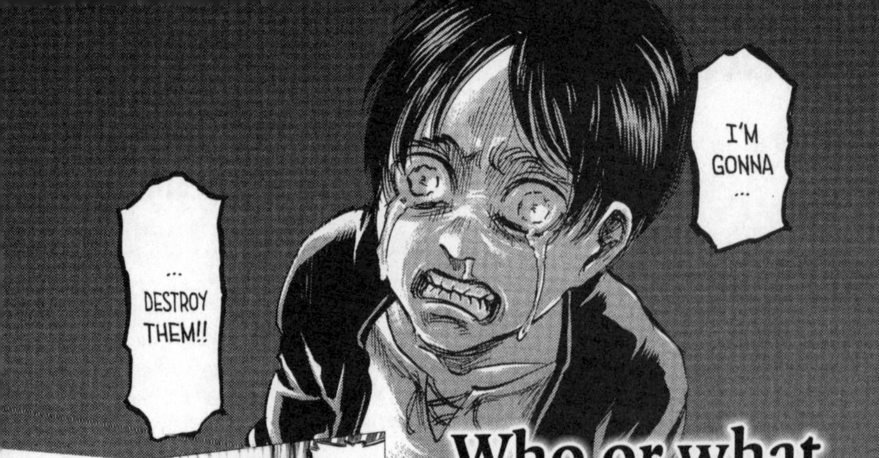
I'M GONNA ...
... DESTROY THEM!!

Who or what is on the other side of EREN's changing **SCREAM**?

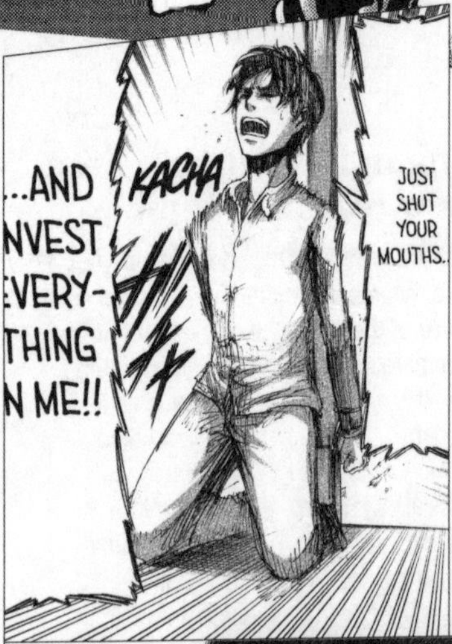
JUST SHUT YOUR MOUTHS.
KACHA
...AND NVEST EVERY-THING N ME!!

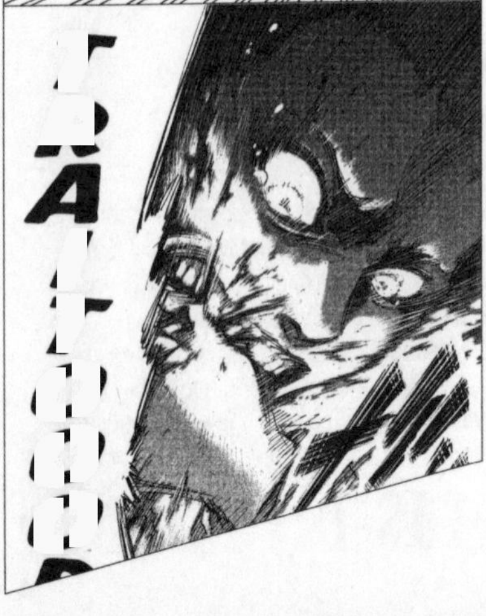

RAGE

In the year 845, Eren's scream first forms out of the anger he feels towards the citizens who sling curses at the Survey Corps, but later, it turns into a wail of sadness for the death of his mother, Carla. At times, Eren's cries are born from the rage he feels at the Titans, and sometimes, they are caused by rage against humanity—a collective Eren can never fully feel a part of. Ultimately, though, they are pointed at Reiner and all others who wish to exterminate mankind.

It was once thought that Eren's fury would never be exhausted until he defeated his enemies. However, after many twists and turns brought him closer to the truth of the world, his fury begins to turn into despair. Then, after Eren overcomes this despair, he comes upon something new…

What does Eren feel after he learns of his HOPELESS REALITY and PAST ...?

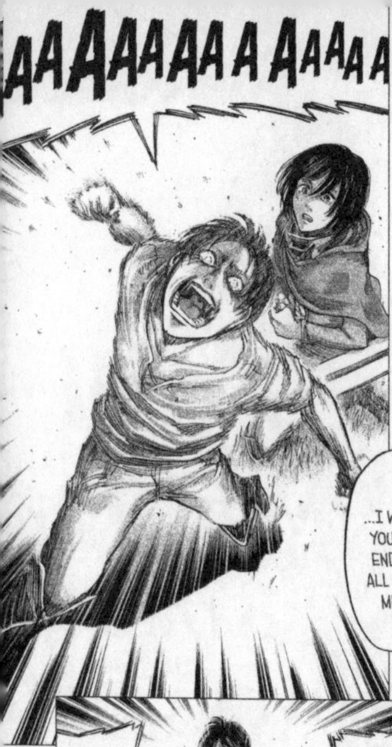
AAAAAAAA AAAAA

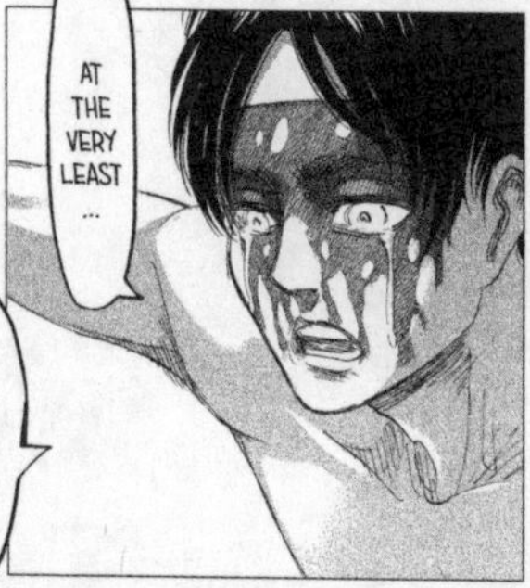
AT THE VERY LEAST ...
...I WANT YOU TO END IT ALL FOR ME.

DESPAIR

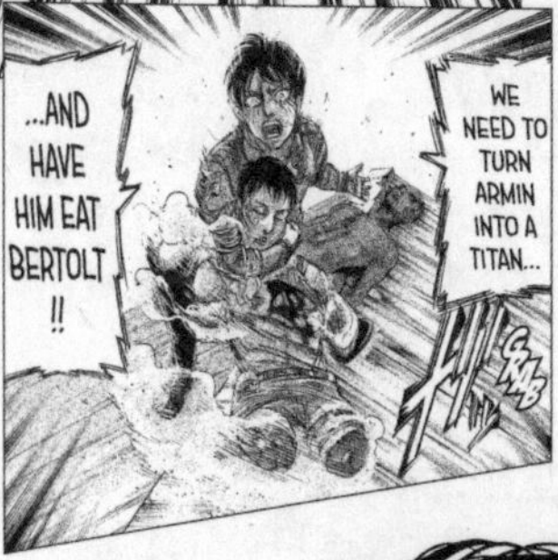
WE NEED TO TURN ARMIN INTO A TITAN...
...AND HAVE HIM EAT BERTOLT !!

First, the death of Hannes, a man who had been close to Eren since his youngest days… Then, Armin's near-death experience during the decisive battle in Shiganshina District… To top it all off, Eren meets the Marleyans, a new, massive enemy… Now that Eren keenly feels just how powerless he is, what goes through his heart and mind as he looks across the sea? The young man who once said he would "Destroy every last one of them!" now stands at a crossroads.

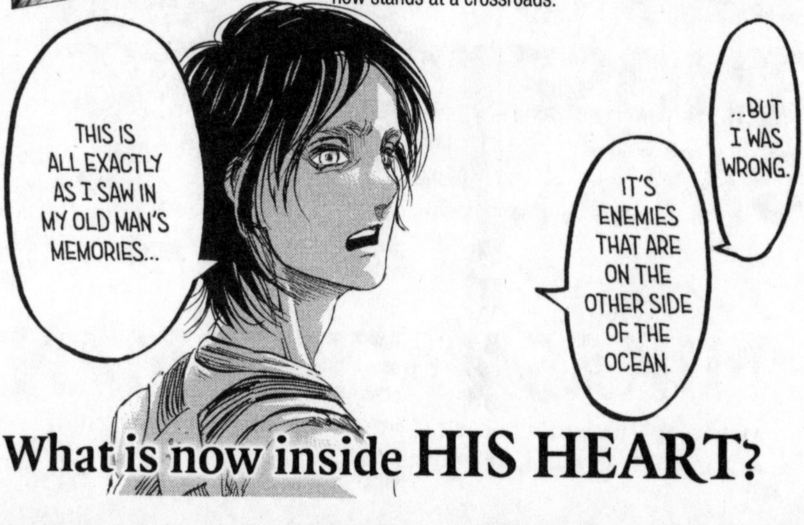
...BUT I WAS WRONG.
IT'S ENEMIES THAT ARE ON THE OTHER SIDE OF THE OCEAN.
THIS IS ALL EXACTLY AS I SAW IN MY OLD MAN'S MEMORIES...

What is now inside HIS HEART?

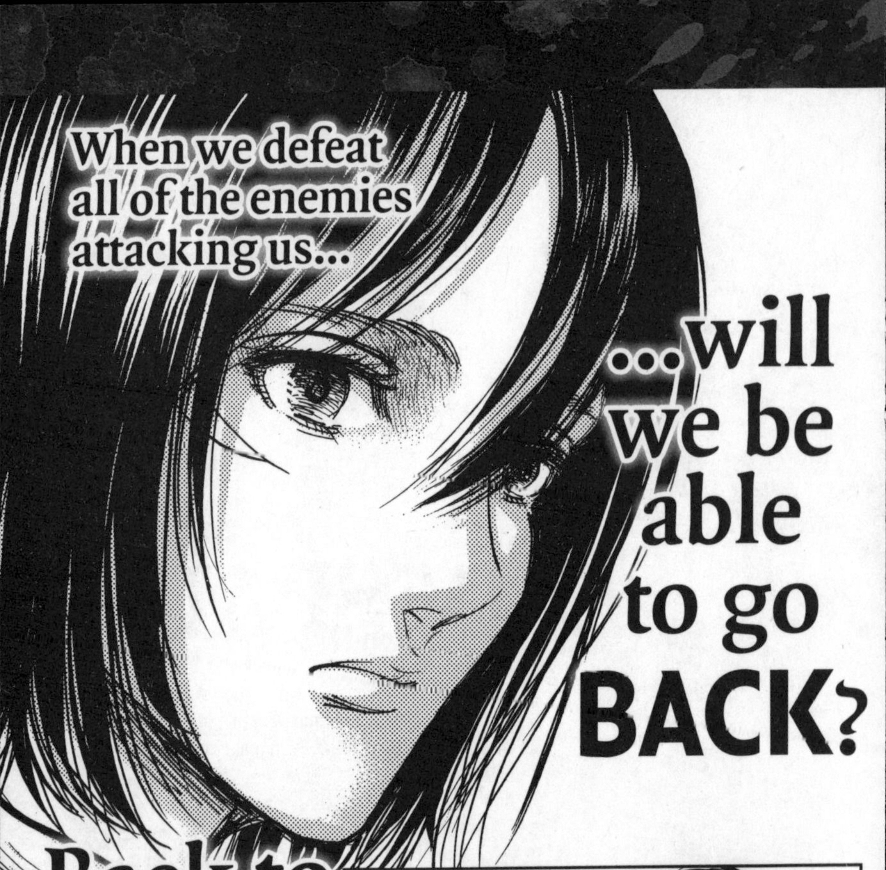
When we defeat all of the enemies attacking us...
...will we be able to go BACK?

Back to THOSE DAYS...

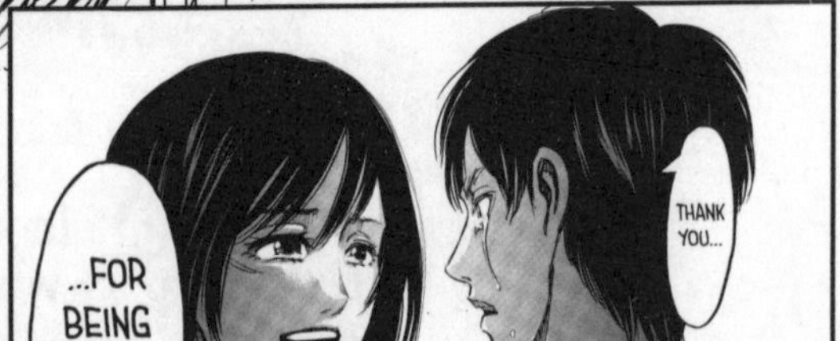
THANK YOU...
...FOR BEING WITH ME.

MIKASA ACKERMAN

BIRTHDAY: **February 10** • HEIGHT: **170 cm (5'7")** • WEIGHT: **68 kg (150 lbs)**
AFFILIATION: **Survey Corps, New Squad Levi**

THAT BOY IS FOOLHARDY...
...SO HELP HIM OUT IF HE GETS IN TROUBLE.
WITHOUT ME AROUND, YOU'LL DIE AN EARLY DEATH.

She fights her enemies and swings her blades for the sake of the one person she can call family: Eren

The Yeagers raised Mikasa, and as someone who has lost all of her blood relatives, they are her only family. After losing Grisha and Carla, Mikasa takes up her blades in order to protect Eren, the only one she has left. Part of what underlies it all may be Carla's words while she was still alive, "Help each other out when you're in trouble." (Volume 1, Episode 1 and more).

...FOR WRAPPING THIS SCARF...
...AROUND ME...

Her scarf, a sign of her bond with Eren

The scarf that Eren gave to Mikasa as a present when she was adopted by the Yeagers is one of her prized possessions. Mikasa most likely sees it as an item that symbolizes the beginning of her bond with her new family. When she faces the Titans and is prepared to die, she finally finds the opportunity to give Eren her thanks (Volume 12, Episode 50).

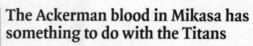

The Ackerman blood in Mikasa has something to do with the Titans

The Ackerman family was a clan of warriors who served the first king, the creator of the Walls, approximately a century ago. Mikasa's family seems to be related to this Ackerman family (Volume 16, Episode 65). The Ackermans say that they have experienced moments in their lives when it felt as though they had suddenly awakened to a new power (Volume 16, Episode 63).

ONE DAY...
...ALL AT ONCE...
...HE FELT A STUPID AMOUNT OF STRENGTH SURGE THROUGH HIS BODY...
...AND HE KNEW EXACTLY WHAT TO DO.

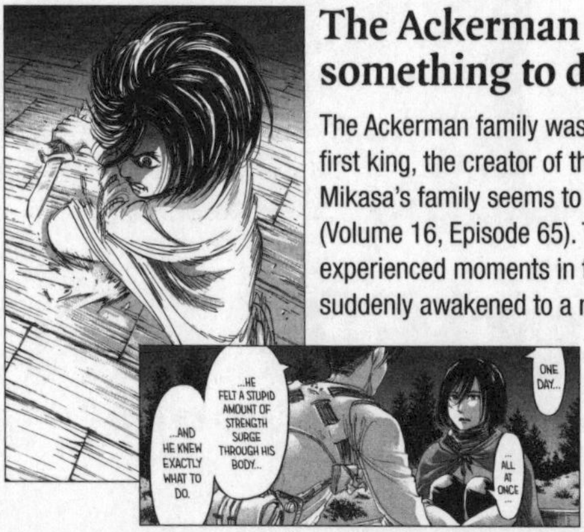

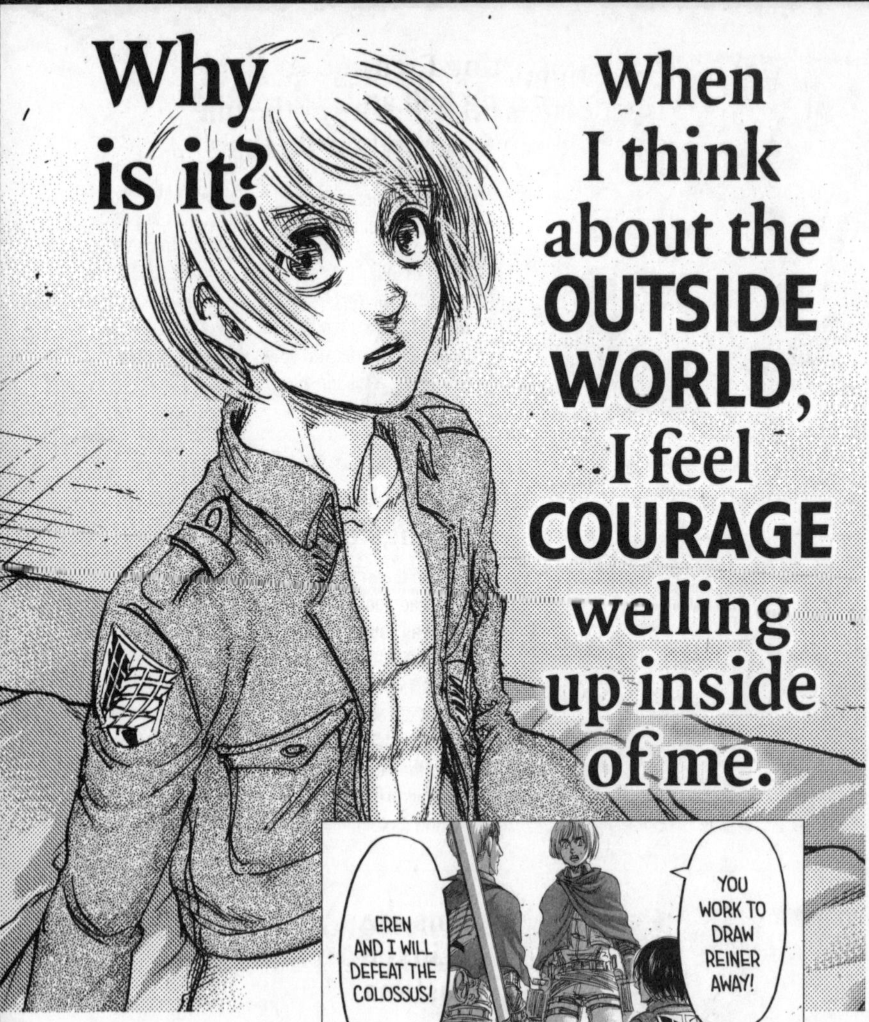

Why is it?
When I think about the OUTSIDE WORLD, I feel COURAGE welling up inside of me.
YOU WORK TO DRAW REINER AWAY!
EREN AND I WILL DEFEAT THE COLOSSUS!

ARMIN ARLERT

BIRTHDAY: November 3 • **HEIGHT:** 163 cm (5'4") • **WEIGHT:** 55 kg (121 lbs)
AFFILIATION: Survey Corps, New Squad Levi

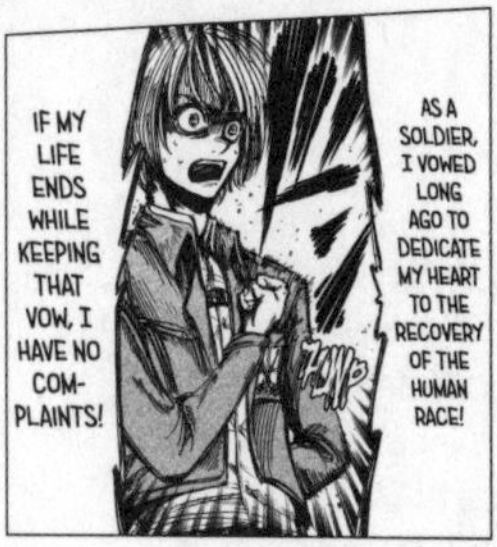
AS A SOLDIER, I VOWED LONG AGO TO DEDICATE MY HEART TO THE RECOVERY OF THE HUMAN RACE!
IF MY LIFE ENDS WHILE KEEPING THAT VOW, I HAVE NO COM-PLAINTS!

Supporting Eren and the others with his strong will and clear mind

Armin has had a strong will from the time he was a child and often found himself standing up against bullies. Though Eren and Mikasa always had to come to his rescue back then, everything changed once he became a soldier. Using his intelligence as a weapon, he saves Eren and the others from many near-disaster situations, as seen in the fight with the Female Titan (Volume 8, Episode 32 and more).

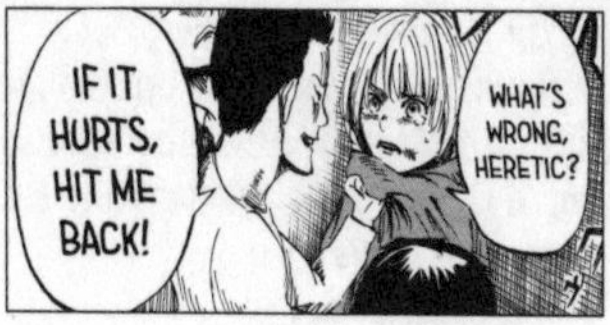
WHAT'S WRONG, HERETIC?
IF IT HURTS, HIT ME BACK!

Dreaming of the world outside the Walls, he walks alongside Eren

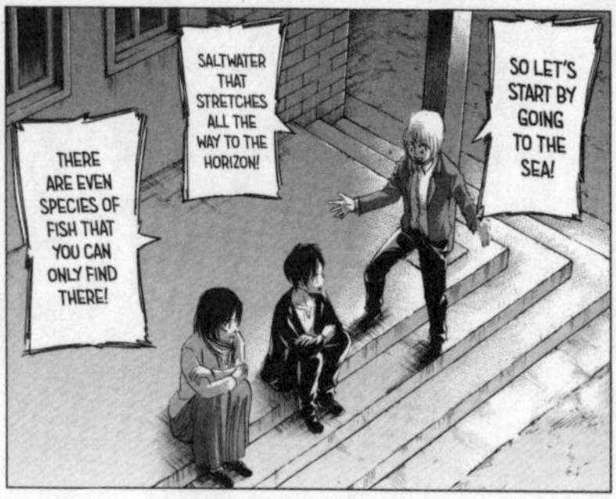
SALTWATER THAT STRETCHES ALL THE WAY TO THE HORIZON!
THERE ARE EVEN SPECIES OF FISH THAT YOU CAN ONLY FIND THERE!
SO LET'S START BY GOING TO THE SEA!

Armin dreams of the world beyond the Walls that he read about in his grandfather's books when he was young. Armin sees the outside world as a symbol of freedom, because as long as the Titans exist, he knows he can never go there. This is what drives him to battle. Lands of ice, plains of sand, seas of salt water that stretch all the way into the horizon... Armin walks alongside Eren believing that one day, he will see this unknown world (Volume 4, Episode 14 and more).

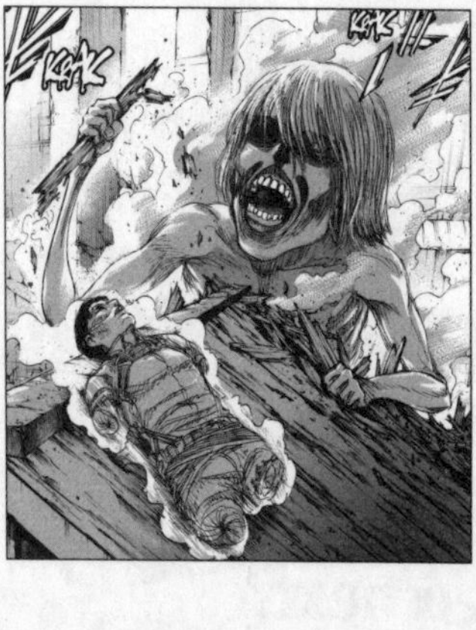

He gains the power of the Titans in the decisive battle in Shiganshina District, but...

After Bertolt transforms into the Colossus Titan in the decisive battle in Shiganshina District, Armin faces off against him and must offer up his life in order to create an opportunity for victory. Barely alive and having suffered critical wounds, Armin is then turned into a Pure Titan by way of an injection and eats Bertolt. Now that he has gained the power of the Colossus Titan, Armin turns back into a human. How does he feel about having eaten someone he once called an ally...? (Volume 21, Episode 84 and more).

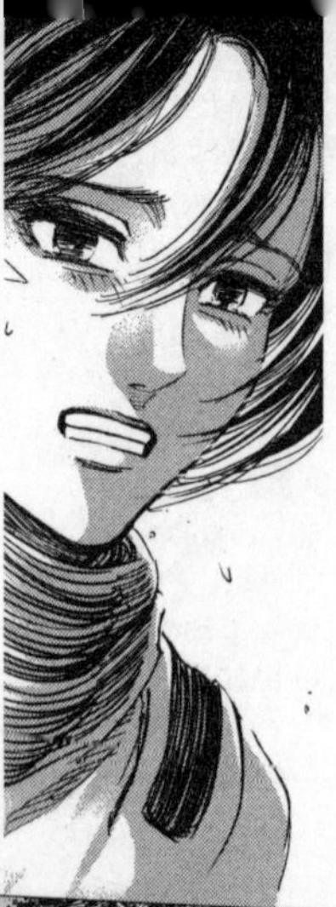

MIKASA, who fought for PRIDE

For Mikasa, battling the Titans was a battle with her pride on the line. After the fall of Shiganshina District, Eren was the only family she had left. She had accepted Eren's decisions and protected him wherever he went in order to be close to him. But after the decisive battle in Shiganshina District, a conflict of opinion arises between them: Eren never gave up on reviving Armin, but Mikasa thought they had no choice but to let him go. Will Mikasa and Eren still be able to keep their eyes on the same goals?

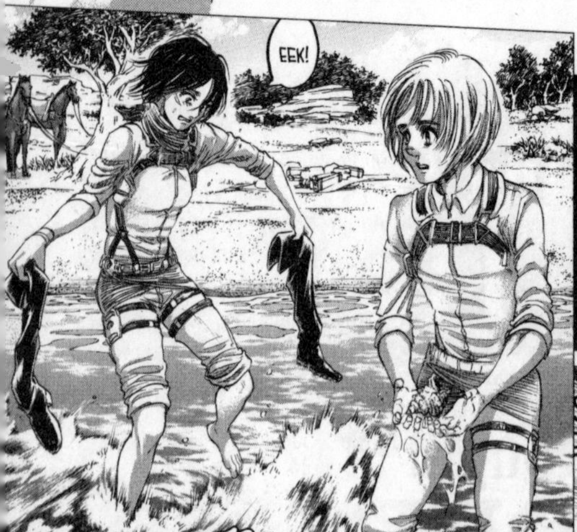
EEK!

WHERE

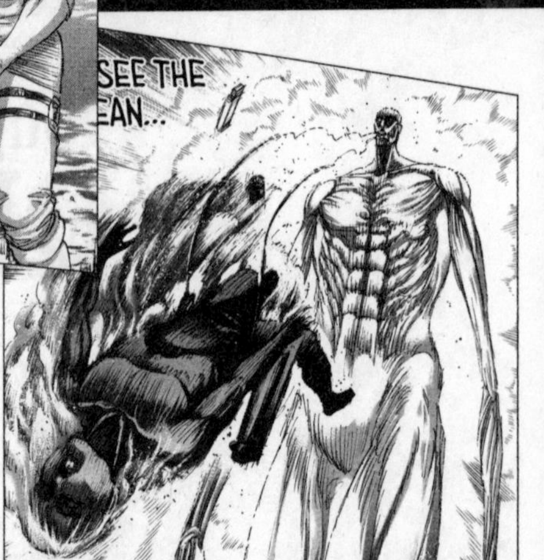
SEE THE

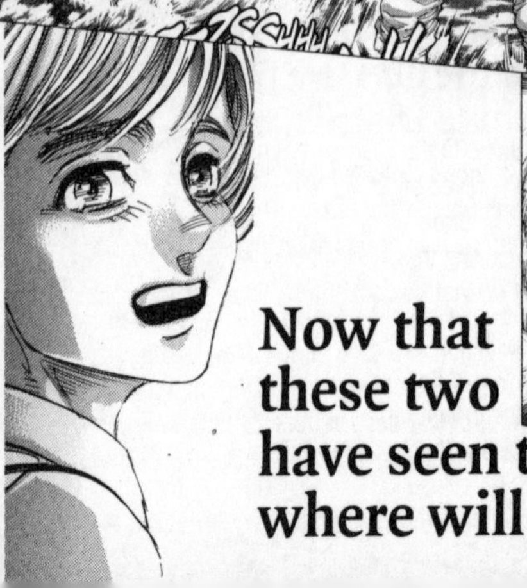

Now that these two have seen the SEA, where will they go next?

YOU'RE STUCK WITH HIM, FOR BETTER OR WORSE.
SHEESH... SO MUCH HAS CHANGED SINCE THEN, BUT YOU'RE STILL DOING THE SAME THINGS YOU DID AS KIDS.

MIKASA and ARMIN:
Are They Headed?

ARMIN, who fought for DREAMS

Armin kept fighting the Titans so that one day he could go to the sea with Eren. In order to defeat the Titans, he was even willing to carry out a plan that preyed on Bertolt's human weakness. "The people capable of changing things are the ones who can throw away everything dear to them." Armin's belief in these words was strengthened from seeing the way Commander Erwin lived his own life. After all that, Armin abandoned his humanity so that he could be the one to change the world and gain the freedom to see the sea.

After retaking Shiganshina District from the Titans, Armin at last reaches the sea he had always dreamed of. What will Armin fight for next, now that the dream that propelled him alongside Eren has come true? How will he use the power of the Colossus that now dwells within his body?

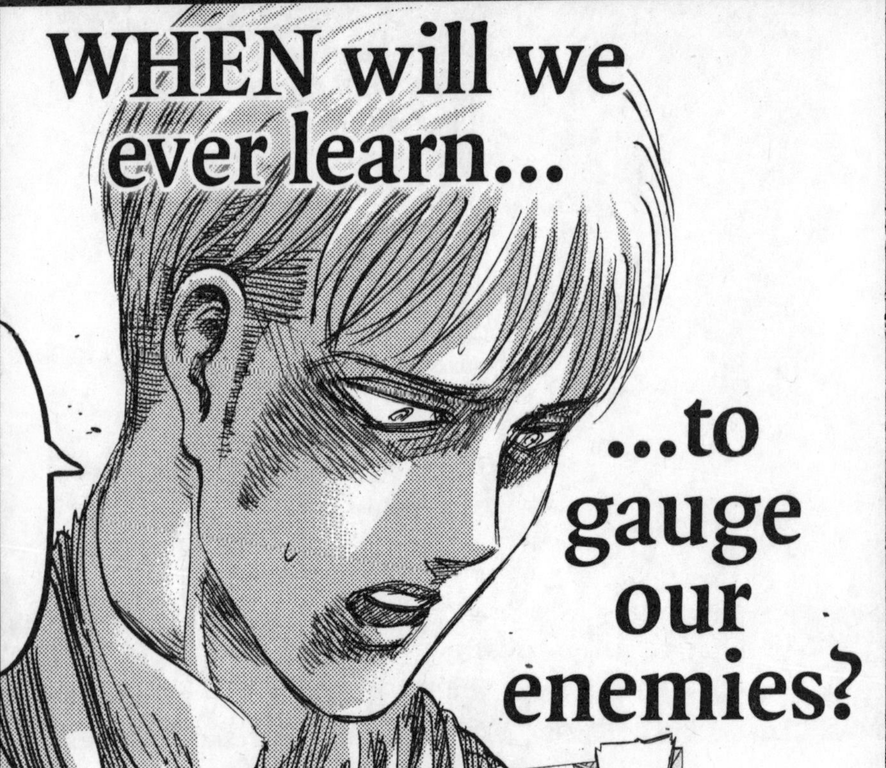
WHEN will we ever learn...
...to gauge our enemies?

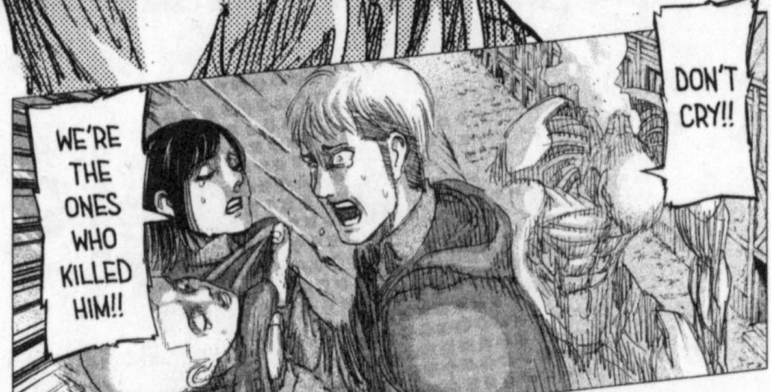
DON'T CRY!!
WE'RE THE ONES WHO KILLED HIM!!

JEAN KIRSTEIN

BIRTHDAY: April 7 • **HEIGHT:** 175 cm (5'9") • **WEIGHT:** 65 kg (143 pounds)
AFFILIATION: Survey Corps, New Squad Levi

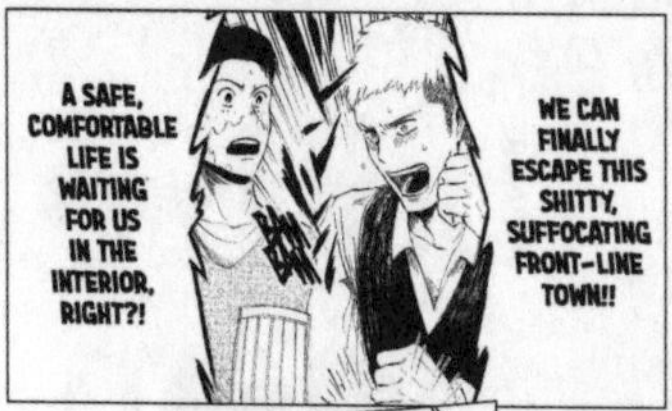
WE CAN FINALLY ESCAPE THIS SHITTY, SUFFOCATING FRONT-LINE TOWN!!
A SAFE, COMFORTABLE LIFE IS WAITING FOR US IN THE INTERIOR, RIGHT?!

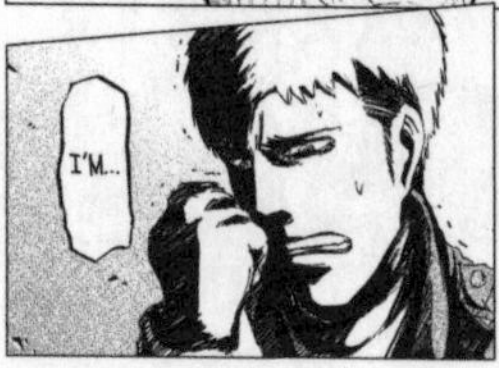
I'M...

A self-centered boy who grows into a leader of his class after experiencing the death of a friend

"Who cares about anyone else so long as I can get into the Military Police Brigade, away from the Titans?" While this was once the philosophy held by Jean as a young, self-centered boy, the death of his Training Corps squadmate, Marco, changes his outlook. Now he accepts that he lives in a reality where he must do something and fight if he wants to survive (Volume 4, Episode 18).

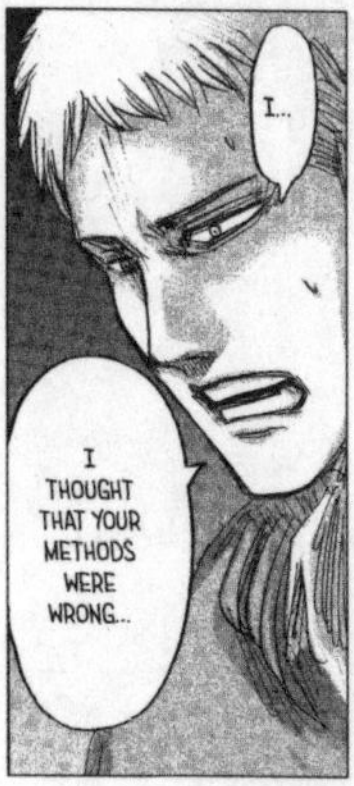
I...
I THOUGHT THAT YOUR METHODS WERE WRONG...

In order to survive with his friends, he prepares to get his hands dirty

Jean thought he was heading into a battle with the Titans, but when he learns that he must also defeat other people in order to gain his freedom, he hesitates. Still, when faced with the reality that his friends will die unless his enemies are defeated, Jean prepares to get his hands dirty (Volume 15, Episode 59).

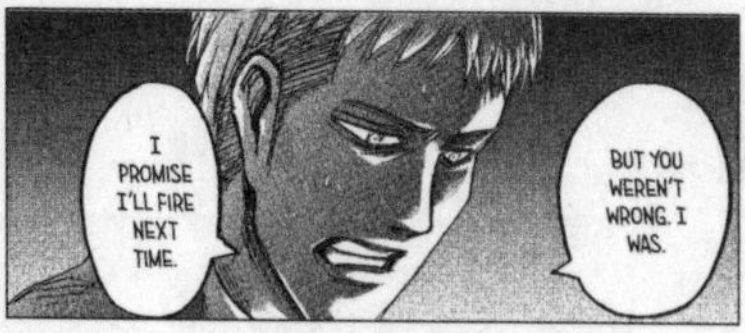
BUT YOU WEREN'T WRONG. I WAS.
I PROMISE I'LL FIRE NEXT TIME.

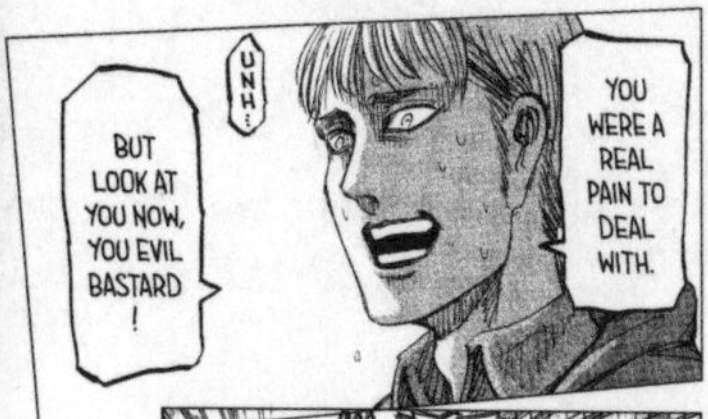
UNH...
YOU WERE A REAL PAIN TO DEAL WITH.
BUT LOOK AT YOU NOW, YOU EVIL BASTARD!

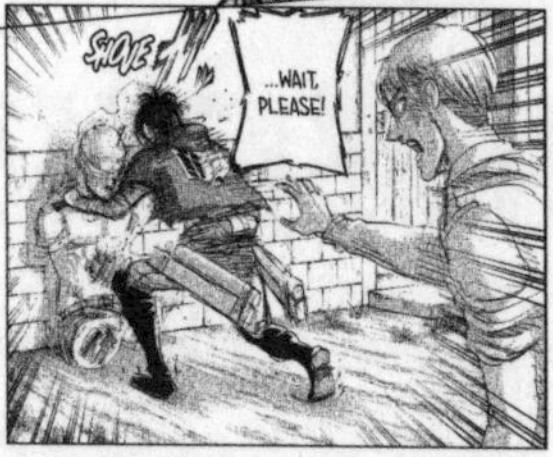
...WAIT, PLEASE!
SHOVE

Mixed and wavering emotions when facing off against Reiner and the others

When Hange tries to finish off the traitorous Reiner, Jean begs Hange to have a change of heart. Jean says that Reiner may be able to give them information on the enemy, or even the power of the Titans. Inside his heart, though, Jean grapples with other emotions he can't quite understand… Reiner was someone he once trained and fought alongside—Jean thought he had thrown away those bonds of friendship, but it's never that easy… (Volume 21, Episode 83)

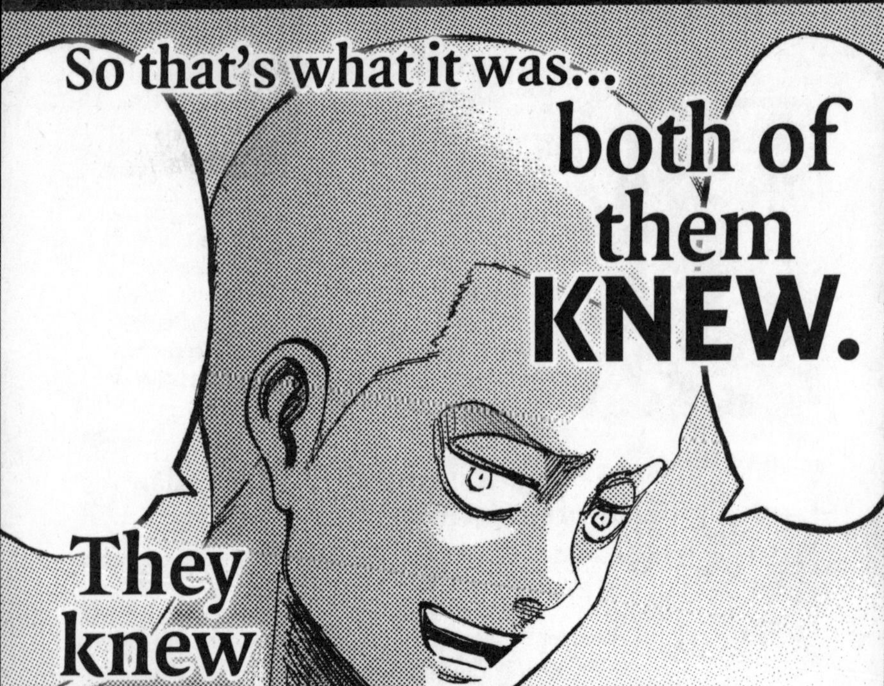
So that's what it was... both of them KNEW.
They knew WHAT had hap-pened...

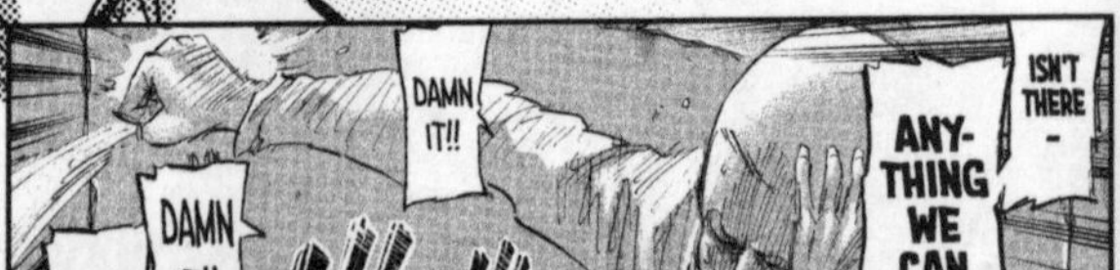
ISN'T THERE -
ANY-THING WE CAN DO?!
DAMN IT!!
DAMN IT!!
DAMN IT!!
BANG BANG

CONNIE SPRINGER

BIRTHDAY: May 2 • **HEIGHT:** 158 cm (5'2") • **WEIGHT:** 58 kg (128 lbs)
AFFILIATION: Survey Corps, New Squad Levi • **BIRTHPLACE:** Ragako Village

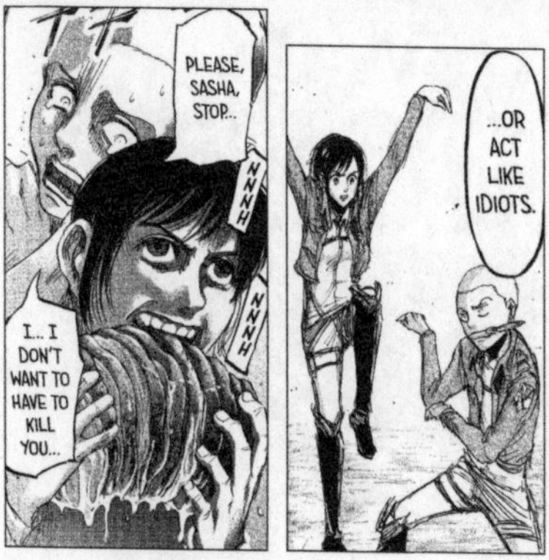
...OR ACT LIKE IDIOTS.
PLEASE, SASHA, STOP...
NNNH
NNNH
I... I DON'T WANT TO HAVE TO KILL YOU...

An airheaded idiot who teams up to form a comedy duo (?!) with Sasha

Ever since their days in the Training Corps, Connie and Sasha have always gotten along well, even showing each other mysterious martial arts techniques during hand-to-hand combat training (Volume 4, Episode 17). This relationship continues, and Connie sometimes even finds himself swept up in some of Sasha's rampages (Volume 18, Episode 72 and more).

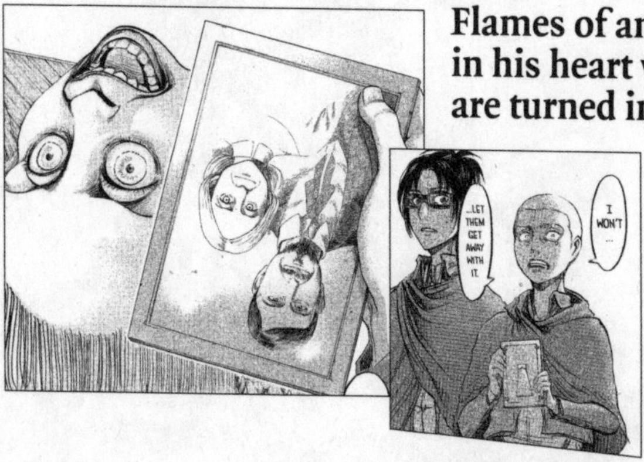
I WON'T...
...LET THEM GET AWAY WITH IT.

Flames of anger are stoked in his heart when his parents are turned into Titans

Connie's hometown, Ragako Village, is destroyed when the Beast Titan appears within Wall Rose. Once he finds out that his own mother was turned into a Titan, his rage burns against Reiner and all the others who must have played a major part in her transformation (Volume 13, Episode 51).

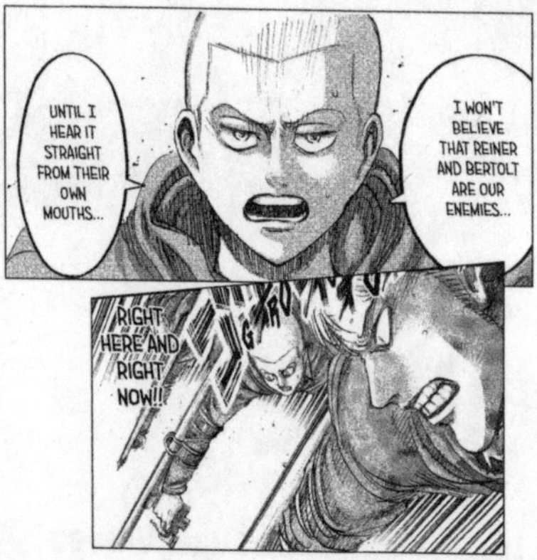
I WON'T BELIEVE THAT REINER AND BERTOLT ARE OUR ENEMIES...
UNTIL I HEAR IT STRAIGHT FROM THEIR OWN MOUTHS...
RIGHT HERE AND RIGHT NOW!!

He was once lost, unsure of how to take Reiner's betrayal...

Though incensed by Reiner and the other traitors, Connie still had trouble tossing out his feelings of friendship for them. But during the decisive battle in Shiganshina District, he recognizes that he cannot survive unless he defeats his enemies. He steels himself before wielding the Thunder Spears against them, with tears running down his cheeks (Volume 19, Episode 77 and more).

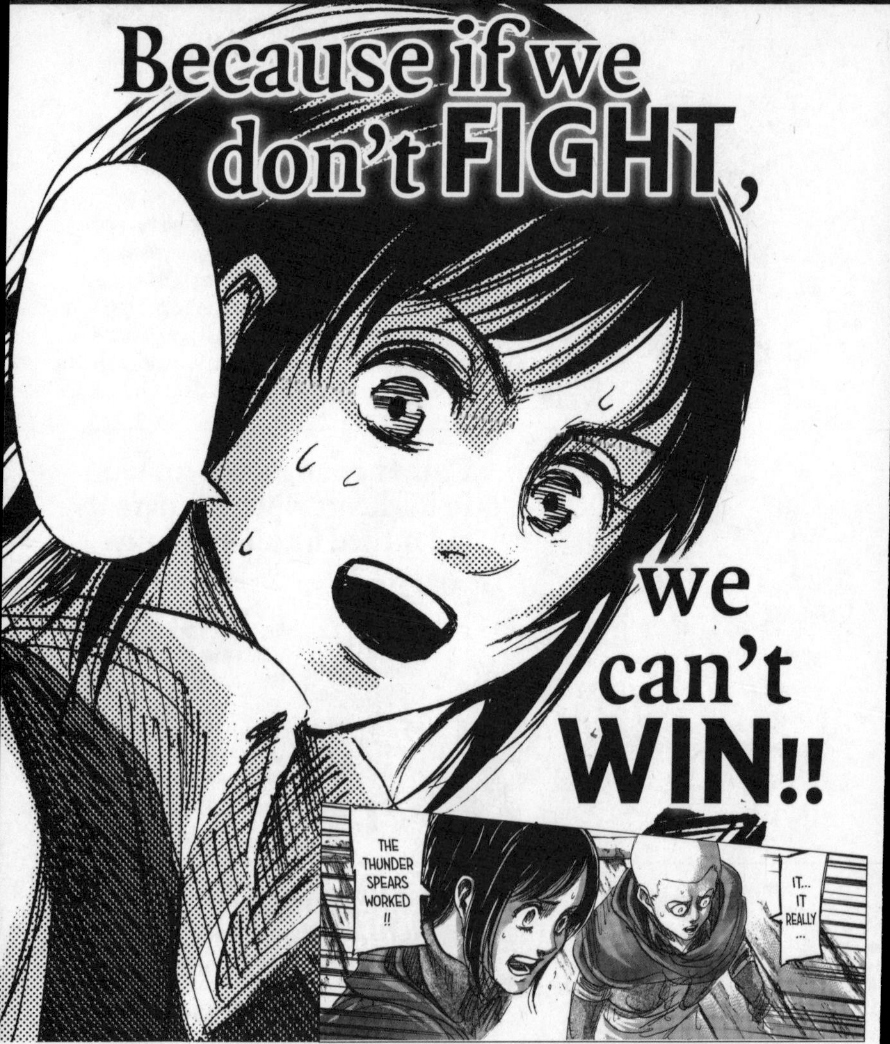
Because if we don't FIGHT,
we can't WIN!!
IT... IT REALLY ...
THE THUNDER SPEARS WORKED !!

SASHA BLOUSE

BIRTHDAY: July 26 • **HEIGHT:** 168 cm (5'6") • **WEIGHT:** 55 kg (121 lbs)
AFFILIATION: Survey Corps, New Squad Levi • **BIRTHPLACE:** Dauper Village

NNNH
WHAT THE HELL DO YOU THINK YOU'RE DOING, POTATO GIRL?!?!
HAVE YOU GONE TOTALLY CRAZY ?!
A STEAMED POTATO, SIR!
I HAPPENED TO SEE THEM IN THE KITCHEN AND COULDN'T HELP MYSELF!

Her obsession with food is still alive and well

Sasha has caused a lot of "trouble" regarding food, even when she was in the Training Corps. During the dinner before the decisive battle in Shiganshina District, Sasha is faced with her first piece of meat in a long time. She loses control and goes on a rampage, even putting Jean's hand at risk of being eaten (Volume 18, Episode 72). Her obsession with food is still alive and well.

GIT MOVIN' !!
GRR

Now that she's back to being her authentic self, she's prepared to defeat her enemies

During the battle inside Wall Rose, Sasha decides that she will fight in order to stay alive. Furthermore, during the battle with the Military Police Brigade's Interior Squad, she accepts the fact that she must defeat her enemies in order to survive, even if they are people (Volume 16, Episode 64).

...THIS MISSION...
...OUR LIVES...

The decisive battle in Shiganshina severs her ties to her former squadmates

Sasha confronts the traitorous Reiner during the decisive battle in Shiganshina District. Initially uncertain of fighting her former squadmate, she ultimately overcomes her hesitation, saying, "If we don't fight, we can't win!!" (Volume 20, Episode 82).

Humanity's strongest soldier, capable of going toe-to-toe with the Beast Titan

Due to his exceptional strength, Levi is able to live up to his title as humanity's strongest soldier. These extraordinary capabilities in battle are said to be a byproduct of Titan science and seem to come from the blood of the Ackermans, a family of warriors who once served the king. He is even able to stand toe-to-toe with Marley's Beast Titan (Volume 20, Episode 80 and more).

As a member of the Ackerman family, he learns how to survive from Kenny

When Levi was young and living in a brothel in the underground city with his mother, Kuchel, he gets taken in by his uncle Kenny. Ever since that day, Levi learned the techniques needed to survive in the underground city, as well as the power needed to fight, from Kenny. When Levi is reunited with his old guardian, they are on opposite sides of the same conflict. After a fierce battle, he shows that the student has surpassed his master (Volume 17, Episode 69).

One step away from ending Zeke during the decisive battle in Shiganshina District

With Erwin's wishes in his heart, Levi goes off to defeat Zeke, the Beast Titan, in a one-on-one fight during the decisive battle in Shiganshina District. Through this grisly confrontation, he shows that he is worthy of being called humanity's strongest soldier. Seconds away from finishing Zeke, Levi allows Zeke to escape. Ultimately, Levi demonstrates that he is more than a match for the Beast Titan in combat (Volume 20, Episode 80 and more).

Levi's **FAREWELLS**

When he lost his mother in the underground city, Kenny was the one who taught a young Levi how to live his life. To Levi, this would have made Kenny more like a father than just an uncle. But when Kenny appears in his life again, this time as an enemy, Levi fights him with everything he has in order to survive—displaying exactly what Kenny taught him as a child and cementing the belief that "Being the most important person in the world means that you're the most powerful person in it."

The battle between Levi and Kenny comes to an end when the underground area collapses and Kenny dies. Before, Kenny had only disappeared from Levi's side when he was young, but this time, Levi witnesses his death. What was Levi thinking and feeling...?

WHAT does Levi FIGHT for after losing Erwin?

In the Survey Corps, Levi put his absolute trust in Erwin, making use of his power to serve his Commander. But when Erwin shows that he is lost between his duty to ensure humanity's future, and the realization of his own dreams, Levi tells him to "Give up on your dreams and die for us." Was this his way of telling Erwin to sacrifice everything and fight if the Commander truly wanted to change the world?

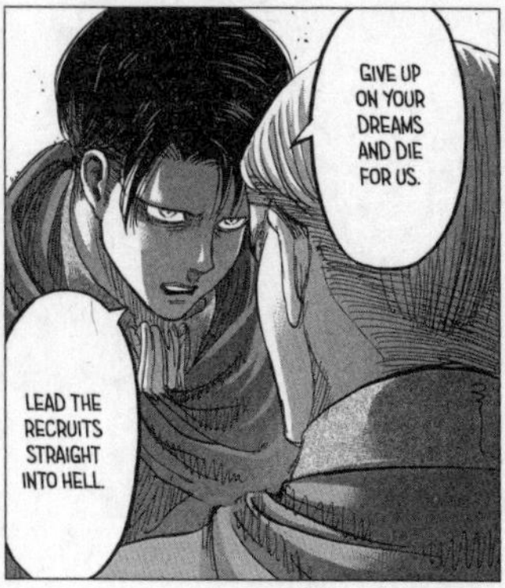
GIVE UP ON YOUR DREAMS AND DIE FOR US.
LEAD THE RECRUITS STRAIGHT INTO HELL.

Levi later goes to revive Erwin with the syringe that will transform Erwin into a Titan, but then stops. Perhaps there was a certain kindness in Levi's actions—Erwin had thrown away his dreams and fought, and now Levi would let him rest in peace with those dreams.

Kenny once served Uri, and when Uri died, Kenny tried to gain the same powers as his master to see what Uri saw. With Kenny and Erwin both gone, what will Levi choose to do next…?

What does this farewell MEAN…?

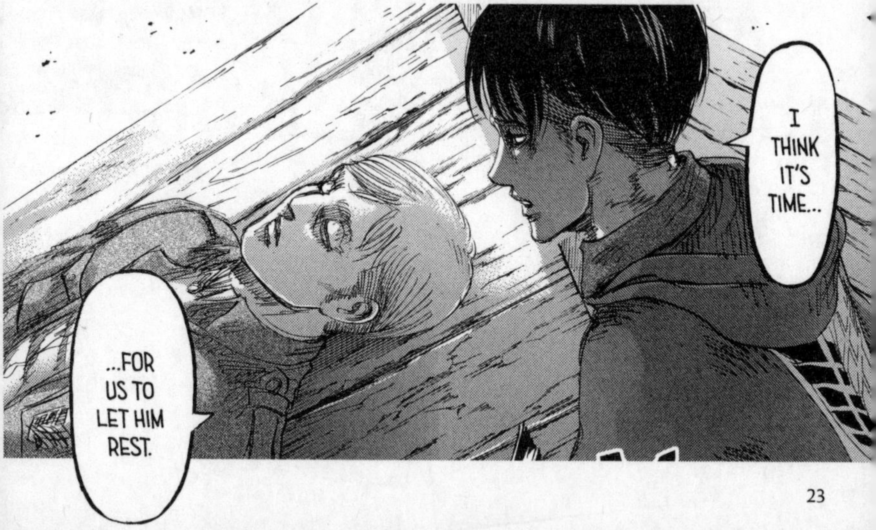
I THINK IT'S TIME...
...FOR US TO LET HIM REST.

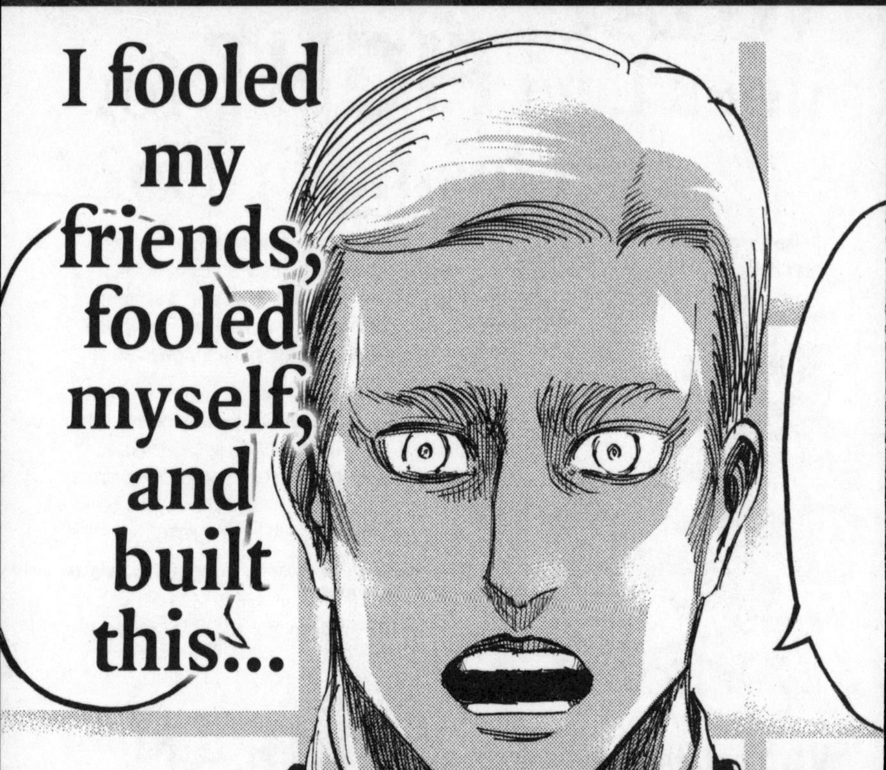
I fooled my friends, fooled myself, and built this...
...mountain of CORPSES that I now stand on.

DECEASED

ERWIN SMITH

BIRTHDAY: October 14 • HEIGHT: 188 cm (6'2") • WEIGHT: 92 kg (203 lbs)
AFFILIATION: Survey Corps Commander (previously)

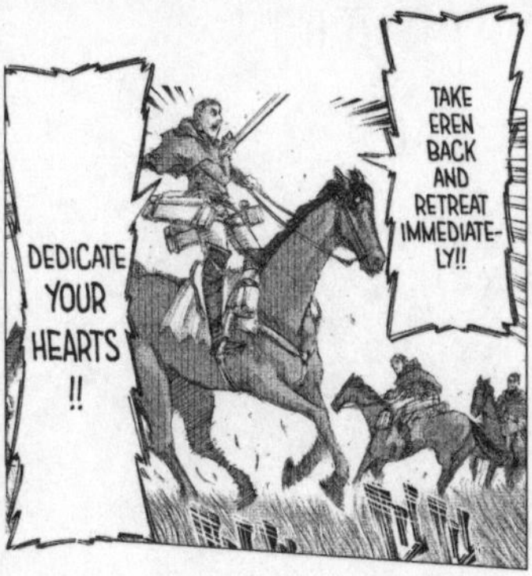
TAKE EREN BACK AND RETREAT IMMEDIATE-LY!!
DEDICATE YOUR HEARTS !!

Devoted his life for the sake of humanity as he led the Survey Corps

As Commander of the Survey Corps, Erwin had earned the absolute trust of his soldiers. He was also the one who introduced the Long-Distance Enemy Scouting Formation to expeditions. His incomparable insight allowed him to come up with strategies on the spot, and he also possessed the decisiveness to put them into action. If it meant winning the battle against the Titans, he was a man capable of throwing away his humanity and being wholly merciless (Volume 7, Episode 27 and more).

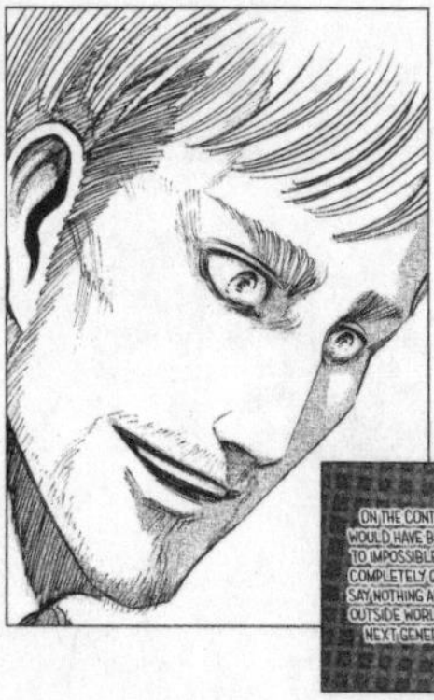

Dove headfirst into the battle in search of his father's dream

How were they able to find out that no humans lived outside the Walls? Erwin's father was punished by the Royal Government for answering this question posed by a young Erwin. Erwin fought the Titans not only to ensure that humanity had a future, but also to grant his father's wish of learning about the truth of their world (Volume 13, Episode 51 and more).

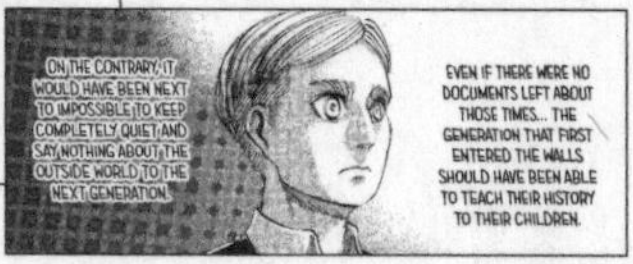
EVEN IF THERE WERE NO DOCUMENTS LEFT ABOUT THOSE TIMES... THE GENERATION THAT FIRST ENTERED THE WALLS SHOULD HAVE BEEN ABLE TO TEACH THEIR HISTORY TO THEIR CHILDREN.
ON THE CONTRARY, IT WOULD HAVE BEEN NEXT TO IMPOSSIBLE TO KEEP COMPLETELY QUIET AND SAY NOTHING ABOUT THE OUTSIDE WORLD TO THE NEXT GENERATION.

Erwin entrusted everything to the next generation during the decisive battle in Shiganshina District

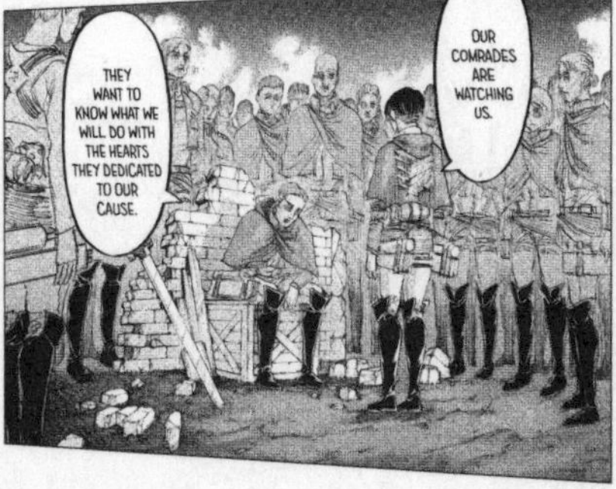
OUR COMRADES ARE WATCHING US.
THEY WANT TO KNOW WHAT WE WILL DO WITH THE HEARTS THEY DEDICATED TO OUR CAUSE.

When the Survey Corps was in danger of being annihilated during the decisive battle in Shiganshina District, the desire to follow his own dreams and head to the basement crossed Erwin's mind. But when Levi's words caused him to give up on these dreams, he then came up with a plan premised on his own death. This is the moment when he entrusted the future to the next generation (Volume 20, Episode 80).

...MY MIND KEEPS DRIFTING...

...BACK TO THAT BASEMENT.

...ON WHICH I NOW STAND.

DREAMS and the Future:
The TRUTH that Erwin CHASED

Throughout his many battles, Erwin was always after the truth. He uncovered the secrets behind Titan biology, and he pinned down the truth about the first king and the Founding Titan that had been concealed by the Royal Government. Erwin fought for the future of humanity.

But while it may have seemed as though Erwin fought for the sake of the people, he also had a personal motive: The dream he chased together with his father of uncovering the truth of the world. When Erwin learned about the basement—with secrets about the Titans hidden within—Erwin must have begun to think of it as the final destination that would make his dreams come true.

AND THAT'S WHEN ERWIN ASKED THE QUESTION.

"HOW DO WE KNOW..."

"...THAT THERE AREN'T ANY HUMANS OUTSIDE THE WALLS?"

...HE SAID.

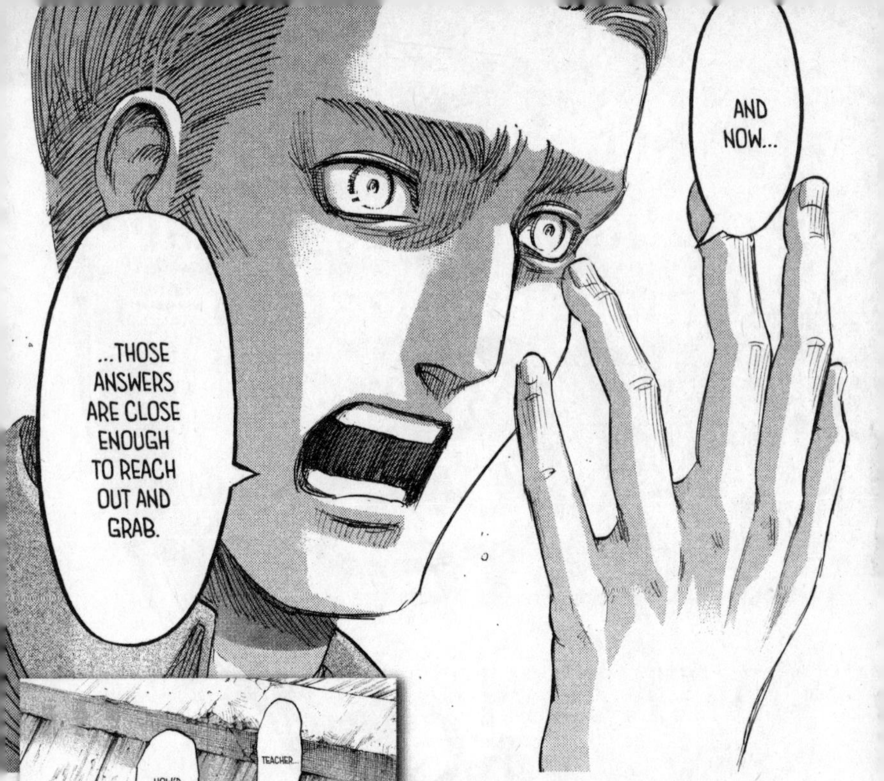
AND NOW...
...THOSE ANSWERS ARE CLOSE ENOUGH TO REACH OUT AND GRAB.

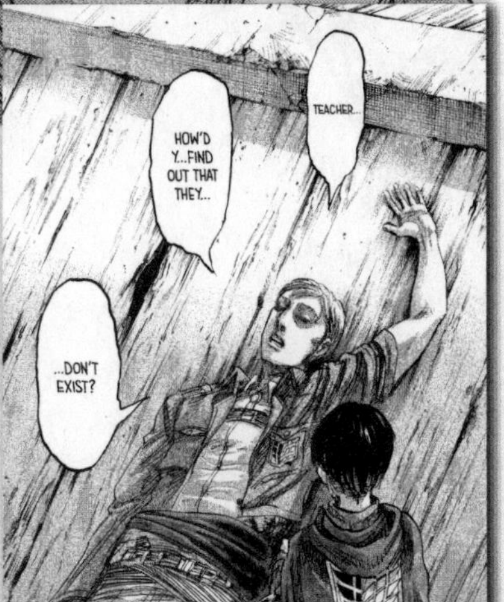
TEACHER...
HOW'D Y...FIND OUT THAT THEY...
...DON'T EXIST?

Though he inspired his fellow soldiers with talk about acting for humanity's sake, Erwin was secretly pursuing his own dreams. He must have even believed himself that he was someone who was acting for humanity's sake. In his final moments, though, Erwin did choose humanity's future. After the Beast Titan's attack left him with critical injuries, while he faded in and out of consciousness, Erwin recalled his time as a child when he spoke to his father about their dreams. His journey began with a dream, then led him down a path of pursuing that dream, and ultimately ended with a dream. Such was Erwin's life…

Was he able to acquire what he SOUGHT?!

The true identity of the enemies we face: men, civilization—

and if I must, THE WORLD.

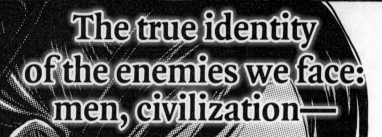

HANGE ZOË

BIRTHDAY: September 5 • **HEIGHT:** 170 cm (5'7") • **WEIGHT:** 60 kg (132 lbs)
AFFILIATION: Survey Corps Commander

A Titan researcher whose rampages cannot be stopped

WHOOOAH! MOBLIT, LOOK AT THIS! EREN'S FACE IS SERIOUSLY MESSED UP!!
AAHH!!
HURRY!! GET A SKETCH OF THIS!! IS HE GOING TO GET HIS OLD FACE BACK?!
WE'LL NEED IT FOR COM-PARISON LATER! HURRY!
SQUAD LEADER!! DO YOU HAVE ANY HUMAN COMPAS-SION AT ALL?!

Though Hange conducted countless experiments on Titans that could nearly be classified as mad, Hange shudders after learning that Titans are in fact, humans (Volume 13, Episode 51). In order to end the fighting as soon as possible, they research Eren's Titan and create a new weapon to defeat the Armored Titan (Volume 13, Episode 53 and more).

ROY.
YOU CAN KEEP FOLLOWING THE ROYAL GOVERN-MENT'S ORDERS...

Willing to fight anything or anyone if it means getting to the truth

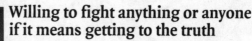

As someone who values the truth more than anything else, Hange cannot turn an ignorant eye to the Royal Government as it deceives the people and hides the reality of the Titan crisis. Hange decides to fight against the Royal Government in order to convey a message to the people inside the walls: The fight for humanity is on (Volume 15, Episode 60)!

THE NEXT COMMANDER OF THE SURVEY CORPS WLL BE HANGE ZOË.
YOU.
IN EXCHANGE FOR THE LOSS OF MANY HEROES, INCLUDING ERWIN SMITH, WE, THE SURVEY CORPS...
...WERE ABLE TO SUCCESSFULLY RETAKE WALL MARIA, DEFEAT THE COLOSSUS TITAN, AND TAKE ITS POWER.

The new Commander of the Survey Corps, upon Erwin's dying wishes

After Erwin is put in grave danger during the battle with the Royal Government, Hange is named the next Commander of the Survey Corps (Volume 14, Episode 57). After Erwin's death during the decisive battle in Shiganshina District, Hange takes up his dying wishes and becomes the leader of the Survey Corps (Volume 22, Episode 89).

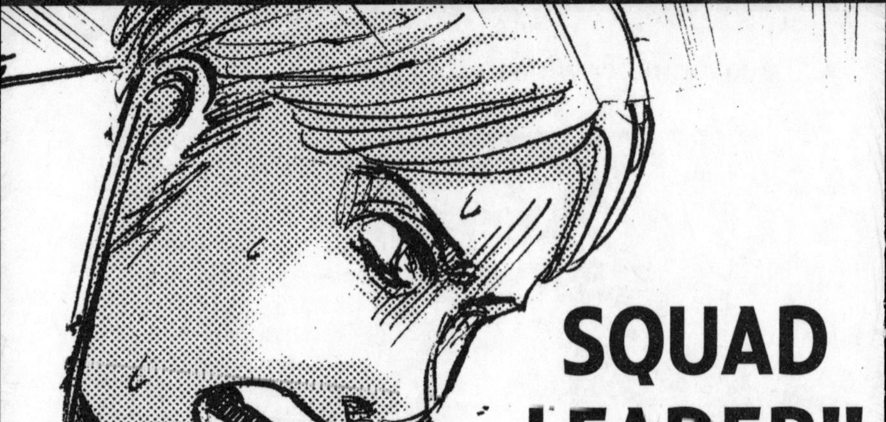
SQUAD LEADER!! You're being reckless!!

DECEASED

MOBLIT BERNER

BIRTHDAY: April 24 • **HEIGHT:** 176 cm (5'9") • **WEIGHT:** 65 kg (143 lbs)
AFFILIATION: Survey Corps, 4th Squad Vice Captain

A vice captain who fretted over Hange's recklessness

Moblit was like Hange's strange partner in crime, always fretting over Hange's recklessness. He ultimately sacrifices himself in order to save Hange from the Colossus Titan (Volume 19, Episode 78).

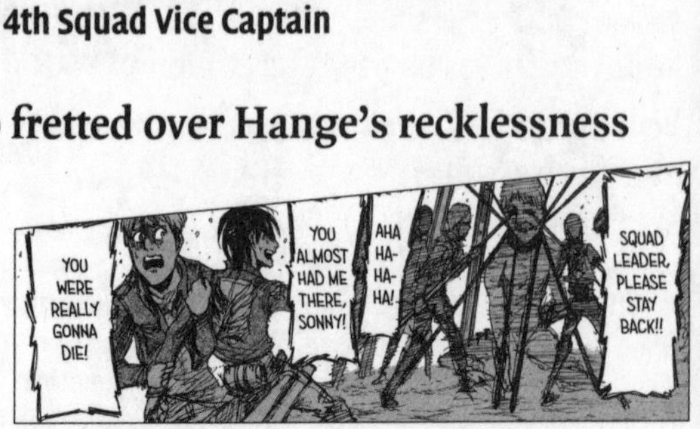
SQUAD LEADER, PLEASE STAY BACK!!
AHA HA-HA-HA!
YOU ALMOST HAD ME THERE, SONNY!
YOU WERE REALLY GONNA DIE!

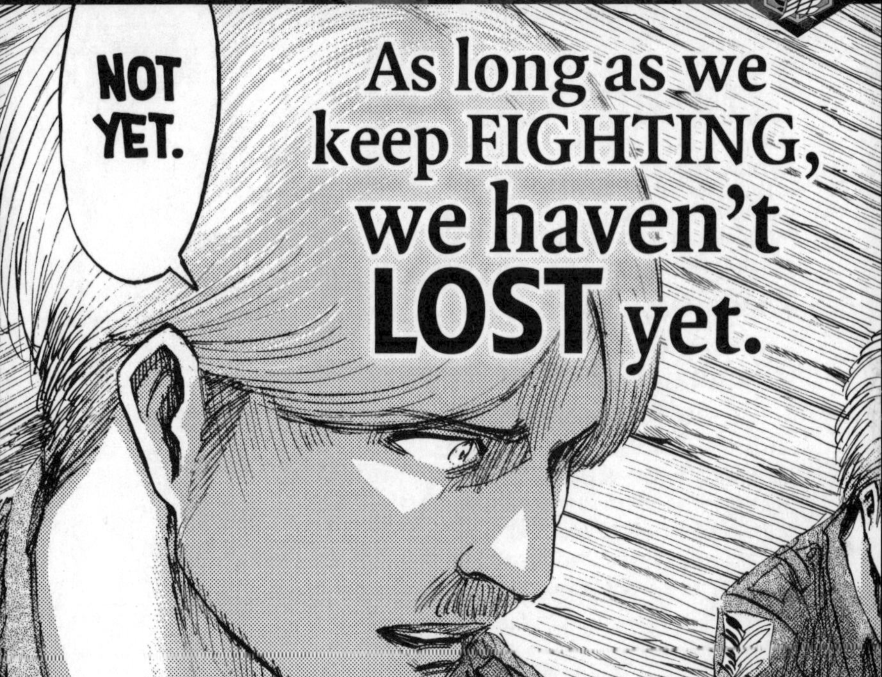
NOT YET.

As long as we keep FIGHTING, we haven't LOST yet.

DECEASED

MIKE ZACHARIAS

BIRTHDAY: November 1 • **HEIGHT:** 196 cm (6'5")
WEIGHT: 102 kg (225 lbs)
AFFILIATION: Survey Corps Squad Leader

Followed his convictions to the end, even when facing the Beast Titan

With his ability to detect Titans using his sense of smell, Mike was the second, most skilled member of the Survey Corps behind Levi. He faced off against the Beast Titan, believing that "Man doesn't lose until the moment he stops fighting." Even when he suffered a fatal wound, he did not let fear overcome him and continued to try to fight back (Volume 9, Episode 35).

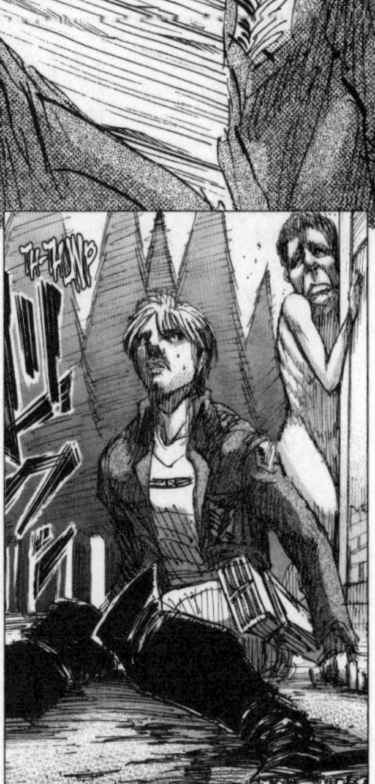

DECEASED

OLUO BOZADO

BIRTHDAY: January 6
HEIGHT: 173 cm (5'8")
WEIGHT: 61 kg (134 lbs)
AFFILIATION: Survey Corps, Squad Levi

Known best for his sarcastic remarks meant to "imitate" Levi

...!!
HEH... WHAT, ARE YOU TRYING TO REIN ME IN, PETRA? IF YOU WANNA ACT LIKE MY WIFE, THERE ARE A COUPLE STEPS YOU SKIPPED.

Oluo was a member of the Survey Corps Special Operations Squad (also known as Squad Levi) led by Levi and designed to observe Eren. While he tried too hard to act like Eren's senior, he was capable when he needed to be. Though he personally thought he was imitating Levi's cool tone, he unfortunately just came off as sarcastic. He met his end during the battle with the Female Titan in the Forest of Giant Trees (Volume 7, Episode 28).

DECEASED

PETRA RAL

BIRTHDAY: December 6
HEIGHT: 158 cm (5'2")
WEIGHT: 55 kg (121 lbs)
AFFILIATION: Survey Corps, Squad Levi

A female soldier who advised Eren, creating a bond with him

PETRA !!
NOW!

The lone woman in Squad Levi. Having entered the Survey Corps at the same time as Oluo, she seemed fed up with Oluo's poor attempts to imitate Levi. She advised Eren when he was on the verge of letting his emotions take control. Petra taught him the importance of trusting his fellow soldiers. However, she died immediately after, during the Female Titan's counterattack (Volume 7, Episode 28).

ELD JINN

DECEASED

BIRTHDAY: January 30
HEIGHT: 182 cm (6'0")
WEIGHT: 75 kg (165 lbs)
AFFILIATION: Survey Corps, Squad Levi

An elite Survey Corps member who knew Oluo during his Training Corps days

A member of Squad Levi and a more senior soldier than Oluo and Petra. He knew about their first deployment and the blunders they committed during it. He was also a brave man, treating Eren humanely, rather than like a monster. While he nearly had the Female Titan cornered in the Forest of Giant Trees, he was unable to finish her off and died in battle (Volume 7, Episode 28).

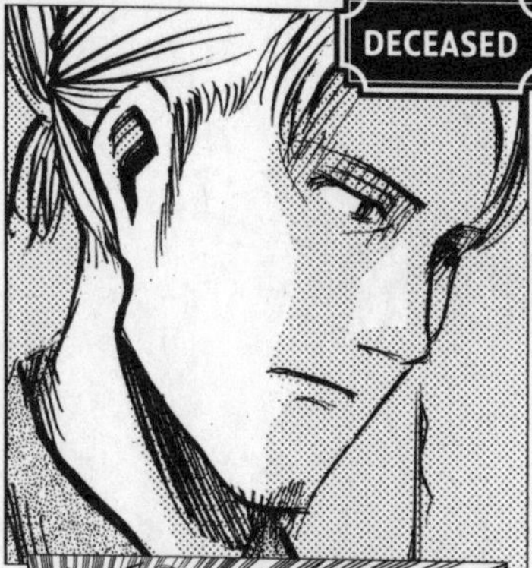

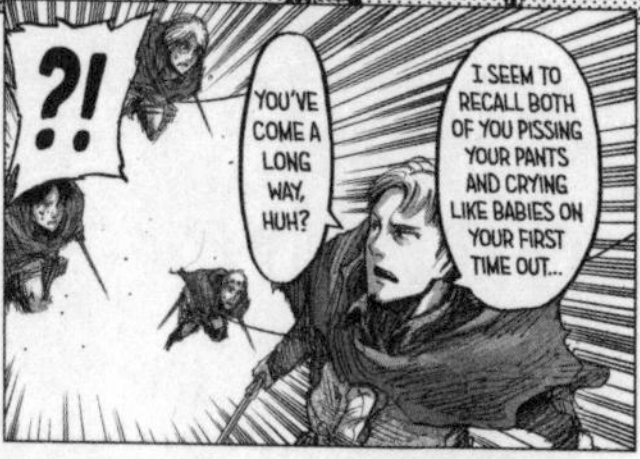
?!
YOU'VE COME A LONG WAY, HUH?
I SEEM TO RECALL BOTH OF YOU PISSING YOUR PANTS AND CRYING LIKE BABIES ON YOUR FIRST TIME OUT...

GÜNTHER SCHULTZ

DECEASED

BIRTHDAY: July 30
HEIGHT: 183 cm (6'0")
WEIGHT: 82 kg (181 lbs)
AFFILIATION: Survey Corps, Squad Levi

The man responsible for assembling Squad Levi

Like Eld, Günther was an elite soldier who played a central role in Squad Levi. When Eren was doubtful about what meaning the 57th expedition outside the Walls had, Günther told him to believe in the Commander, focusing Eren on their purpose. During the Expedition, though, he is defeated by Annie's blades when she returns to human form (Volume 7, Episode 28).

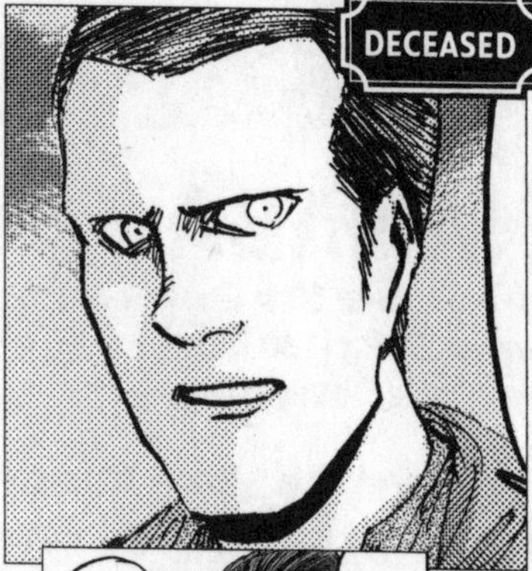

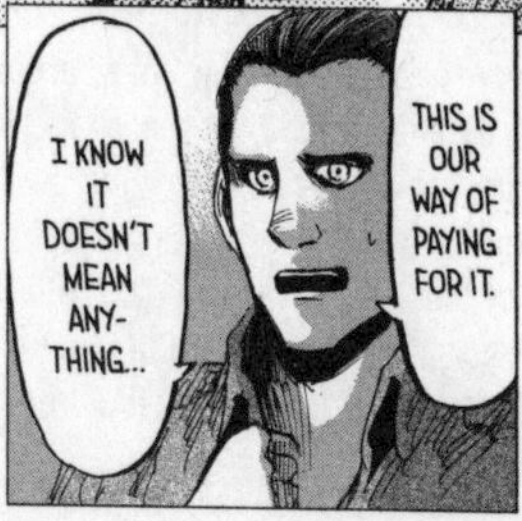
I KNOW IT DOESN'T MEAN ANY-THING...
THIS IS OUR WAY OF PAYING FOR IT.

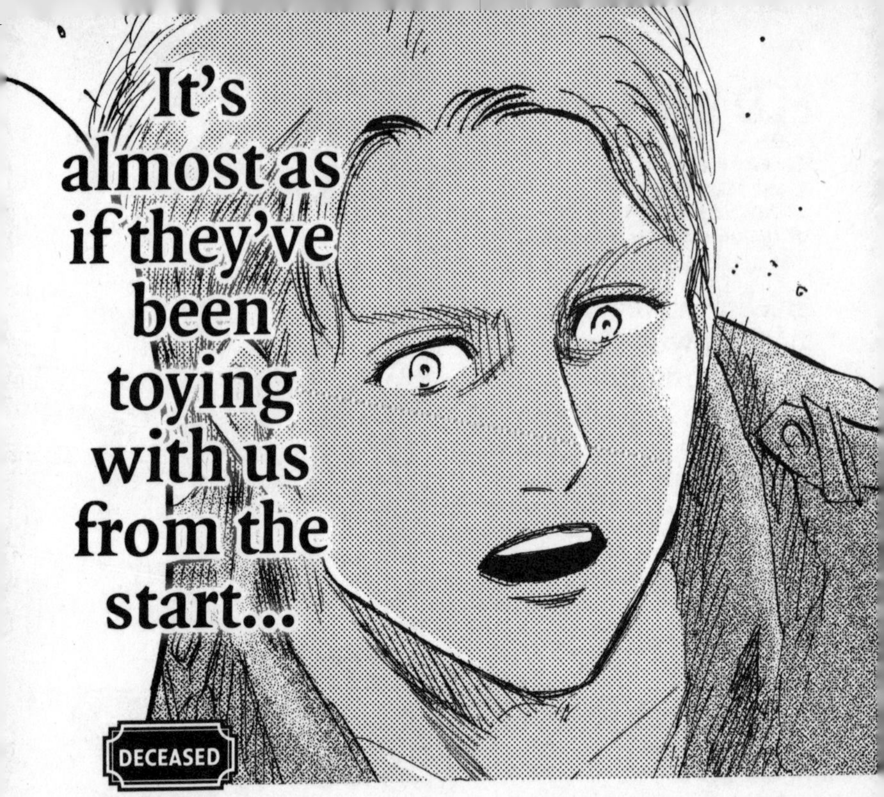
It's almost as if they've been toying with us from the start...
DECEASED

NANABA

BIRTHDAY: June 30 • **HEIGHT:** 172 cm (5'8")
WEIGHT: 59 kg (130 lbs)
AFFILIATION: Survey Corps

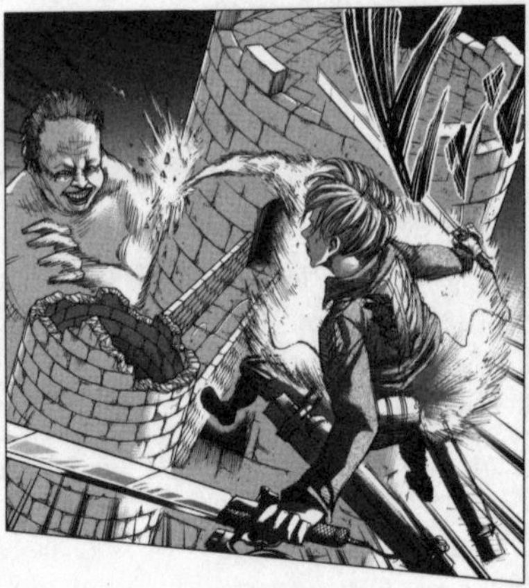

Protected the 104th during the struggle at Utgard Castle

An elite Survey Corps member who participated in the 57th expedition outside the Walls and other campaigns. She fought valiantly at the ruins of Utgard Castle in order to protect the members of the 104th. Nanaba dies after trying to save Gelgar after running out of gas in her Vertical Maneuvering Equipment (Volume 10, Episode 40).

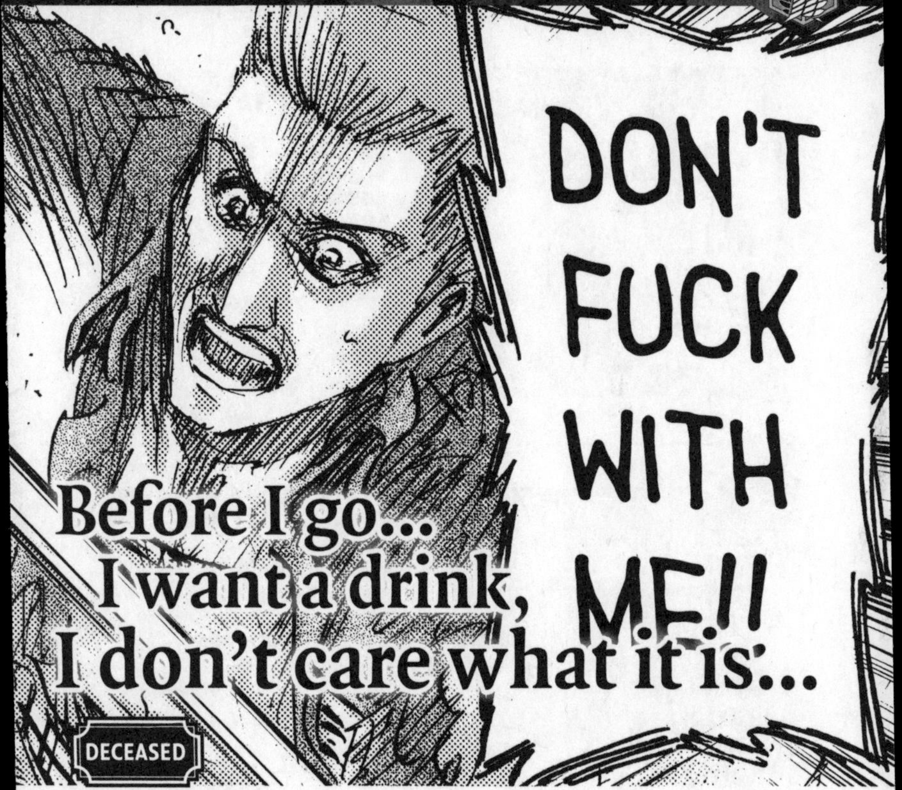
DON'T FUCK WITH ME!!
Before I go...
I want a drink,
I don't care what it is...
DECEASED

GELGAR

BIRTHDAY: October 9 • **HEIGHT:** 179 cm (5'10") • **WEIGHT:** 75 kg (165 lbs)
AFFILIATION: Survey Corps

A man who could not forget about his liquor, even when on the cusp of death

Gelgar had a certifiable love for alcohol, even putting his hands on an old bottle in the ruins of Utgard Castle. While he was made leader of the South Team by Mike, he used all of his gas and blades and ended up as Titan food. The one thing he wanted most when he was on the verge of being snatched by a Titan was his beloved liquor (Volume 10, Episode 40).

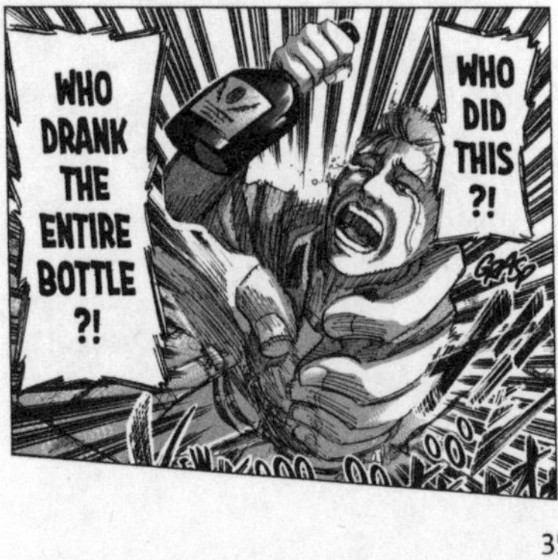
WHO DID THIS ?!
WHO DRANK THE ENTIRE BOTTLE ?!

BUT... THAT'S WHAT IT WOULD MEAN.

THOMAS

BIRTHDAY: April 20
HEIGHT: 175 cm (5'9")
WEIGHT: 61 kg (134 lbs)
AFFILIATION: Survey Corps

The Survey Corps member to inform Ehrmich District of the Titans that had appeared in the interior. After arriving in Ehrmich, he forces himself back on the fastest horse he can find and returns to Erwin (Volume 9, Episode 36).

DECEASED

YES... THE NUMBER OF TITANS DOES APPEAR TO BE SMALL.
BE HARD TO SAY FOR SURE THAT THEY'VE REALLY BROKEN THROUGH THE WALL.

HENNING

BIRTHDAY: January 31
HEIGHT: 175 cm (5'9")
WEIGHT: 72 kg (158 lbs)
AFFILIATION: Survey Corps

Like Nanaba and Gelgar, Henning was a member of the Survey Corps who found himself besieged in the ruins of Utgard Castle. While he attempted to stop the Titans' attack, he took a direct hit from a rock thrown by the Beast Titan and died in battle (Volume 10, Episode 39).

DECEASED

LYNNE

BIRTHDAY: February 17
HEIGHT: 170 cm (5'7")
WEIGHT: 57 kg (126 lbs)
AFFILIATION: Survey Corps

A soldier who helped defend the inside of the ruins of Utgard Castle alongside Reiner, and who also told the others to take shelter on the roof. Alongside Henning, she died instantly when hit by a flying rock (Volume 10, Episode 39).

HAJIME ISAYAMA Reveals

How His CHARACTERS WERE BORN: Part 1

EREN YEAGER

Since Eren is a character who thrashes around in the story, I gave him black hair because I wanted to be able to do things like put speed lines through his otherwise fully inked hair. I also paid a lot of attention to his eyes. I wanted to make them feel different from the other characters', so I made his eyebrows thinner. While Eren gives off a strong impression of being an angry character, it would feel too artificial if I were to draw his eyebrows thick to make that more apparent. He would become a character created out of the needs of the work, making him no longer realistic. This also goes for Levi. I feel that when you want to make a strong, cool character, it's not all about adding elements. You need to subtract something, too.

Though the name "Eren" might sound like a woman's name, I decided on it because I thought that the out-of-place feeling would make it easier to remember. The name Yeager comes from the German for "hunter."

Eren is the polar opposite of the chosen, talented protagonist you so often see in films and other media. I was also skeptical about the importance of one's bloodline when coming up with Eren, which is why I made him someone who was not blessed with natural talent.

ARMIN ARLERT

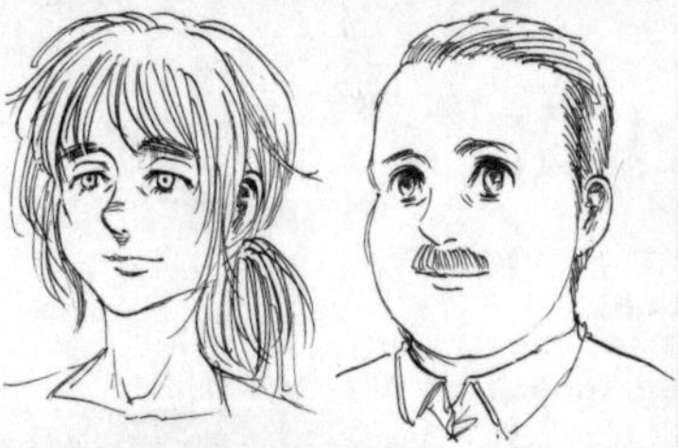

I gave Armin a round nose to make him seem mild-mannered and weak while also giving him some kind of unique trait. But since identifiable character traits in manga often take the form of easily noticed accessories like hats, it was hard to get people to realize that his nose is one of his distinguishing features. Aside from that, I guess there's the fact that Armin's body is smaller than Eren's and Mikasa's.

I chose the name Armin Arlert because of the way it causes you to think of the word "aluminum," and because it seemed like starting both names with the same letter would make it easier to remember.

Speaking of Armin, his parents once created a hot air balloon in the anime, but I guess I never got a chance to depict that in the manga. I actually even prepared rough sketches of his parents, and Armin takes more after his father.

How Armin resembles his parents

MOTHER:
Hair, nose, eyebrows

FATHER:
Eyes

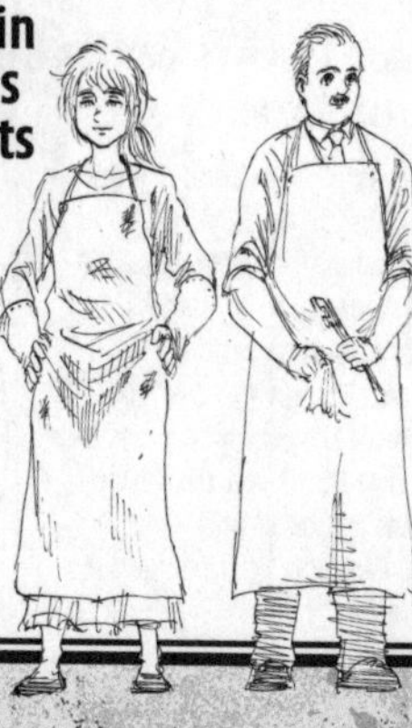

DECEASED

KLAUS

BIRTHDAY: October 20
HEIGHT: 172 cm (5'8")
WEIGHT: 75 kg (165 lbs)
AFFILIATION: Survey Corps Team Leader

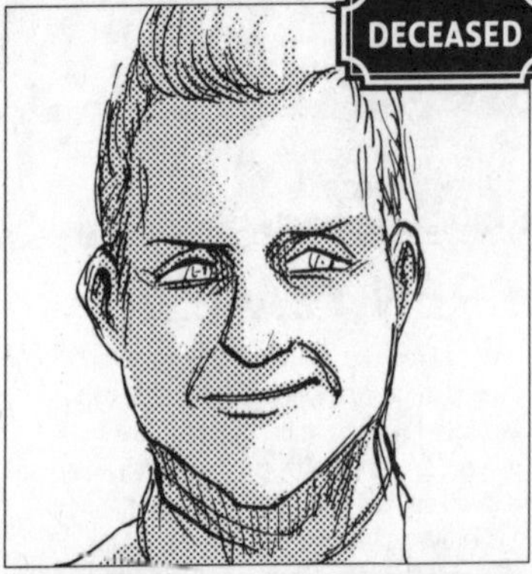

Gave everything he had to defend the Corps's horses during the battle for Shiganshina!

Klaus was the leader responsible for the team stationed inside the gate during the decisive battle in Shiganshina District. After the Beast Titan appeared, his team came together with Dirk's and Marlene's to defend the horses from the smaller Titans with everything they had. He died in battle from rocks thrown by the Beast Titan (Volume 20, Episode 79 and more).

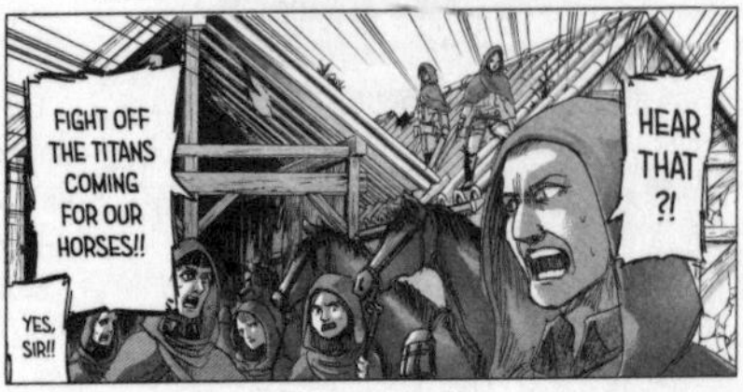
HEAR THAT ?!
FIGHT OFF THE TITANS COMING FOR OUR HORSES!!
YES, SIR!!

DECEASED

DIRK

BIRTHDAY: December 26
HEIGHT: 175 cm (5'9")
WEIGHT: 72 kg (159 lbs)
AFFILIATION: Survey Corps Team Leader

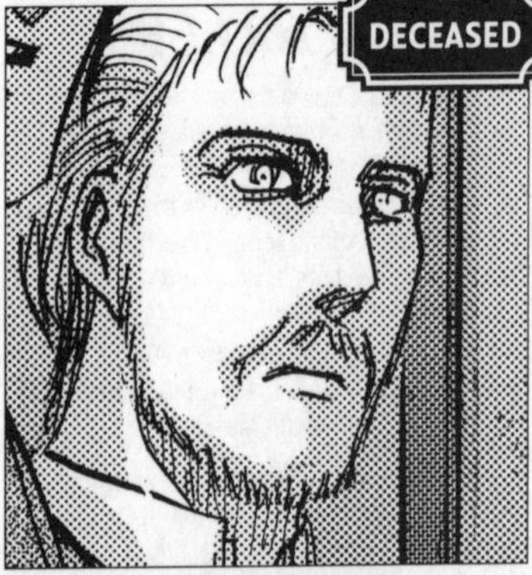

Loses his life to the Beast Titan's rock volley

Dirk was a Team Leader who fought in the decisive battle in Shiganshina District. He called Erwin's decision to entrust Armin with the command of some of his forces as a "big gamble." His death came at the hands of the Beast Titan when he was attacked with flying rocks (Volume 20, Episode 79 and more).

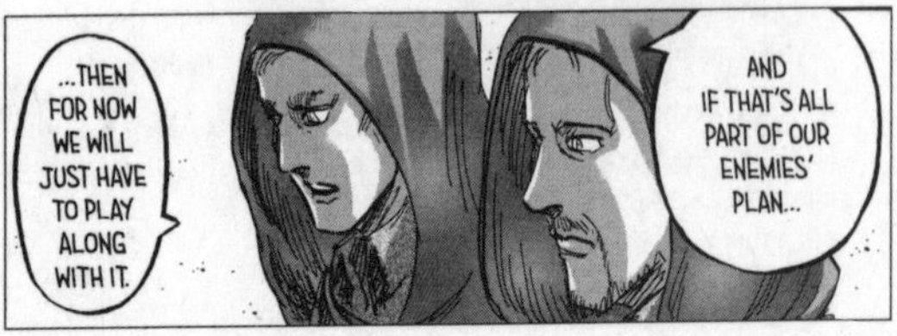
AND IF THAT'S ALL PART OF OUR ENEMIES' PLAN...
...THEN FOR NOW WE WILL JUST HAVE TO PLAY ALONG WITH IT.

MARLENE

BIRTHDAY: December 27
HEIGHT: 165 cm (5'5")
WEIGHT: 55 kg (121 lbs)
AFFILIATION: Survey Corps Team Leader

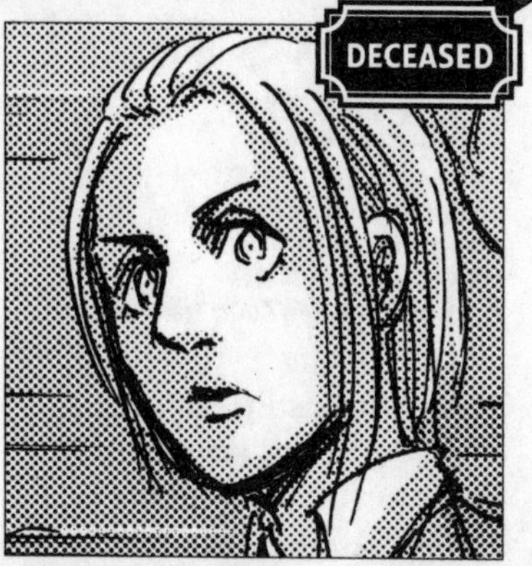
DECEASED

A Team Leader who was close to Hange

Marlene was a Team Leader who participated in the decisive battle in Shiganshina District. She seems to have known Hange for quite some time and even talked to Hange in a familiar way during the strategy meeting before the battle. She died in battle from rocks thrown by the Beast Titan.

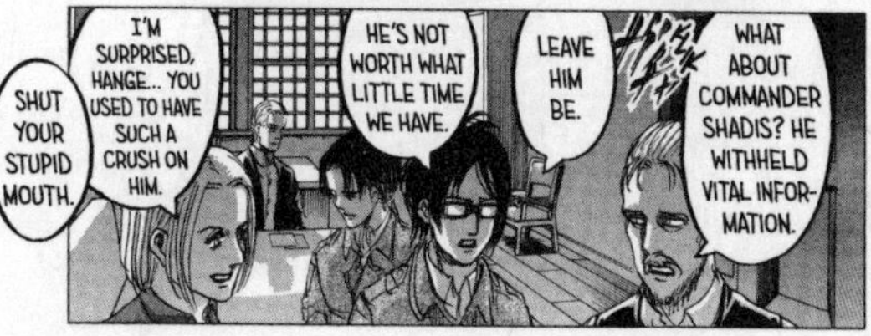
WHAT ABOUT COMMANDER SHADIS? HE WITHHELD VITAL INFORMATION.
LEAVE HIM BE.
HE'S NOT WORTH WHAT LITTLE TIME WE HAVE.
I'M SURPRISED, HANGE... YOU USED TO HAVE SUCH A CRUSH ON HIM.
SHUT YOUR STUPID MOUTH.

BLACK-HAIRED SOLDIER

BIRTHDAY: August 8
HEIGHT: 175 cm (5'9")
WEIGHT: 60 kg (132 lbs)
AFFILIATION: Survey Corps Team Leader

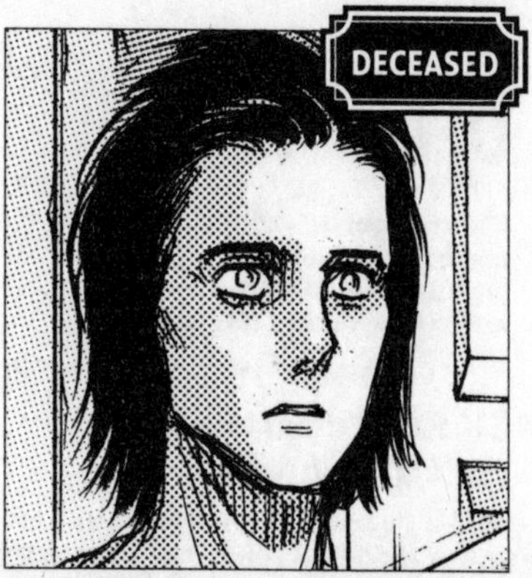
DECEASED

The Team Leader who gave meat to the recruits

A Team Leader who spent two months' worth of food costs to give meat to the soldiers during the celebration held on the night before the decisive battle (Volume 18, Episode 72 and more). He fought using the Thunder Spears during the battle for Shiganshina District.

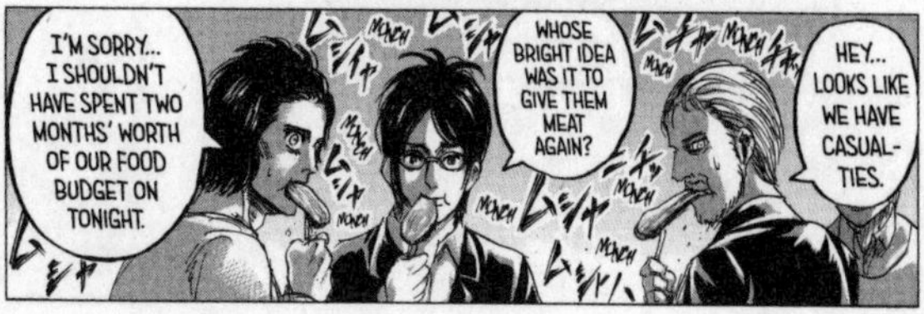
HEY... LOOKS LIKE WE HAVE CASUALTIES.
WHOSE BRIGHT IDEA WAS IT TO GIVE THEM MEAT AGAIN?
I'M SORRY... I SHOULDN'T HAVE SPENT TWO MONTHS' WORTH OF OUR FOOD BUDGET ON TONIGHT.

SASHA'S TEAM LEADER

BIRTHDAY: January 28
HEIGHT: 177 cm (5'10")
WEIGHT: 87 kg (192 lbs)
AFFILIATION: Survey Corps Team Leader

Understands Erwin's intentions and goes around the Forest of Giant Trees

This Team Leader rescues Sasha when she is chased by a Titan and panics during the 57th expedition outside the Walls. When he sees the central column enter the Forest of Giant Trees, he understands Erwin's intentions and gives the order to go around it (Volume 6, Episode 24 and more).

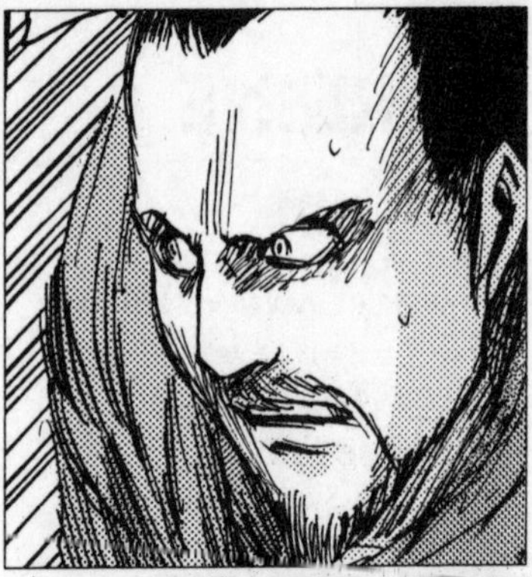

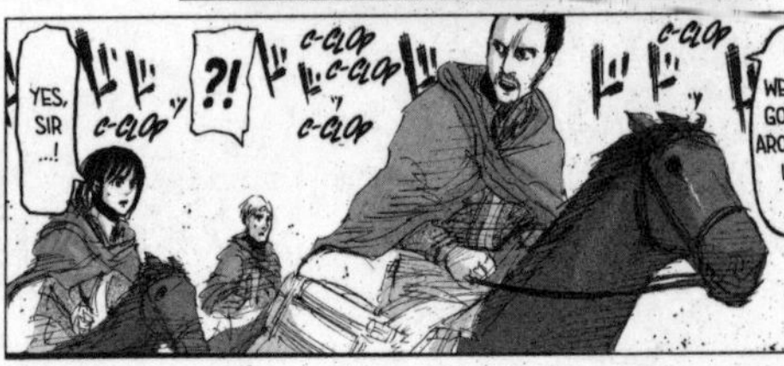
WE'RE GOING AROUND IT.
?!
YES, SIR ...!

DECEASED

DITA NESS

BIRTHDAY: September 20
HEIGHT: 178 cm (5'10")
WEIGHT: 84 kg (185 lbs)
AFFILIATION: Survey Corps Team Leader

Falls to the Female Titan protecting Armin

Dita was the leader responsible for the team that included Armin. During the courses meant for the recruits, he taught the new soldiers the meaning and importance of the Long-Distance Enemy Scouting Formation. Though he successfully teamed up with Siss to take out an Abnormal, he was no match for the Female Titan and died when his wire was grabbed. His favorite horse was named Charlotte (Volume 5, Episode 22).

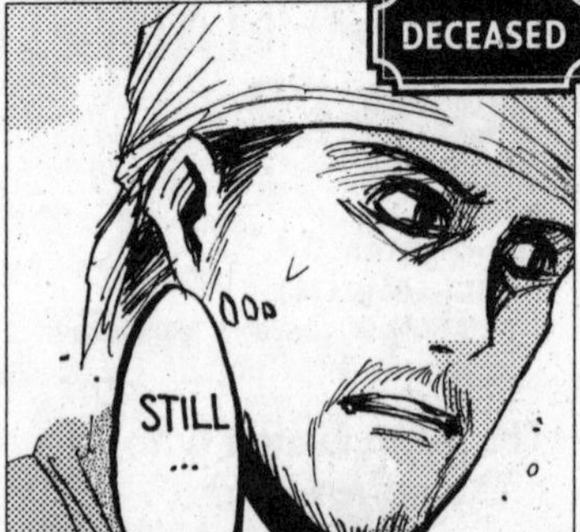
STILL ...

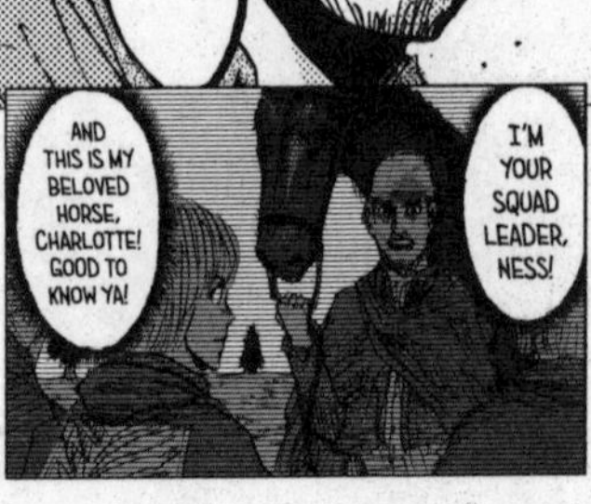
I'M YOUR SQUAD LEADER, NESS!
AND THIS IS MY BELOVED HORSE, CHARLOTTE! GOOD TO KNOW YA!

THE SURVEY CORPS

DECEASED

MOSES BRAUN

BIRTHDAY: December 18
HEIGHT: 187 cm (6'2")
WEIGHT: 88 kg (194 lbs)
AFFILIATION: Survey Corps

Moses encountered a Titan during the expedition led by Keith Shadis that Erwin Smith was also a part of. As he went to slice at it, he screamed, "Let's teach this thing the power of the human race!!" (Volume 1, Episode 1).

DECEASED

LUKE SISS

BIRTHDAY: September 26
HEIGHT: 177 cm (5'10")   WEIGHT: 80 kg (176 lbs)
AFFILIATION: Survey Corps, Team Ness
(57th expedition outside the Walls)

Siss synchronized perfectly with his superior, Ness, to unleash an attack that miraculously defeated an Abnormal running in Armin's direction. However, he died immediately after when the Female Titan grabbed him and crushed him (Volume 5, Episode 22).

BAGGY-PANTS LEON

BIRTHDAY: October 26

A mysterious Survey Corps member who sloppily equips his Vertical Maneuvering Equipment.

LAUDA AND RASHAD

BIRTHDAY: March 12

BIRTHDAY: September 24

Upon Hange's instructions, these two face off against the Colossus Titan as Team Leaders.

DARIUS'S TEAM MEMBERS A, B, AND C

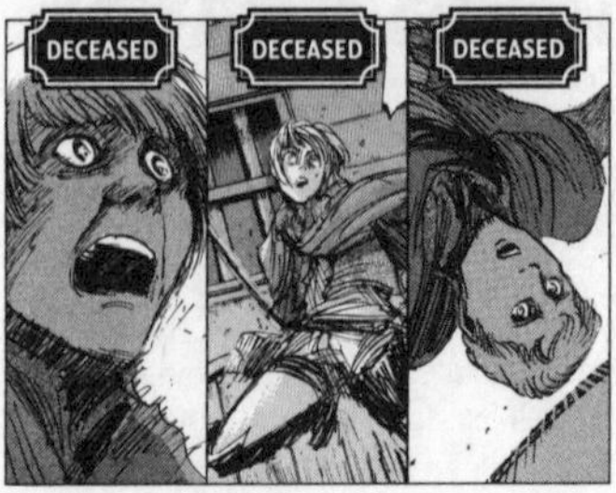
DECEASED
DECEASED
DECEASED

All three fall victim at the same time to the Female Titan's attack.

DARIUS BAER-VARBRUN

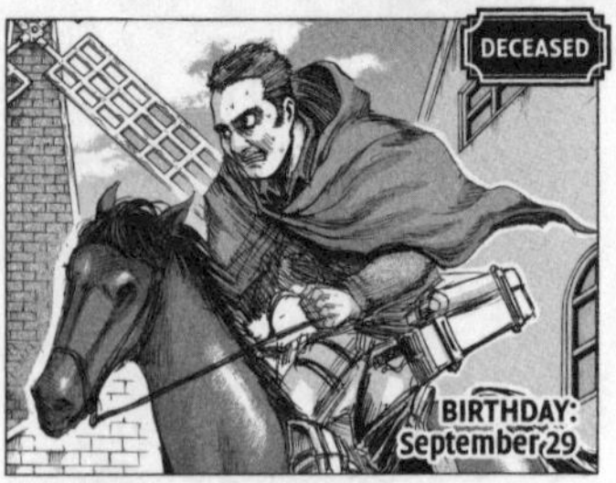
DECEASED
BIRTHDAY: September 29

Though he and his three soldiers valiantly fought the Female Titan, he was kicked to death.

MESSENGER

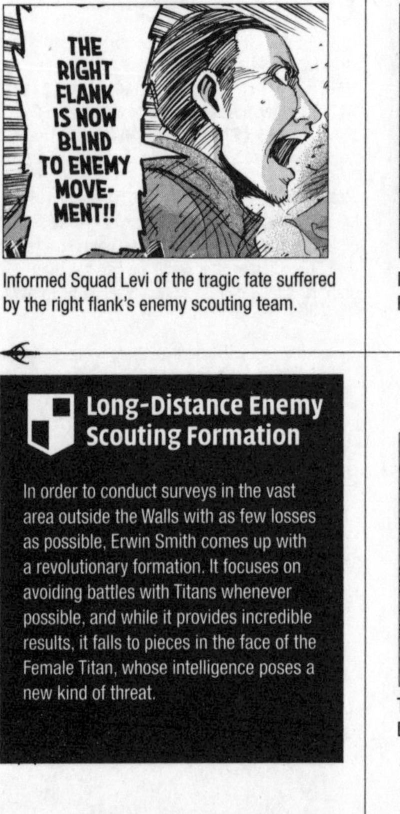
THE RIGHT FLANK IS NOW BLIND TO ENEMY MOVE-MENT!!

Informed Squad Levi of the tragic fate suffered by the right flank's enemy scouting team.

ENEMY SCOUT ON THE RIGHT FLANK'S TEAM

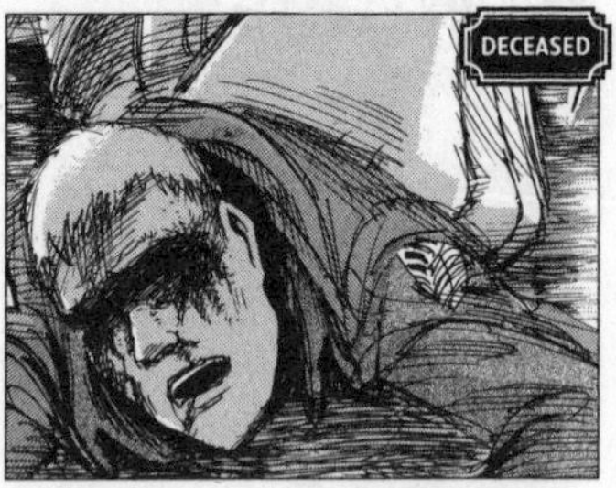
DECEASED

Died to the army of Titans brought by the Female Titan.

Long-Distance Enemy Scouting Formation

In order to conduct surveys in the vast area outside the Walls with as few losses as possible, Erwin Smith comes up with a revolutionary formation. It focuses on avoiding battles with Titans whenever possible, and while it provides incredible results, it falls to pieces in the face of the Female Titan, whose intelligence poses a new kind of threat.

SURVEY CORPSMEN A AND B WHO FIGHT THE FEMALE TITAN

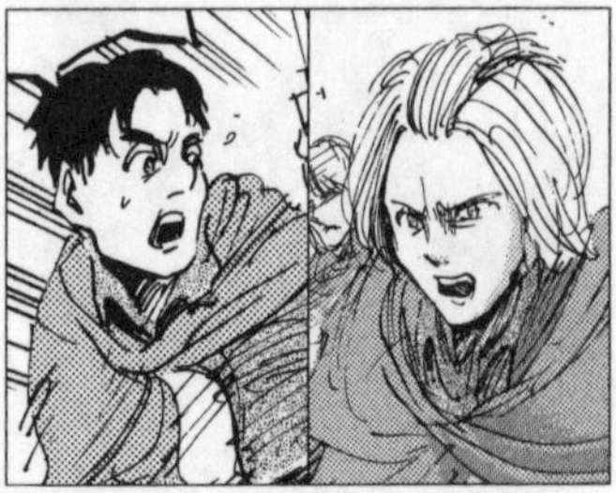

These two go to face the Female Titan after Darius's Team.

ENEMY SCOUTS A AND B FROM FIRST COLUMN, 13TH

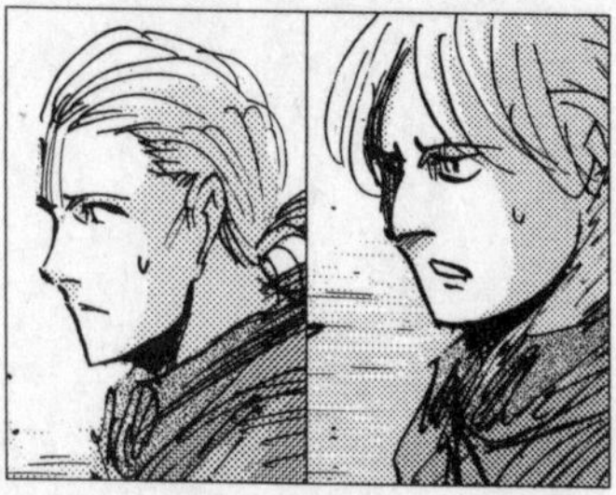

Positioned on the far left flank, these two wonder why their course has not changed.

TRANSPORT TEAM SOLDIER FROM THIRD COLUMN, FIRST

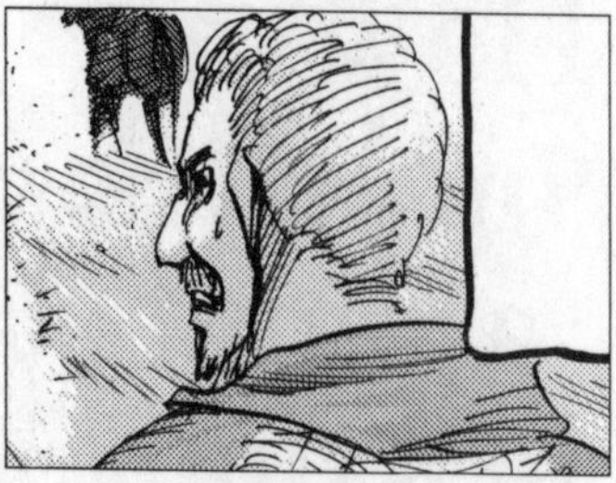

Positioned toward the front-center, this man is responsible for transporting the equipment used to immobilize the Female Titan.

THE LAST REINFORCING MEMBER OF THE TEAM CHASING THE FEMALE TITAN

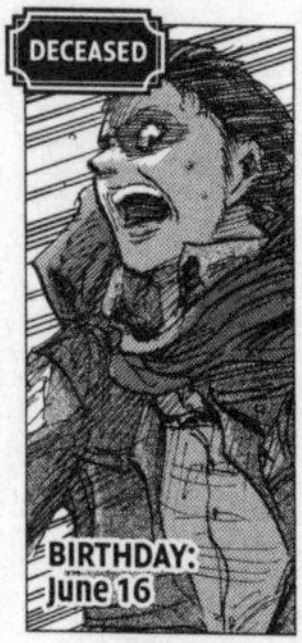
DECEASED
BIRTHDAY: June 16

A fairly elite soldier who fought the Female Titan alone while Eren pondered whether to turn into a Titan and spent a long while reminiscing. He died after being slammed against a giant tree.

ENEMY SCOUTS A AND B FROM FIRST COLUMN, FIFTH

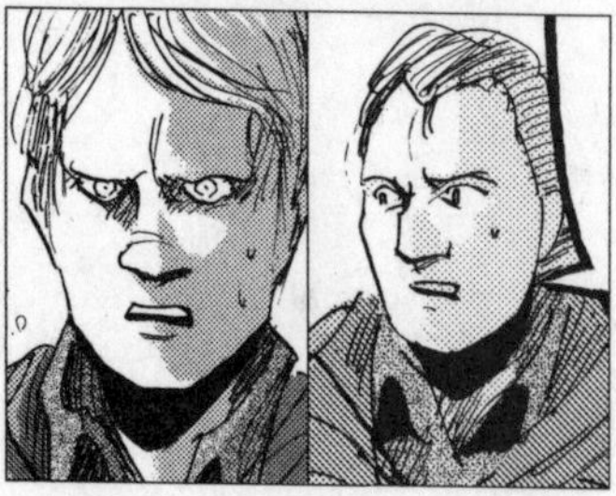

Positioned near the front of the formation, these two mention the Forest of Giant Trees.

WOUNDED SOLDIER ON HORSEBACK

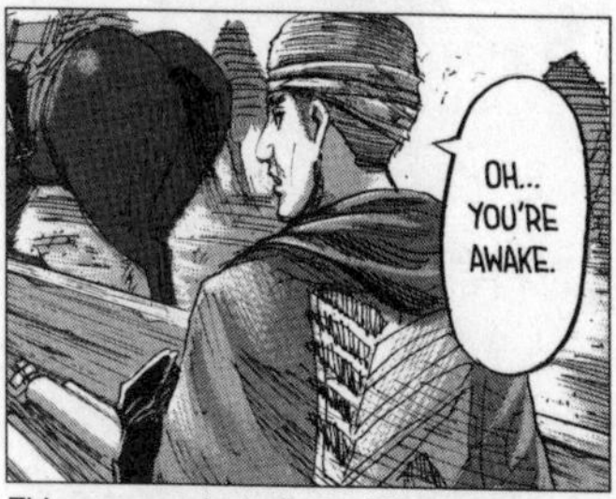
OH... YOU'RE AWAKE.

This man speaks to Eren while he was in a carriage after being saved.

SOLDIERS A AND B ON THE FEMALE TITAN CAPTURE TEAM

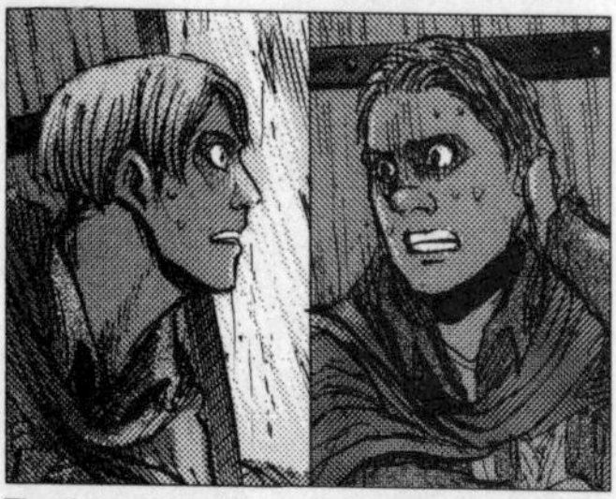

These two stand by and wait to operate the equipment used to immobilize the Female Titan.

How can you JOKE around at a time like this, Captain...?

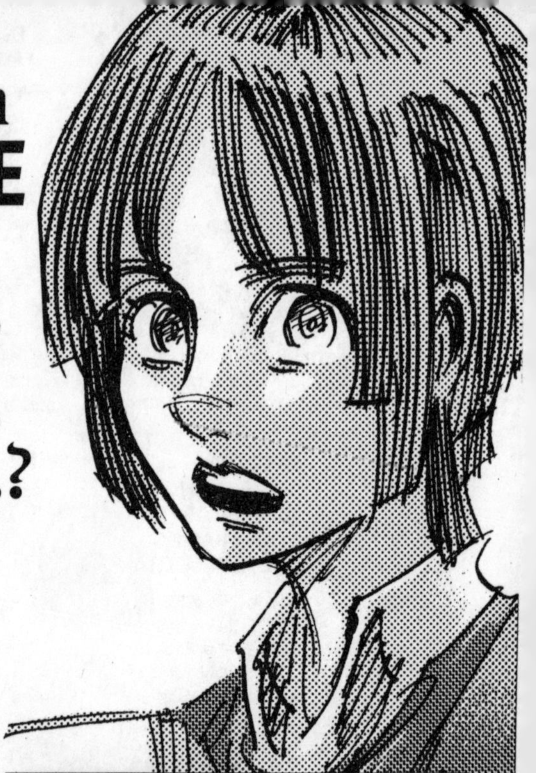

DECEASED

NIFA

BIRTHDAY: April 28
HEIGHT: 165 cm (5'5")
WEIGHT: 58 kg (128 lbs)
AFFILIATION: Survey Corps

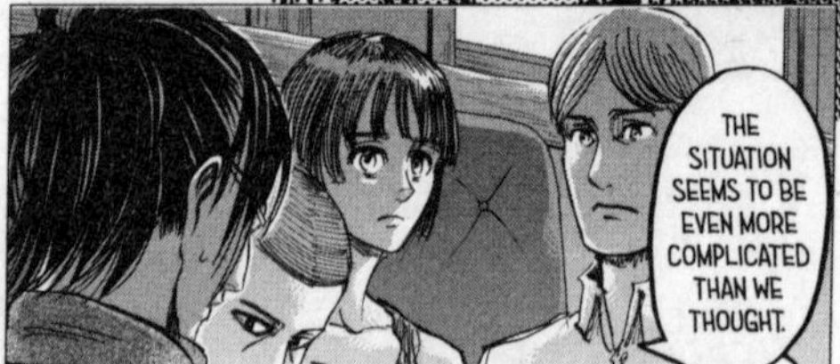
THE SITUATION SEEMS TO BE EVEN MORE COMPLICATED THAN WE THOUGHT.

A long-serving assistant

Together with Hange, Nifa rushed to the ruins of Utgard Castle to rescue Krista and the others. While she worked alongside Levi during the battle with the First Interior Squad, she fell victim to Kenny's surprise attack and died (Volume 14, Episode 57 and more).

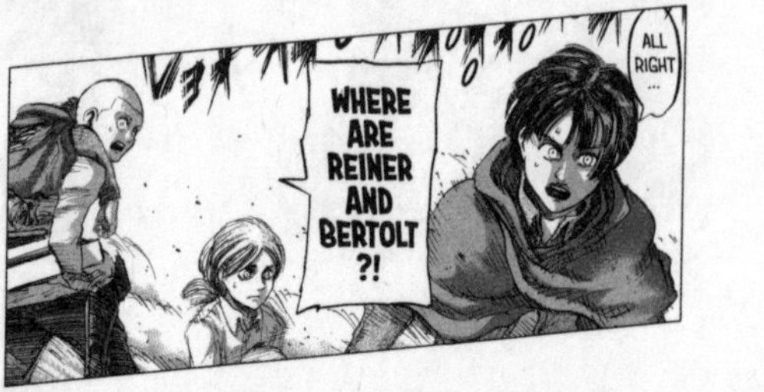
ALL RIGHT ...
WHERE ARE REINER AND BERTOLT ?!

KEIJI

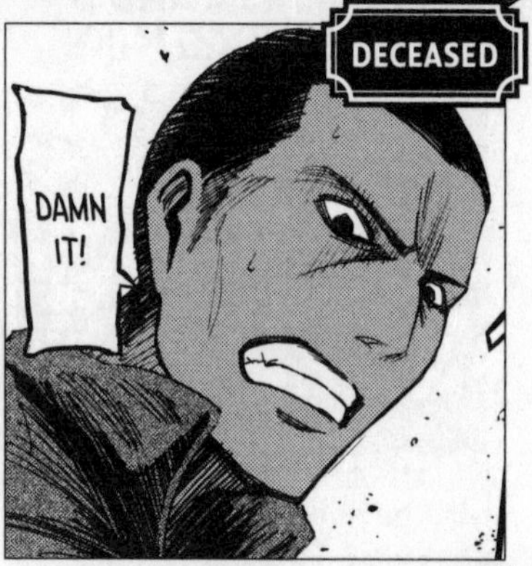
DECEASED
DAMN IT!

BIRTHDAY: January 8
HEIGHT: 178 cm (5'10")
WEIGHT: 59 kg (130 lbs)
AFFILIATION: Survey Corps

A veteran soldier who experienced the battle in the Forest of Giant Trees

Keiji participated in the battle against the Female Titan during the 57th expedition outside the Walls. He later took out his anger on the crystal that surrounds Annie while in Stohess District. Unable to avoid Kenny's attack during the battle with the First Interior Squad, he died in battle (Volume 14, Episode 57 and more).

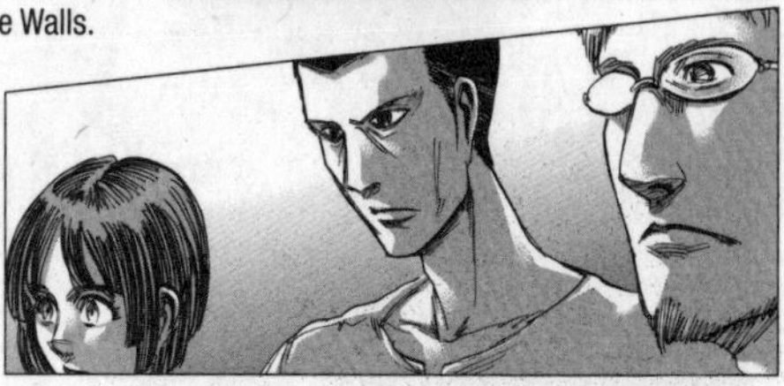

GOGGLED SOLDIER

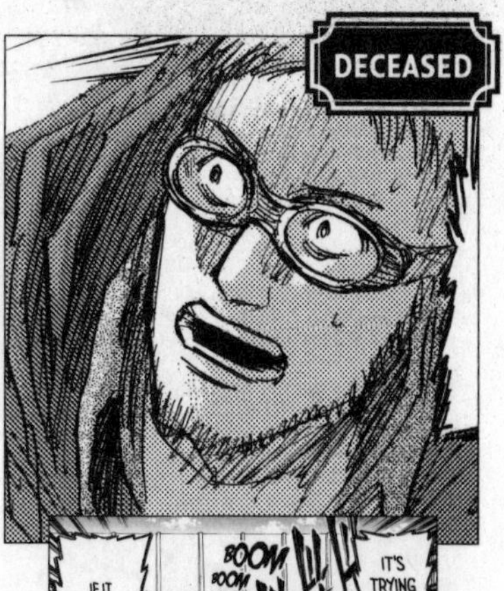
DECEASED

BIRTHDAY: December 15
HEIGHT: 175 cm (5'9")
WEIGHT: 62 kg (137 lbs)
AFFILIATION: Survey Corps

Experienced many fierce battles alongside Keiji

An elite Survey Corps member who participated in the 57th expedition outside the Walls. He worked alongside Keiji under Levi during the battle against the First Interior Squad. While he had been a long-active Survey Corps member like Keiji and Nifa, he died after being attacked by Kenny (Volume 14, Episode 57 and more).

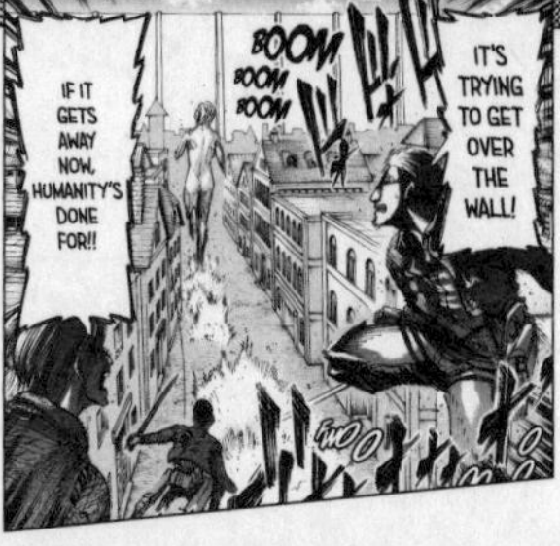
IT'S TRYING TO GET OVER THE WALL!
BOOM BOOM BOOM
IF IT GETS AWAY NOW, HUMANITY'S DONE FOR!!

SOLDIERS A AND B FROM SQUAD MIKE

When Mike decides to fight the Titans on his own, these two notice.

LONG-HAIRED SURVEY CORPSMAN

...HE LOOKS LIKE HE'S SLEEPING PEACEFULLY.

DECEASED

I MEAN...

Found peace on his deathbed thanks to Levi's words.

POMPADOURED CORPSMAN

Looks after Mikasa after she returns with injured ribs.

MESSAGE RUNNER

Informs others of the appearance of Titans inside Wall Rose.

SURVEY CORPSMAN B

Informs Erwin that there are suspicions about a murder.

SURVEY CORPSMAN A

States that there are currently no Titans when asked by Jean.

BAIT CORPSMAN

Responsible for luring the Titans into the "Titan Gallows."

SURVEY CORPSMAN C

Discovers the near-dead Kenny together with Levi.

SURVEY CORPSMAN WHO DISCOVERED THE CAVITY

DECEASED

Discovered the cavity that Reiner hid inside during a survey of the Wall.

GORDON AND SANDRA

DECEASED

BIRTHDAY: November 19

DECEASED

BIRTHDAY: April 10

Together with Floch, these two were transferred from the Garrison into the Survey Corps.

SURVEY CORPSMAN D

DECEASED

BIRTHDAY: March 9

Though he shook with fear, he never stopped charging the Beast Titan.

THUNDER SPEAR SOLDIERS A AND B

DECEASED

DECEASED

Both of these soldiers stood against the Armored Titan on Hange's orders to finish the Titan. They were equipped with Thunder Spears, but met their end because of the blast generated by the Colossus Titan.

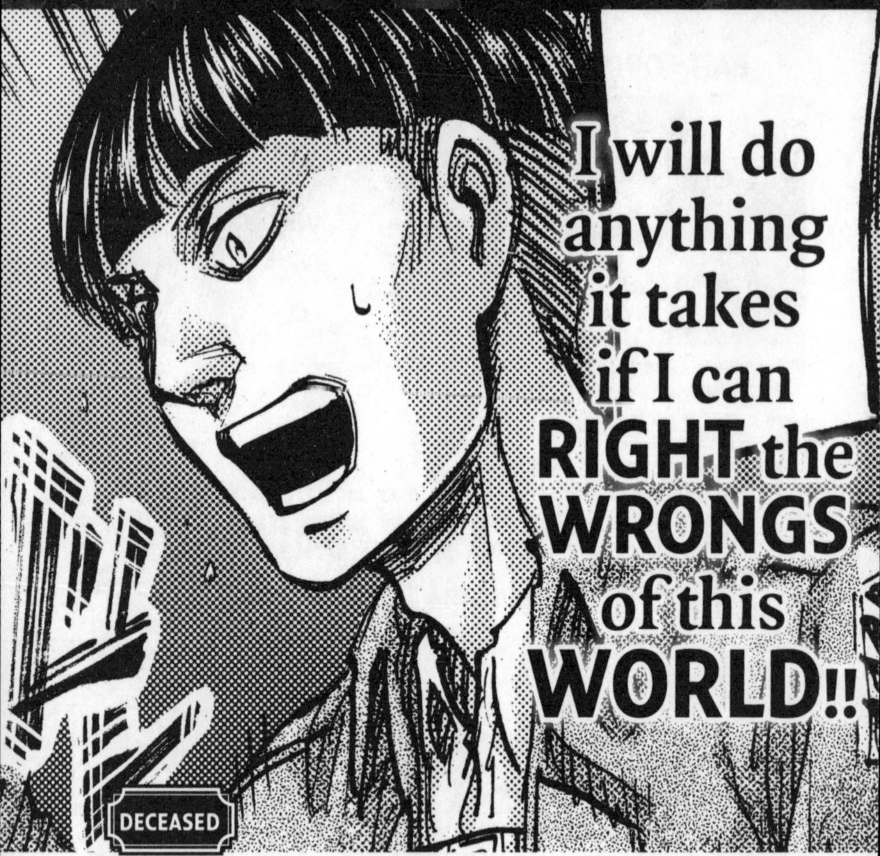
I will do anything it takes if I can RIGHT the WRONGS of this WORLD!!
DECEASED

MARLOWE FREUDENBERG

BIRTHDAY: February 28 • **HEIGHT:** 178 cm (5'10") • **WEIGHT:** 66 kg (146 lbs)
AFFILIATION: Survey Corps

Gave up his life to the Survey Corps, objecting to the way the Royal Government acted

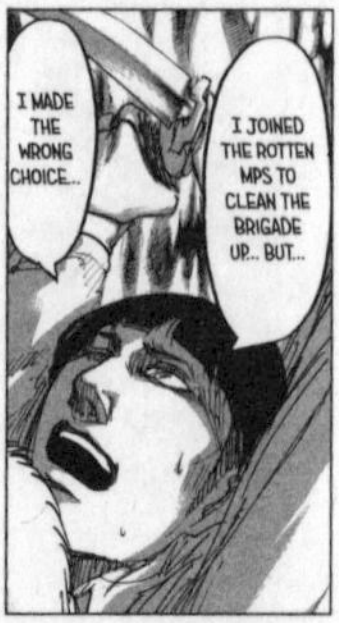
I JOINED THE ROTTEN MPS TO CLEAN THE BRIGADE UP... BUT...
I MADE THE WRONG CHOICE...

Marlowe was a recruit who joined the Military Police Brigade in order to pursue his ideals of righting the injustices of the world. But when the Royal Government falsely accused the Survey Corps of going around and killing civilians, he decided to cooperate with Levi. He later transferred into the Survey Corps, but died in battle before reaching his goals in the struggle for Shiganshina District (Volume 20, Episode 81).

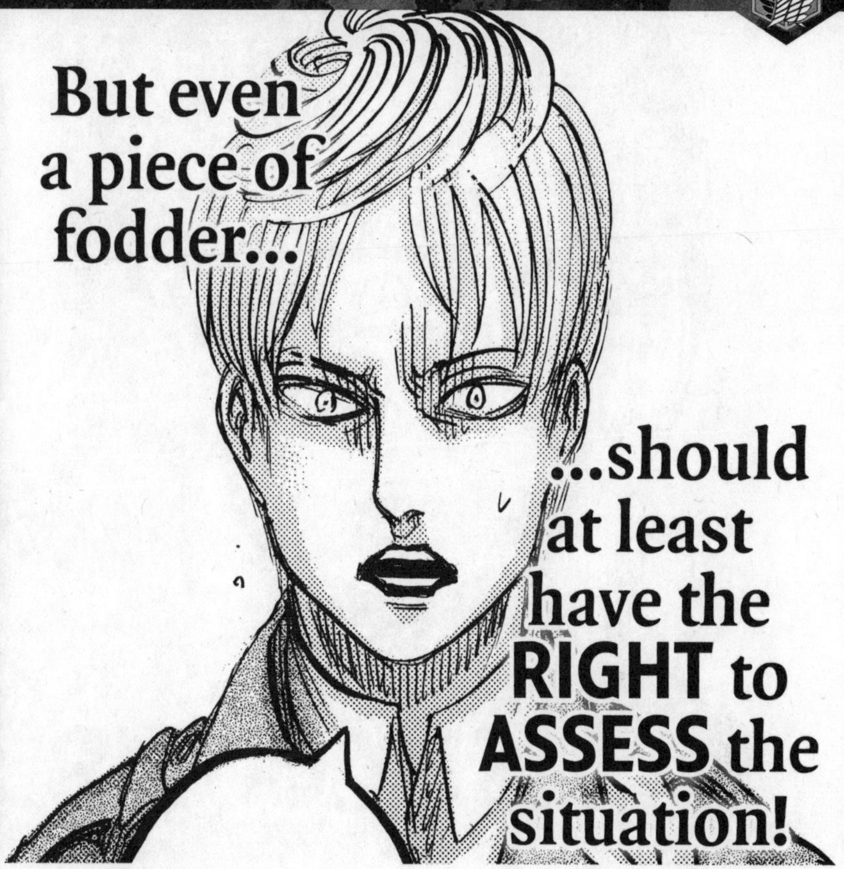
But even a piece of fodder...
...should at least have the RIGHT to ASSESS the situation!

FLOCH

BIRTHDAY: October 8 • **HEIGHT:** 175 cm (5'9")
WEIGHT: 65 kg (143 lbs)
AFFILIATION: Survey Corps

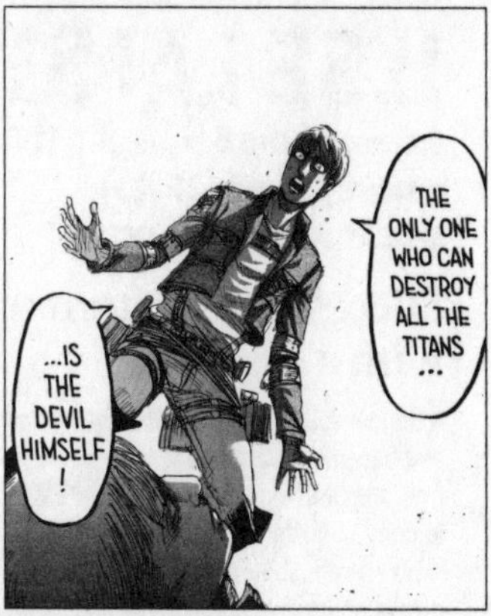
THE ONLY ONE WHO CAN DESTROY ALL THE TITANS...
...IS THE DEVIL HIMSELF!

A new recruit who stands against Eren and the others after being faced with Erwin's death

Floch is a new Survey Corps recruit who participates in the decisive battle in Shiganshina District. When he survives, he confronts Eren during the debate to revive a critically wounded Erwin, saying that "The only one who can destroy all the Titans is the devil!" (Volume 21, Episode 84 and more).

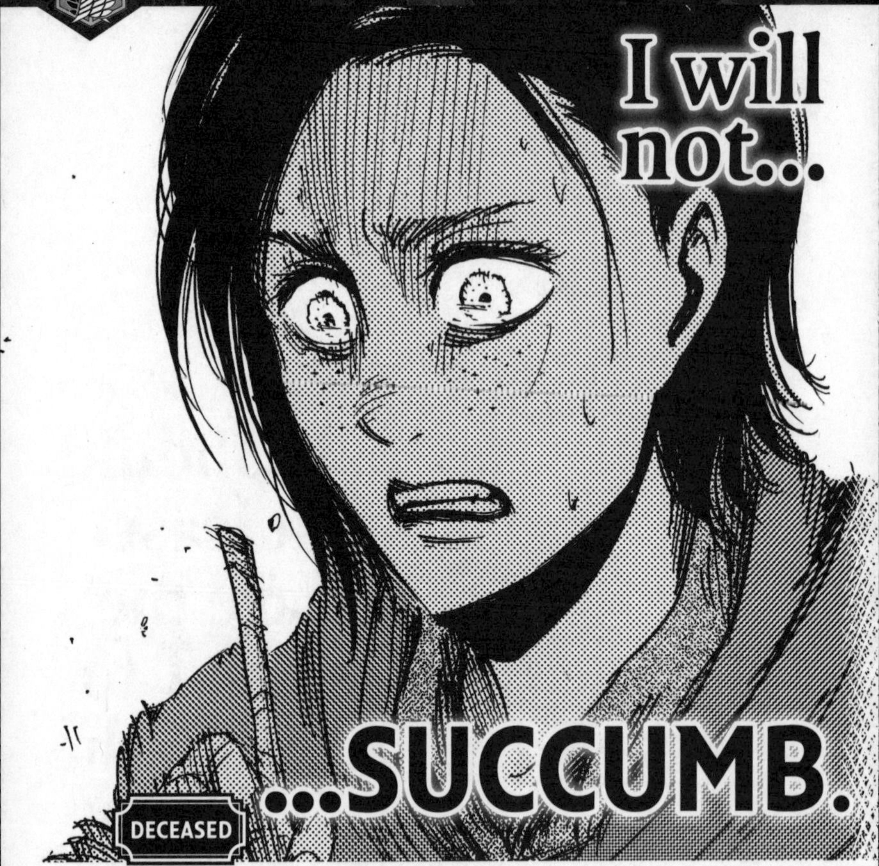
I will not...
...SUCCUMB.

DECEASED

ILSE LANGNAR

BIRTHDAY: June 6 • **HEIGHT:** 160 cm (5'3")
WEIGHT: 58 kg (128 lbs)
AFFILIATION: Survey Corps

Successfully communicates with a Titan

A female soldier who lost track of her fellow Corpsmen and became isolated from her team while returning from the 34th expedition outside the Wall. She was able to communicate her intentions with the 6-meter-class Titan she encountered in the forest, and she recorded the details of the incident in her notebook (Special Episode in Volume 5).

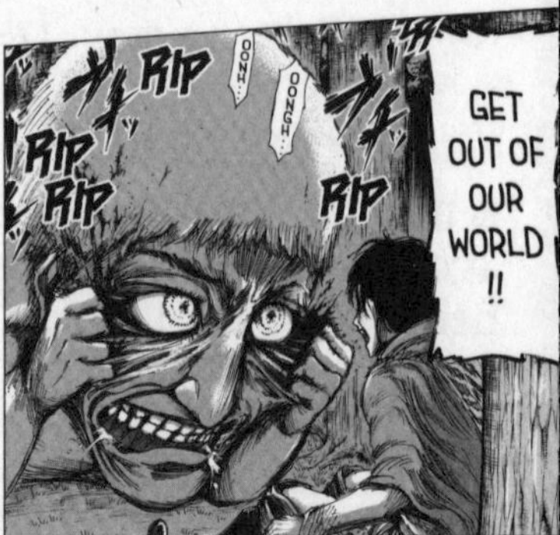
GET OUT OF OUR WORLD !!
OONGH...
OONH...
RIP
RIP
RIP
RIP

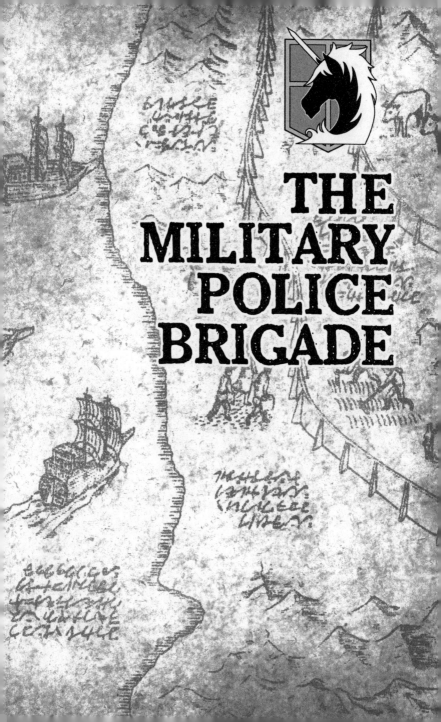

THE
MILITARY
POLICE
BRIGADE

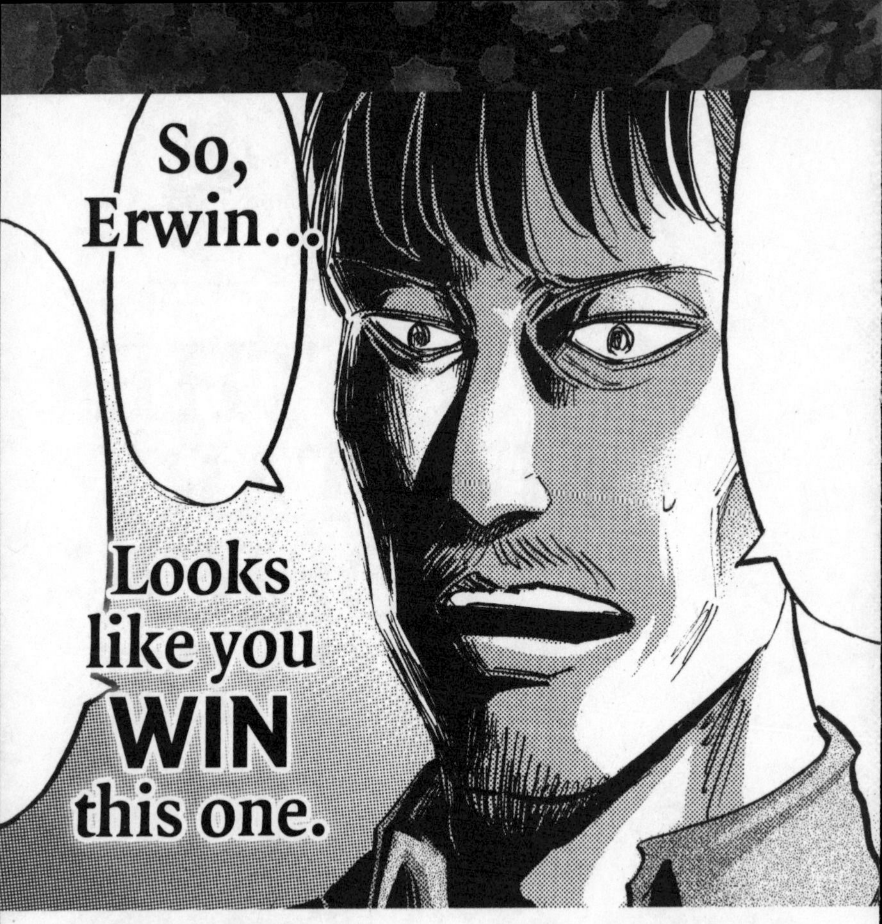
So, Erwin...
Looks like you WIN this one.

NILE DOK

BIRTHDAY: November 1 • **HEIGHT:** 177 cm (5'10")
WEIGHT: 80 kg (176 lbs)
AFFILIATION: Chief of the Military Police Brigade

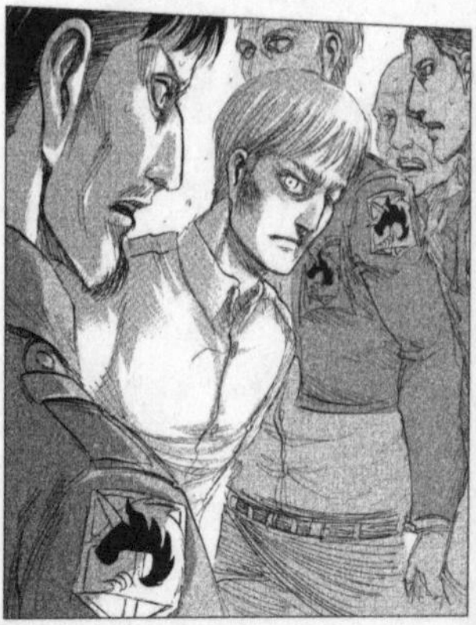

Joins the forces opposing the Royal Government after seeing Erwin's determination

Nile was friends with Erwin during their days together in the Training Corps. However, after he was assigned to the Military Police Brigade, Nile and Erwin often clashed due to their respective positions. But when Nile sees Erwin's resolve during the coup inside the Walls, along with the dark side of the Royal Government, he decides to help destroy the ruling order (Volume 15, Episode 61 and more).

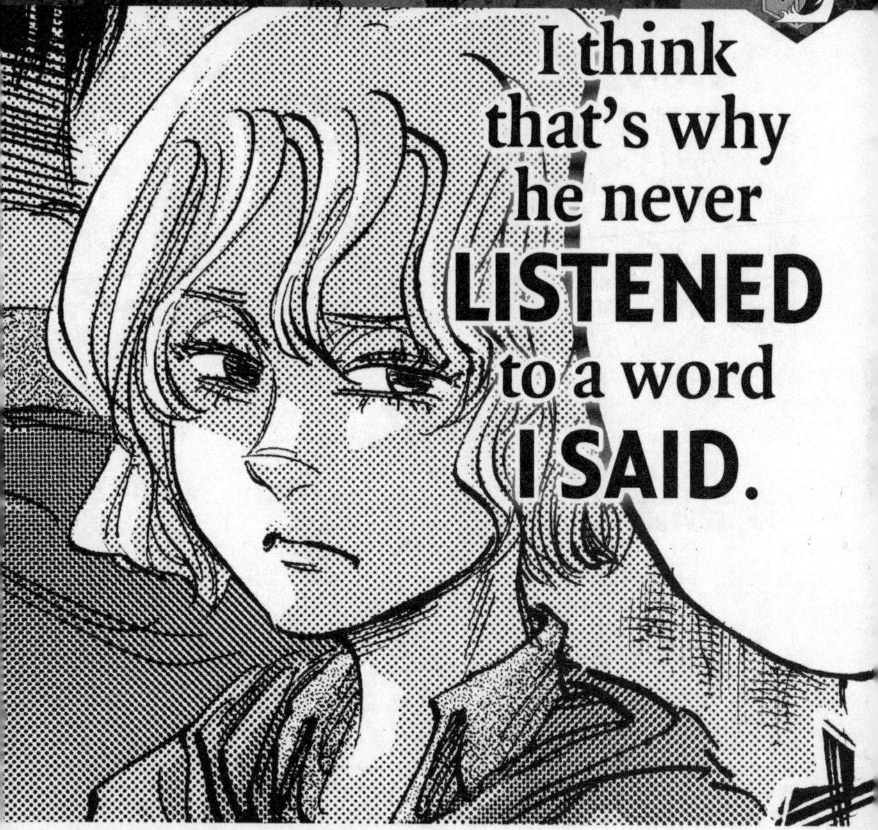
I think that's why he never LISTENED to a word I SAID.

HITCH DREYSE

BIRTHDAY: May 10 • **HEIGHT:** 168 cm (5'6") • **WEIGHT:** 53 kg (117 lbs)
AFFILIATION: Military Police Brigade

Left speechless when Marlowe, a man who lived by his ideals, dies

Hitch is a young female recruit who, unable to let Marlowe go alone, follows him when he cooperates with the Survey Corps. While she returns to the Military Police Brigade after the fall of the Royal Government, she is left speechless after hearing about Marlowe's final moments from Floch (Volume 22, Episode 90 and more).

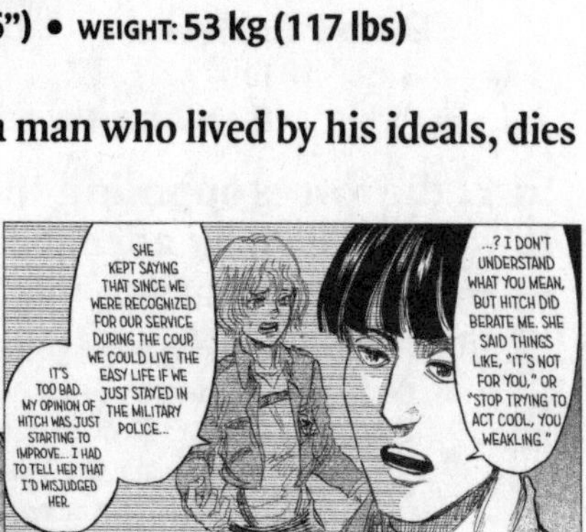
...? I DON'T UNDERSTAND WHAT YOU MEAN, BUT HITCH DID BERATE ME. SHE SAID THINGS LIKE, "IT'S NOT FOR YOU," OR "STOP TRYING TO ACT COOL, YOU WEAKLING."
SHE KEPT SAYING THAT SINCE WE WERE RECOGNIZED FOR OUR SERVICE DURING THE COUP, WE COULD LIVE THE EASY LIFE IF WE JUST STAYED IN THE MILITARY POLICE...
IT'S TOO BAD. MY OPINION OF HITCH WAS JUST STARTING TO IMPROVE... I HAD TO TELL HER THAT I'D MISJUDGED HER.

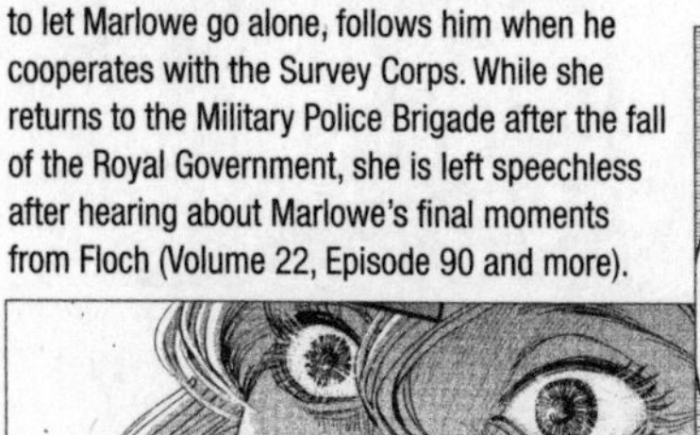

EREN'S JAILER

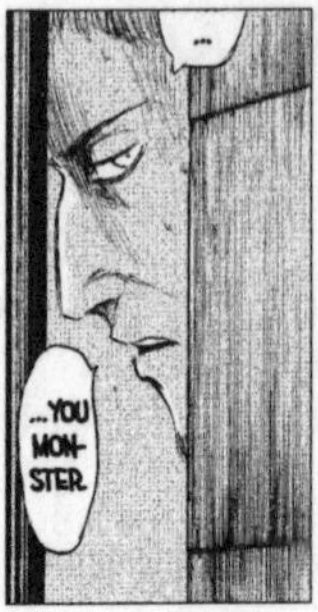
...
...YOU MON-STER

A man who stands watch over Eren, suspected of being an enemy of humanity after turning into a Titan. He treats Eren like a monster and responds to him with cold cruelty.

INVESTIGATING MPS A AND B

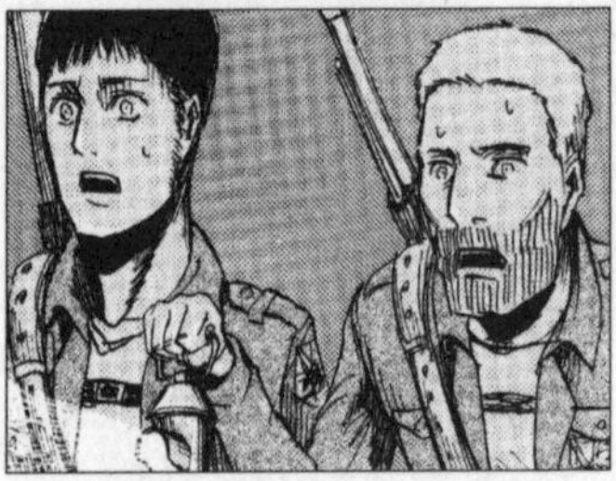

Both are terrified after seeing corpses of the robbers that a young Eren and Mikasa fought off.

MPS A AND B WHO INVESTIGATE THE VERTICAL MANEUVERING EQUIPMENT

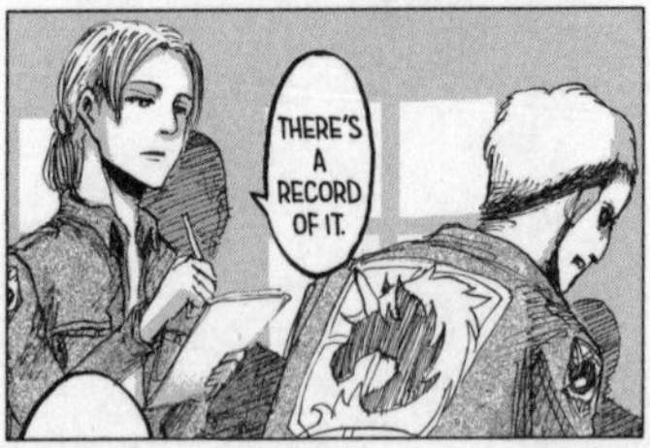
THERE'S A RECORD OF IT.

Both conduct an investigation in order to find the culprit behind Sonny and Bean's murder.

SETTLEMENT MP

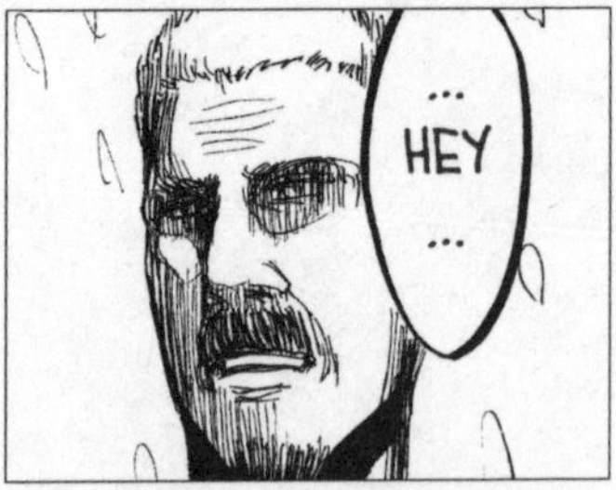
... HEY ...

An MP who supervises the refugees living in a settlement. Arrogant and unpopular.

BORIS FEULNER

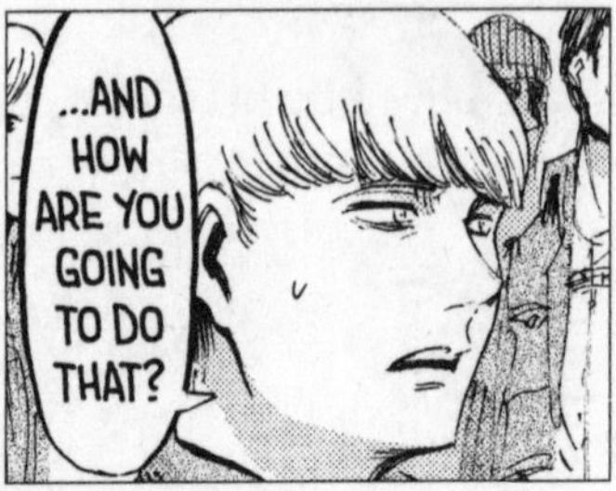
...AND HOW ARE YOU GOING TO DO THAT?

Boris can't help but sneer at Marlowe's upright and sincere attitude.

MARLOWE'S SUPERIOR

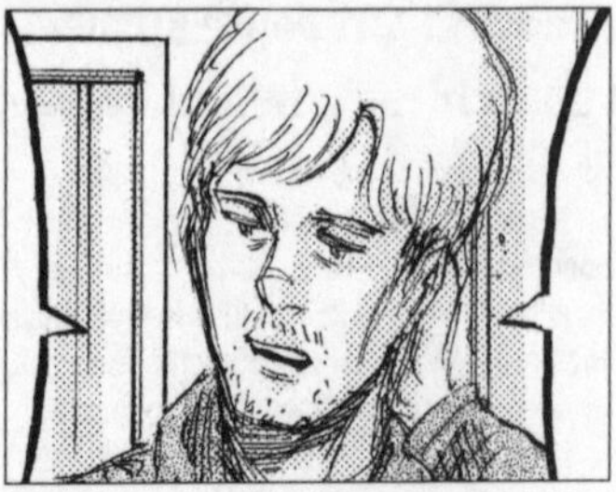

His post in the interior has made him forget the threat of the Titans, and he now lives a life of sloth.

THE MILITARY POLICE BRIGADE

REINFORCING MPS A AND B

These two join up with the Survey Corps after reports that Titans have appeared inside the Walls.

MARLOWE'S SQUADMATE

Shows puzzlement when Marlowe argues for reforming the Military Police Brigade.

FLYER-DISTRIBUTING MP

Distributes flyers announcing the suspicions that Dimo Reeves was murdered.

REINFORCING MP C

DECEASED

Though he boasted that Titans were just prey to him, he dies tragically at their hands.

SENIOR MP OFFICIALS B AND C

Both voice their opposition to publicly announcing the secrets of the Titans

SENIOR MP OFFICIAL A

EARLIER THAN EXPECTED.

Makes critical statements prior to the retaking of Wall Maria.

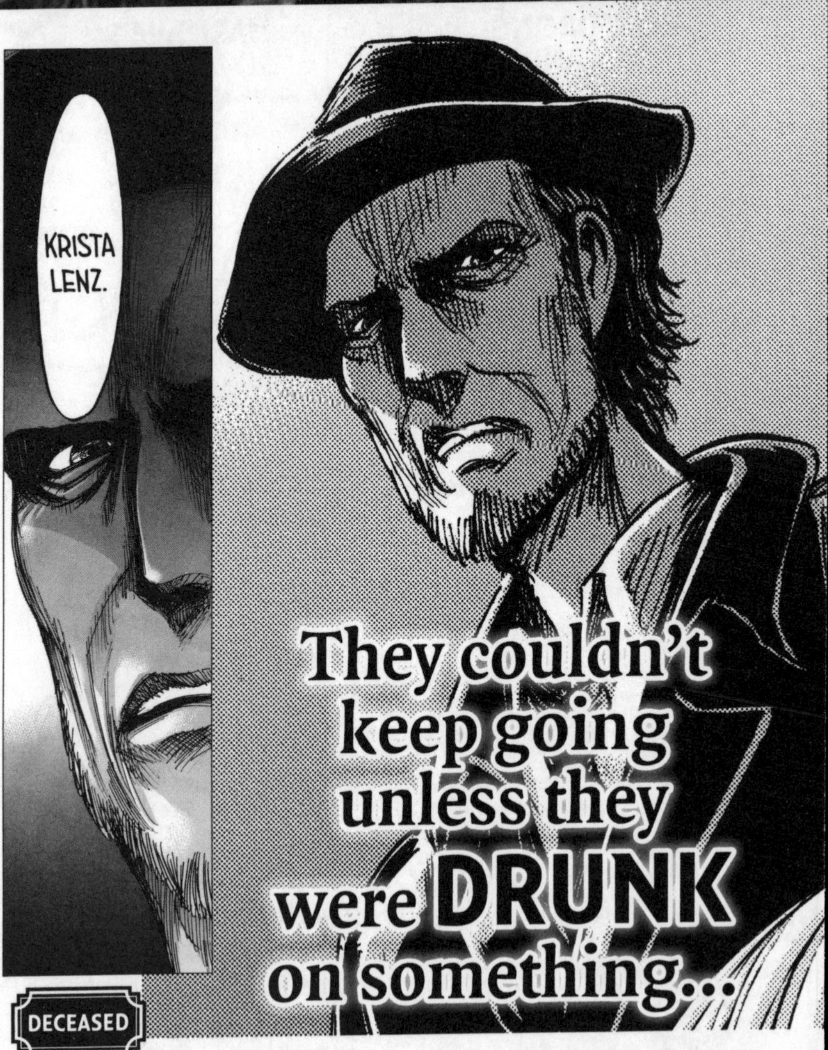
KRISTA LENZ.
They couldn't keep going unless they were DRUNK on something...
DECEASED

KENNY ACKERMAN

BIRTHDAY: February 4 • **HEIGHT:** 190 cm (6'3") • **WEIGHT:** 120 kg (265 lbs)
AFFILIATION: Military Police Brigade First Interior Squad, Anti-Personnel Vertical Maneuvering Unit Captain

THAT'S RIGHT... BEING THE MOST IMPORTANT PERSON IN THIS WORLD MEANS THAT YOU'RE THE MOST POWERFUL PERSON IN IT.
WHAT'S GOIN' ON?
DIDN'T THE ACKERMANS USED TO BE A WARRIOR FAMILY CLOSE TO THE CROWN...?
HOW'D THIS HAPPEN?

Kenny the Ripper, a member of the Ackerman line who raised Levi

To stop the persecution of the Ackerman family, Kenny killed one Reiss family dog after the next, earning himself the feared moniker "Kenny the Ripper." When he was reunited with his missing sister Kuchel, he decided to raise her son Levi (Volume 17, Episode 69 and more).

I WANT TO CREATE A PARADISE...
...FOR THE SURVIVING, WANING REMNANTS OF HUMANITY.
FOUND YA!!
THE LAW'S HERE TO SHOOT DOWN THE BAD GUYS!
BANG!!
BANG!!
STOMP
STOMP

Joined the Interior Squad seeking the same thing that Uri was after

The Reiss family was always a threat to Kenny, so he initially opposed Uri Reiss, the man possessing the immense power of the Founding Titan. However, when the influential Uri bowed his head to a crook like Kenny—in apology for the years of tragedy between their families—Kenny was deeply moved. His odd friendship with Uri was the motivation behind Kenny becoming the leader of the Anti-Personnel Vertical Maneuvering Unit in the Military Police Brigade's Interior Squad (Volume 17, Episode 69 and more).

'CAUSE...
I CAN'T BE SOME KID'S...
...DAD.
THUD

Entrusts Levi with the serum when he realizes he was a slave to power

After losing Uri, Kenny began to seek godlike powers, seeking the same heights as the friend he lost. During his battle with Levi, Kenny realized that he, too, was a slave to power—that he was only waiting for the chance to gain the power of the Titans under Rod Reiss. This moved him to entrust Levi with the syringe containing the power to transform a human into a Titan (Volume 17, Episode 69 and more).

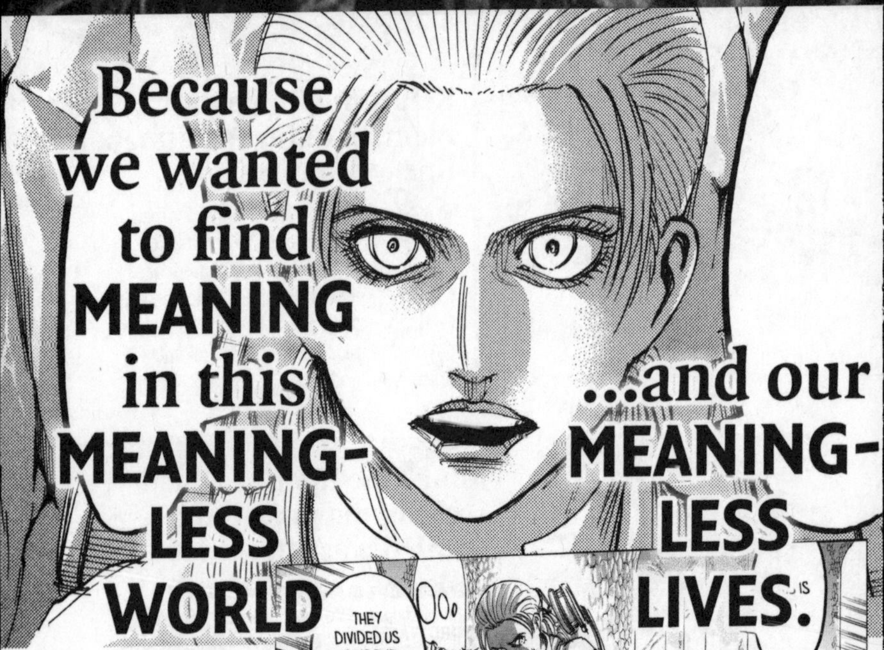
Because we wanted to find MEANING in this MEANING-LESS WORLD...
...and our MEANING-LESS LIVES.

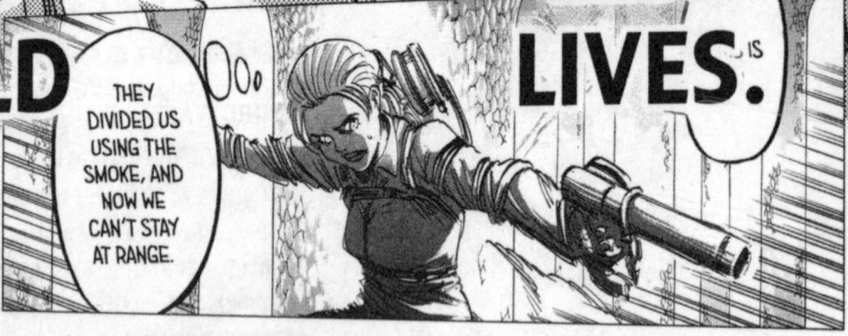
THEY DIVIDED US USING THE SMOKE, AND NOW WE CAN'T STAY AT RANGE.

DECEASED

TRAUTE CAVEN

BIRTHDAY: February 14 • **HEIGHT:** 172 cm (5'8") • **WEIGHT:** 65 kg (143 lbs)
AFFILIATION: Military Police Brigade First Interior Squad, Anti-Personnel Vertical Maneuvering Unit

Aligns herself with Kenny's dream of upending the world, cooperating with him in her own way

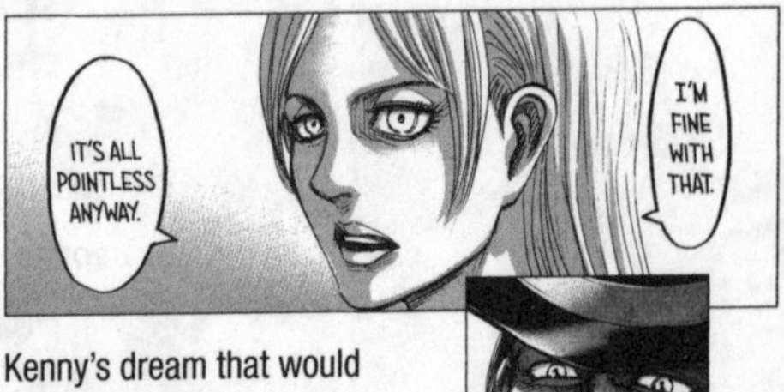
I'M FINE WITH THAT.
IT'S ALL POINTLESS ANYWAY.

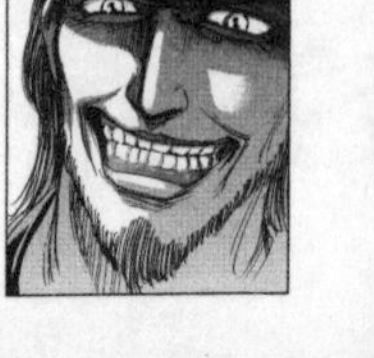

A female soldier who aligned herself with Kenny's dream that would "grab the world by its roots and flip it upside down" and joined the Anti-Personnel Vertical Maneuvering Unit in order to find meaning in a meaningless world. While she acted as the unit's second-in-command, she died when the underground area in Lord Reiss's territory collapsed (Volume 16, Episode 64 and more).

FEMALE SOLDIER SHOT AND KILLED BY ARMIN

DECEASED

Died when her humanity got in the way and she hesitated to kill Jean.

SOLDIER WITH A SHAVED HEAD

DECEASED

A soldier who carried out Kenny's plan together with Traute.

Kenny's Soldiers Who Died in the Fight in the City

KENNY'S SUBORDINATE A

DECEASED

DURAN

DECEASED

KENNY'S SUBORDINATE D

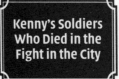

DECEASED

KENNY'S SUBORDINATE C

DECEASED

KENNY'S SUBORDINATE B

DECEASED

Kenny's Soldiers Who Died in the Final Underground Battle

KENNY'S SUBORDINATE F

DECEASED

KENNY'S SUBORDINATE E

DECEASED

The pursuit of Levi kicks off a fierce battle in the city with Jean and Armin that then leads into another encounter in an underground cavern where all of these individuals die.

KENNY'S SUBORDINATE H

DECEASED

KENNY'S SUBORDINATE G

DECEASED

DJEL SANNES

BIRTHDAY: October 28
HEIGHT: 183 cm (6'0")
WEIGHT: 76 kg (168 lbs)
AFFILIATION: Military Police Brigade First Interior Squad

Though he participated in many atrocities in order to preserve the Royal Government...

As a member of the Interior Squad from a young age, Djel tortured and killed many rebellious members in order to preserve the Royal Government. We can tell by his memories that he was involved in the deaths of Erwin's father, Armin's parents, and even Historia's mother (Volume 14, Episode 55).

I HAVE THE KING...
I PROTECTED THE KING TOGETHER WITH MY COMRADES... FOR YEARS...

SANNES'S ASSOCIATE

MISTER SANNES!

BIRTHDAY: April 19
HEIGHT: 175 cm (5'9") WEIGHT: 65 KG (143 LBS)
AFFILIATION: Military Police Brigade First Interior Squad

Falling for Dimo's convincing performance, this soldier requests a search party for Sannes's group when they fall into a valley (Volume 13, Episode 54).

RALPH

BIRTHDAY: August 26
HEIGHT: 177 cm (5'10") WEIGHT: 71 kg (157 lbs)
AFFILIATION: Military Police Brigade First Interior Squad

An MP captured by the Survey Corps at the same time as Sannes. He falls for Hange's trap, which makes him betray Sannes (Volume 14, Episode 55)

THE MUSTACHIOED MAN

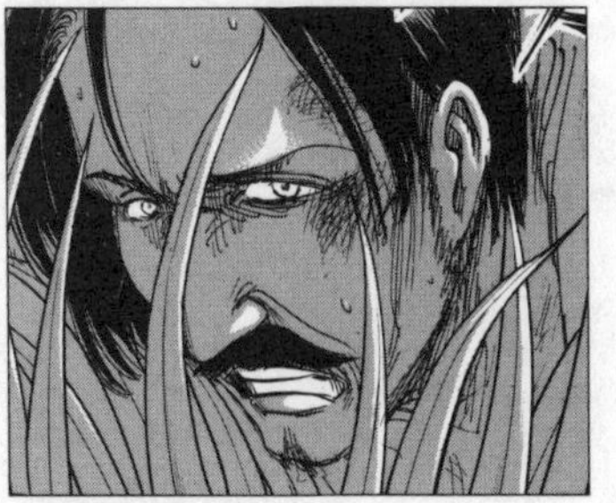

BIRTHDAY: September 21
HEIGHT: 187 cm (6'2") **WEIGHT:** 72 kg (159 lbs)
AFFILIATION: Military Police Brigade First Interior Squad

A man taken out of the Interior Squad's headquarters by Levi and the others. He continues to believe in the Royal Government's superiority, even when tortured (Volume 15, Episode 60 and more).

INTERIOR SQUAD SOLDIER

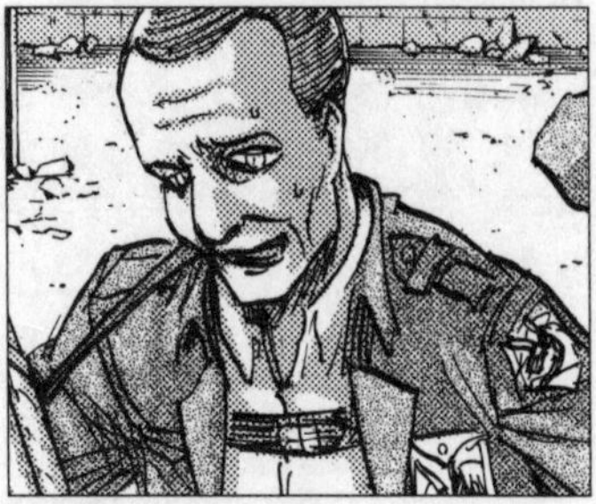

BIRTHDAY: September 21
HEIGHT: 173 cm (5'8") **WEIGHT:** 68 kg (150 lbs)
AFFILIATION: Military Police Brigade First Interior Squad

He is with Kenny when Dimo is murdered. He shows his theatrical side when lured out by Flegel (Volume 15, Episode 60).

COLUMN Sannes, a Man Who Swore His Loyalty, Infatuated With the King

While he was an Interior Squad soldier, Sannes's torture victims included even regular citizens. He respected and revered the crown, and Uri in particular. Though his cruel actions may be hard to comprehend, the fact that he killed the king's enemies gave him a sense of pride. He thought that together with his friends, he was protecting the crown.

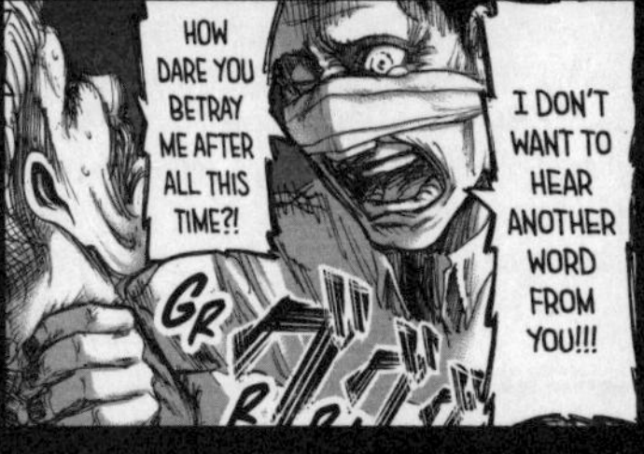
HOW DARE YOU BETRAY ME AFTER ALL THIS TIME?!
I DON'T WANT TO HEAR ANOTHER WORD FROM YOU!!!

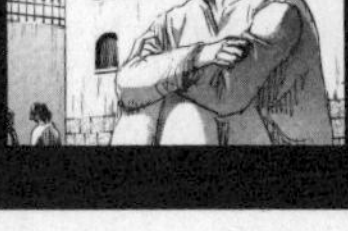

He feels a deep sense of despair at himself after betraying the king. What is going on in his head behind the softened expression he shows while imprisoned?

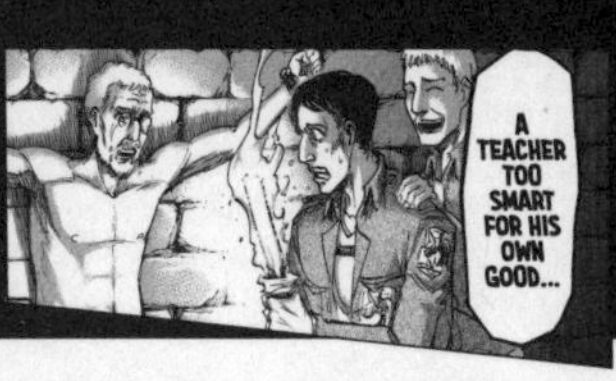
A TEACHER TOO SMART FOR HIS OWN GOOD...

HAJIME ISAYAMA Reveals

How His CHARACTERS WERE BORN: Part 2

MIKASA ACKERMAN

Mikasa is based off of a customer at a store where I used to work part-time. I needed to come up with looks for the characters of *Attack on Titan* back then, and so I was always thinking about my characters while on the job. Just in that moment, we had a customer who made me think, "that's her!" I remember that the moment I saw her, I scribbled her most notable points on the back of a nearby receipt, "scarf, hair like this, slightly thick eyebrows, thin eyes." I had thought that Mikasa would be a Western character until that point, but these characteristics were what caused me to make her an Asian character.

As I had yet to decide on where the story would go, I was still wondering whether the title should have two main characters or one. It ended up being three characters because I wanted to spread the traits of intelligence, bravery, and power to different characters. Mikasa became the character with power because of the feeling I had about how it would be interesting if a *tokusatsu* show had a female character acting as the leading red ranger.

As for her name, I heard that a title will succeed if you name your female lead after a battleship, and so I used the name of the Japanese battleship Mikasa. "Ackerman" is a German word for "someone who works the fields."

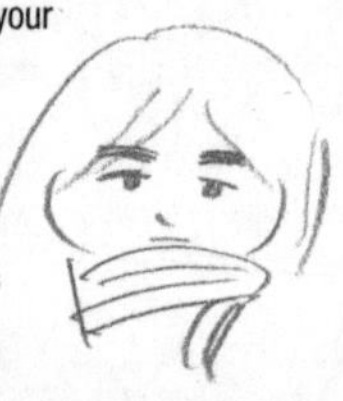

JEAN KIRSTEIN

A character that appeared in the very first *Attack on Titan*, which received an honorable mention in the 2006 Magazine Grand Prix, ended up getting split in two to create Armin and Jean. My original idea was for him to play a heelish role as someone who points out when the protagonists are being deceitful, and this is where Jean's mean face comes from. When Kisho Taniyama, one of my favorite voice actors, agreed to voice him in the television anime, his performance also had a strong effect on Jean's character.

I also really like "Jean" as a name that gives off the sense that he is like a representative of the people. He is the character who has grown the most since the beginning of the series, and while he was hated at first, he is a very true character, thus making him easy to use and fun to draw.

CONNIE SPRINGER

My idea for Connie was that he was like a kid on summer break. At the time, I designed him as a character to just place in the top 10 of the Training Corps. He ended up being a silly goof because he was a young man with an innocent personality.

I picked his first name because "Connie" has a friendly and familiar ring to it. "Springer" comes from the word "spring," which I associate with characteristics like spry and quick.

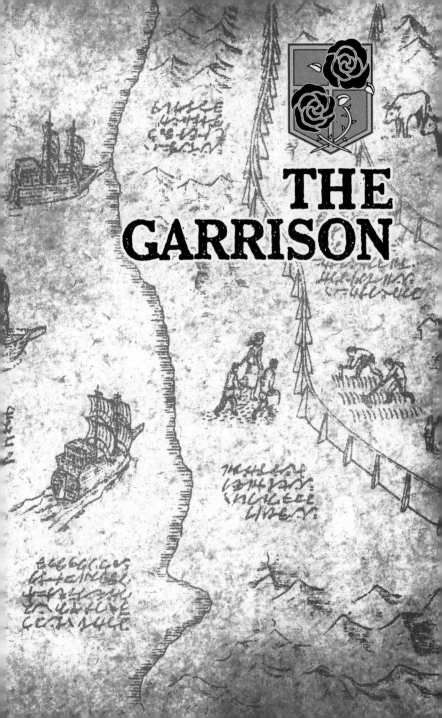

THE
GARRISON

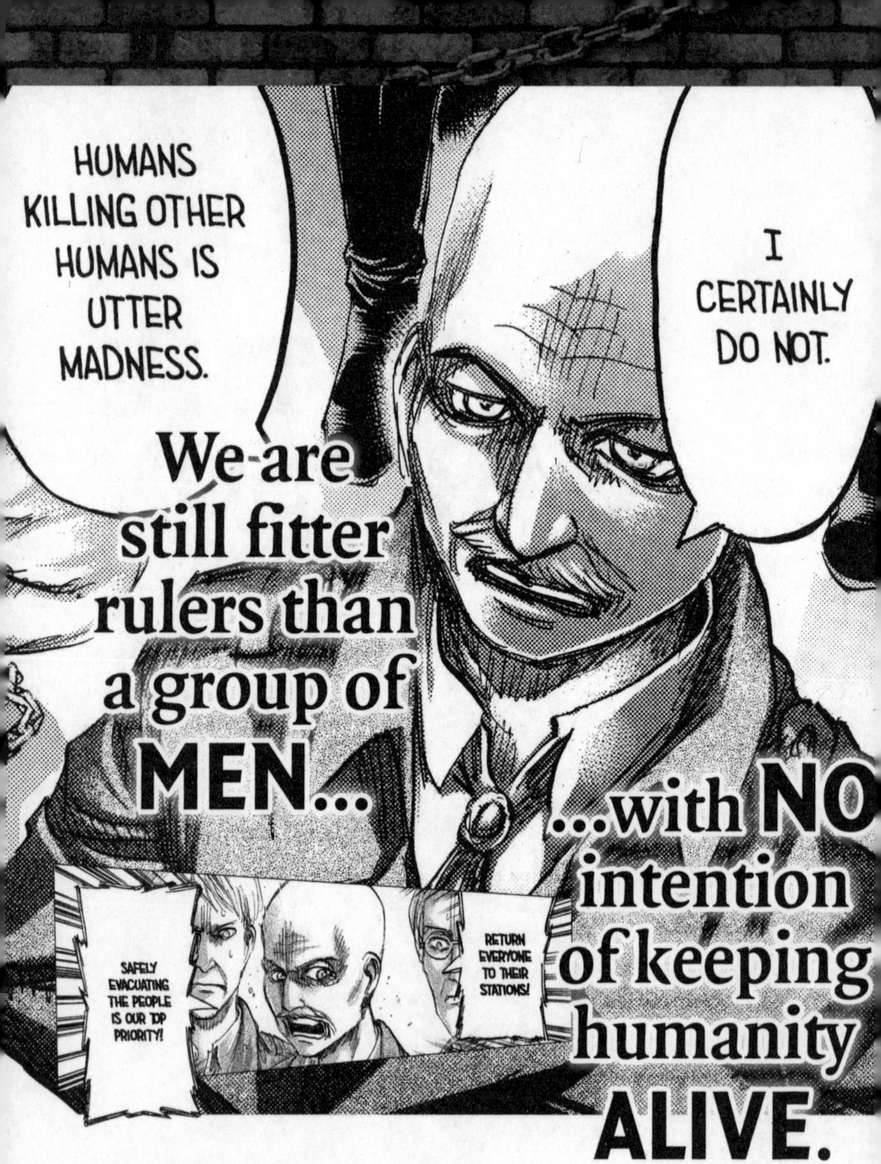
HUMANS KILLING OTHER HUMANS IS UTTER MADNESS.
I CERTAINLY DO NOT.
SAFELY EVACUATING THE PEOPLE IS OUR TOP PRIORITY!
RETURN EVERYONE TO THEIR STATIONS!
We are still fitter rulers than a group of MEN...
...with NO intention of keeping humanity ALIVE.

DOT PIXIS

BIRTHDAY: September 13 • HEIGHT: 180 cm (5'11") • WEIGHT: 73 kg (161 lbs)
AFFILIATION: Garrison, Chief Official of the Southern Territories

The Chief Official of the Southern Territories who takes the future of humanity seriously

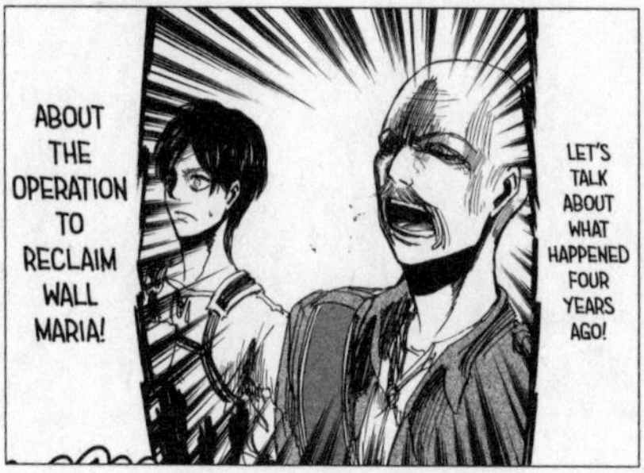
LET'S TALK ABOUT WHAT HAPPENED FOUR YEARS AGO!
ABOUT THE OPERATION TO RECLAIM WALL MARIA!

The most senior officer responsible for the soldiers in the Southern Territories, which falls under Titan attack. He is such a flexible thinker that he is able to take a recruit's opinions (Armin's) into consideration if it means finding a way to victory. He is also a natural eccentric who boasts that he wouldn't mind being eaten by a Titan so long as it is a gorgeous one (Volume 3, Episode 12).

Though he tries to avoid infighting among men...

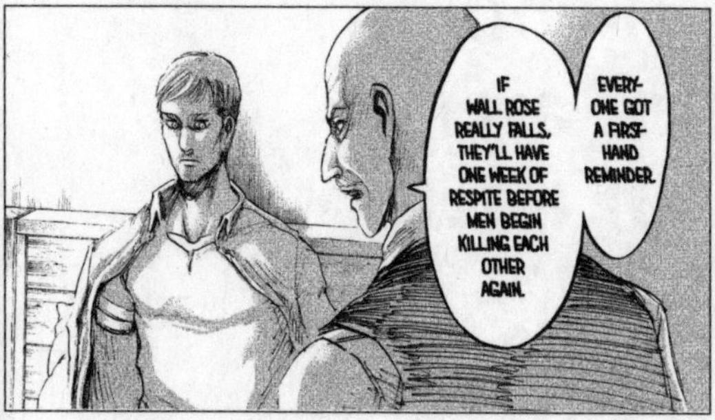
EVERY-ONE GOT A FIRST-HAND REMINDER.
IF WALL ROSE REALLY FALLS, THEY'LL HAVE ONE WEEK OF RESPITE BEFORE MEN BEGIN KILLING EACH OTHER AGAIN.

Pixis wishes for humanity to come together in the face of the Titan threat. However, when the Beast Titan appears inside Wall Rose, he sees the mass confusion that occurs. He is forced to understand that in emergencies, conflict between humans is impossible to avoid (Volume 13, Episode 51).

After seeing Erwin's determination, he becomes a leader in overthrowing the Royal Government

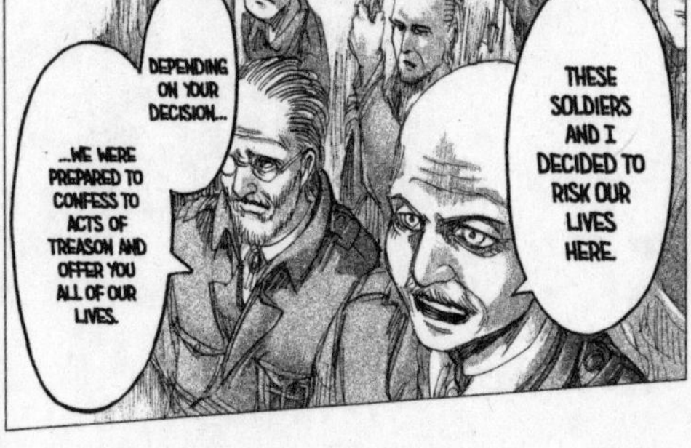
THESE SOLDIERS AND I DECIDED TO RISK OUR LIVES HERE.
DEPENDING ON YOUR DECISION...
...WE WERE PREPARED TO CONFESS TO ACTS OF TREASON AND OFFER YOU ALL OF OUR LIVES.

Pixis is not enthusiastic at first about Erwin's plans for a coup. However, when the Royal Government hears Anka's false report of a Titan attack and begins to make plans to ensure the Royal Capital's safety over the lives of any evacuees, Pixis rises against them in revolt (Volume 15, Episode 61).

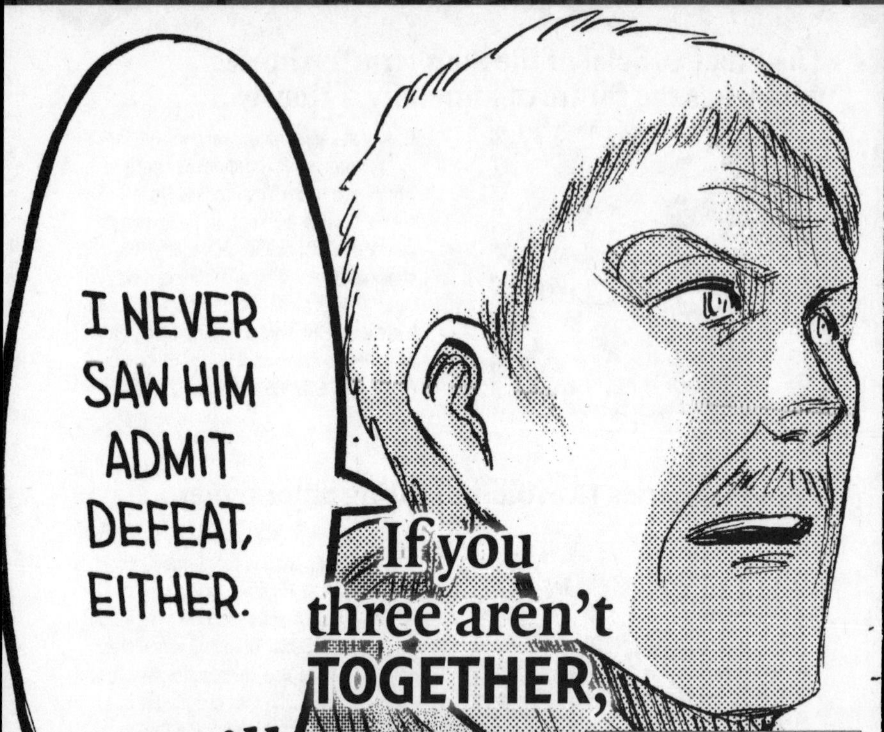
I NEVER SAW HIM ADMIT DEFEAT, EITHER.

If you three aren't **TOGETHER**, we'll never see those old **DAYS** again.

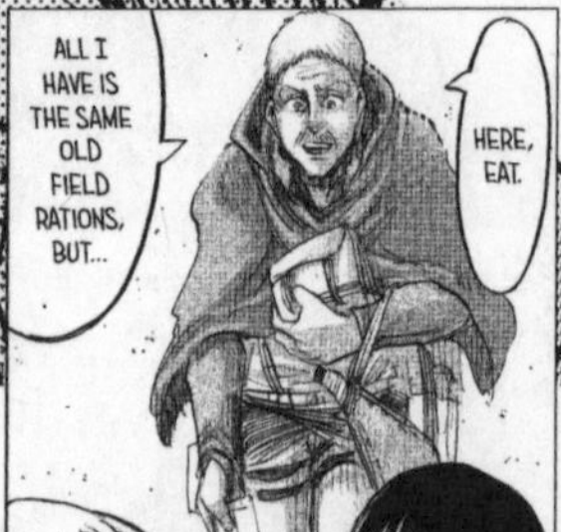
ALL I HAVE IS THE SAME OLD FIELD RATIONS, BUT...
HERE, EAT.

DECEASED

HANNES

BIRTHDAY: January 18 • **HEIGHT:** 190 cm (6'3") • **WEIGHT:** 88 kg (194 lbs)
AFFILIATION: Garrison Captain

UNTIL YOU OR I GET THERE.
EREN'S ALWAYS BEEN LIKE THAT, RIGHT?

A man who watched over Eren and friends since they were little

Before the Colossus Titan appeared in Shiganshina District, Hannes was used to day-drinking and feeling no sense of danger whatsoever (Volume 1, Episode 1). He grew as a soldier after the fall of Shiganshina District, gaining the trust of Eren, Mikasa, and Armin, all while encouraging them (Volume 11, Episode 45 and more).

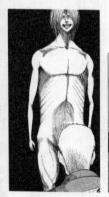

His regret about what happened that day never left his heart

DID MIKASA GET MAD AT YOU FOR SOME-THING?
HUH?! WHAT MAKES YOU THINK I'M CRYING?!
YOU REEK OF LIQUOR !!

Hannes always regretted not being able to save Eren's mother Carla from a Pure Titan. Hannes fought with his life on the line in order to get back those peaceful days when he drunkenly joked around with a young, angry Eren (Volume 11, Episode 45 and more).

When he faced the Pure Titan once more, he fought it with everything he had and died

RAAGH !!
SLICE
HAH!! HOW OFTEN DO YOU GET A CHANCE LIKE THIS?!
RIGHT,
YOU TWO ?!!

When Hannes faced the same Pure Titan from inside Wall Rose, he went to attack it alone. This act may have been his way of saying goodbye to the person he was during the fall of Shiganshina, when he turned his back and fled out of fear (Volume 12, Episode 50).

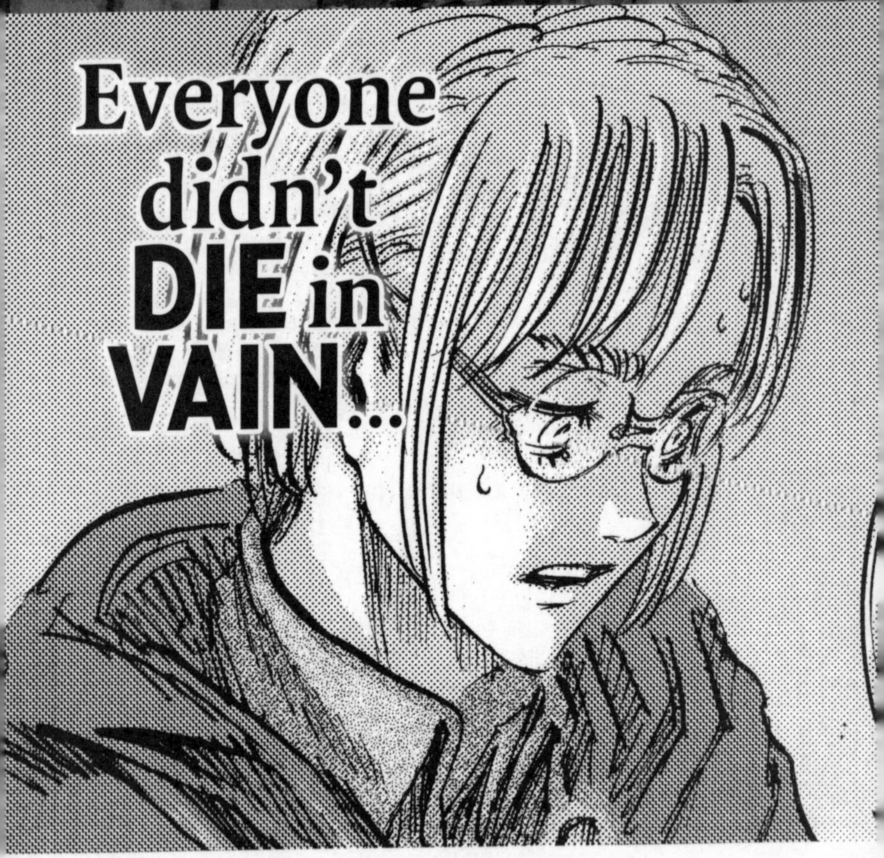
Everyone didn't DIE in VAIN...

RICO BRZENSKA

BIRTHDAY: December 7 • **HEIGHT:** 156 cm (5'1") • **WEIGHT:** 52 kg (115 lbs)
AFFILIATION: Garrison Squad Leader

A Garrison elite who even participated in the battle for Trost District

During the battle for Trost District, Squad Leader Rico shows strong misgivings about the plan that places Eren at its center. She is one of the few survivors of the plan. Later, she meets with survivors who fought the Titans during the melee inside Wall Rose (Volume 13, Episode 51 and more).

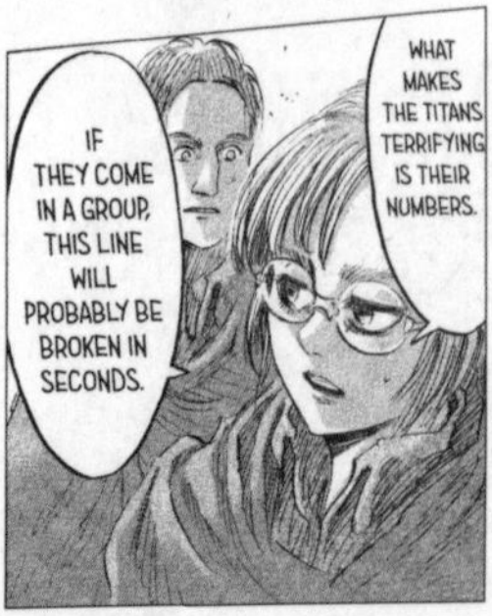
WHAT MAKES THE TITANS TERRIFYING IS THEIR NUMBERS.
IF THEY COME IN A GROUP, THIS LINE WILL PROBABLY BE BROKEN IN SECONDS.

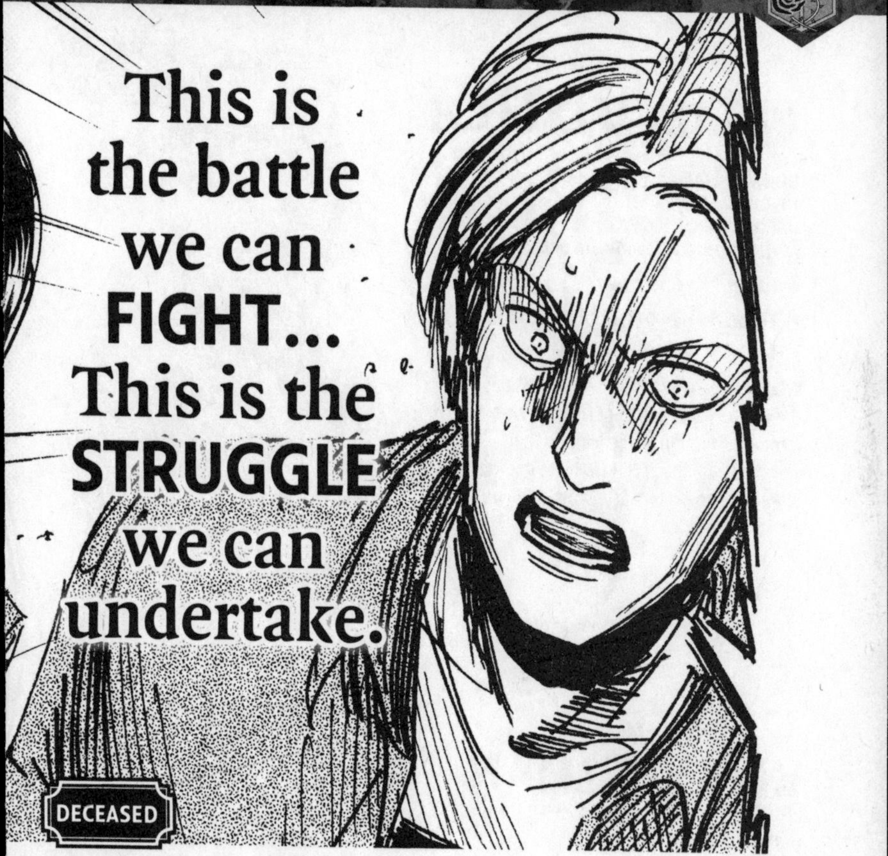
This is the battle we can FIGHT... This is the STRUGGLE we can undertake.
DECEASED

IAN DIETRICH

BIRTHDAY: March 10 • **HEIGHT:** 188 cm (6'2") • **WEIGHT:** 82 kg (181 lbs)
AFFILIATION: Garrison Squad Leader

A man who pulled Rico and the others forward, sacrificing his life for the sake of Trost District

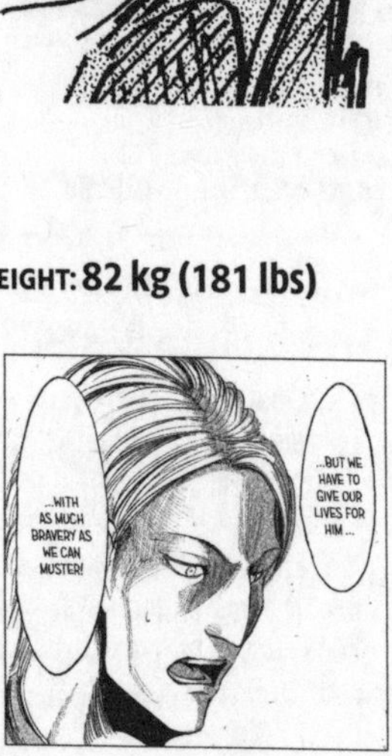
...BUT WE HAVE TO GIVE OUR LIVES FOR HIM...
...WITH AS MUCH BRAVERY AS WE CAN MUSTER!

Ian encouraged Rico and the others when they hesitated to carry out the plan set out for the battle for Trost District. Even though they seemed to be at an overwhelming disadvantage, he stated that to struggle is to fight. He eventually offered himself as bait and died in order to protect Eren's Titan (Volume 4, Episode 14).

MITABI JARNACH

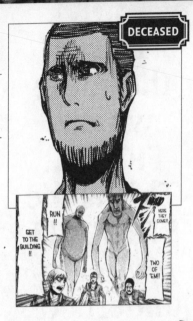

BIRTHDAY: February 20
HEIGHT: 191 cm (6'3")
WEIGHT: 81 kg (179 lbs)
AFFILIATION: Garrison Squad Leader

A man who protected Eren's Titan by acting as bait

When Mitabi saw Eren's immobile Titan during the battle for Trost District, he ordered a retreat from the battlefield. He then screamed curses at the Titans to get their attention and protect Eren's Titan (Volume 4, Episode 14).

DECEASED

HERE THEY COME!!
TWO OF 'EM!!
RUN !!
GET TO THE BUILDING !!

KITZ WEILMAN

BIRTHDAY: August 2
HEIGHT: 195 cm (6'5")
WEIGHT: 110 kg (243 lbs)
AFFILIATION: Garrison Captain

A captain as delicate as a fawn who tries to end Eren

When Kitz learns that the mysterious Titan that appears inside of Trost District is actually Eren, he takes Rico and Ian as he tries to move on his own to eliminate him (Volume 3, Episode 11). Because he is "as delicate as a fawn," according to Pixis, his fear of the Titans causes him to lose his reason and block out Armin's arguments.

I'LL BLOW YOU TO PIECES WITHOUT BATTING AN EYE!
THEY ARE CLEARLY DEFIANT.

GUSTAV

BIRTHDAY: July 20
HEIGHT: 188 cm (6'2")
WEIGHT: 80 kg (176 lbs)
AFFILIATION: Garrison

Participated in the battle for Trost District as Pixis's aide

A soldier who assists Pixis like a second-in-command. He plays an advising role in the battle for Trost District. Along with Armin and Anka, he helped put together the details of the plan to retake the District using Eren's Titan. He is a capable soldier who uses more than simple theory in his plans, considering even the emotional state of the soldiers on the ground (Volume 3, Episode 12 and more).

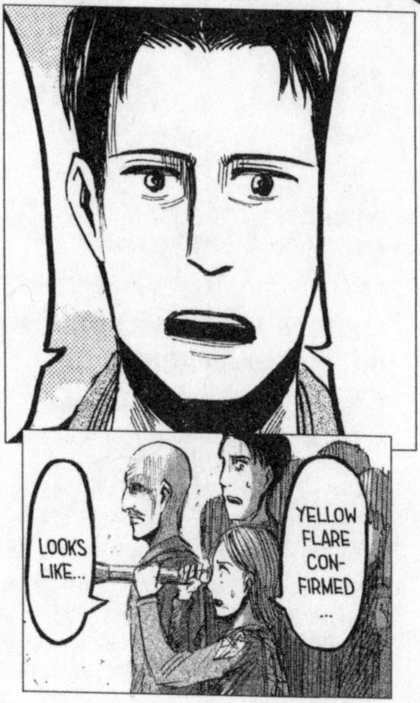
YELLOW FLARE CON-FIRMED ...
LOOKS LIKE...

ANKA

BIRTHDAY: June 1
HEIGHT: 155 cm (5'1")
WEIGHT: 53 kg (117 lbs)
AFFILIATION: Garrison

A female Garrison member who assists Commander Pixis

A soldier who accompanies Pixis, a position she begins to frequently take after helping to plan the battle for Trost District. She even begins to monitor his alcohol intake at times (Volume 13, Episode 51). She plays a role in the overthrow of the Royal Government when she gives the false report about a Titan attack during Erwin's coup attempt (Volume 15, Episode 61).

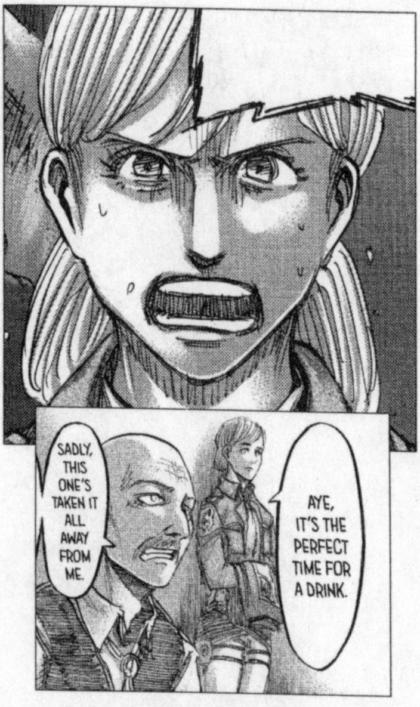
AYE, IT'S THE PERFECT TIME FOR A DRINK.
SADLY, THIS ONE'S TAKEN IT ALL AWAY FROM ME.

PHIL

BIRTHDAY: DECEMBER 28
HEIGHT: 168 CM (5'6")
WEIGHT: 56 KG (123 LBS)
AFFILIATION: GARRISON

Hannes's trusted subordinate, faithful to his mission

Though Phil strongly adheres to the distinction between superiors and subordinates, he shows that he has a compassionate side when he is concerned for the safety of Eren and his friends, who he knows have a deep relationship with Hannes. He acts as a messenger when it is revealed that Reiner, Bertolt, and Ymir from the 104th Training Corps are Titans, communicating the information to Pixis and others (Volume 11, Episode 45).

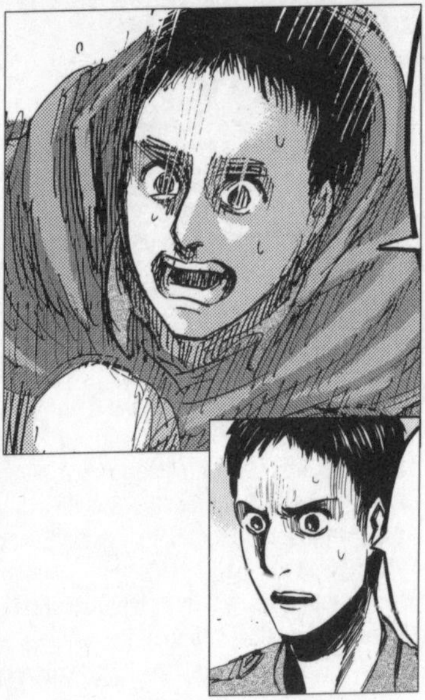

COLUMN: The Cherished Happy Days of the "Wall Construction Corps"

Discipline had grown lax among Hannes and his friends, a group Eren called the "Wall Construction Corps" (Volume 1, Episode 1). However, the world suddenly changed when the Colossus Titan appeared. Hannes later reminisces, saying "I'd do anything to get those quiet, dull days back..." (Volume 11, Episode 45).

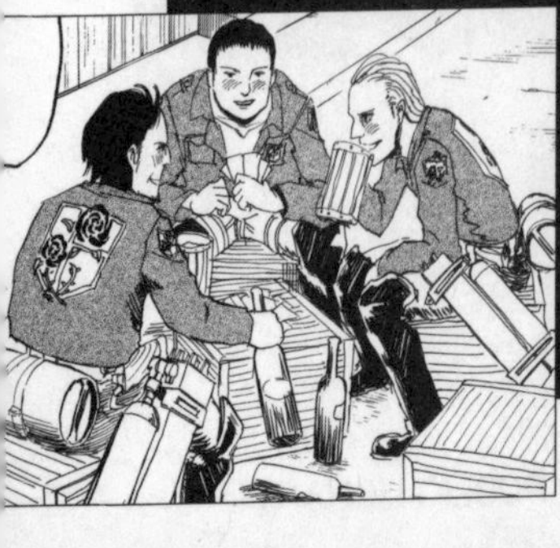

FUGO

This man helped Hannes repair the wall in Shiganshina District before the appearance of the Colossus Titan. Having grown complacent after a hundred-year history of peace within the Walls, drinking on the job was a regular part of life for him (Volume 1, Episode 1).

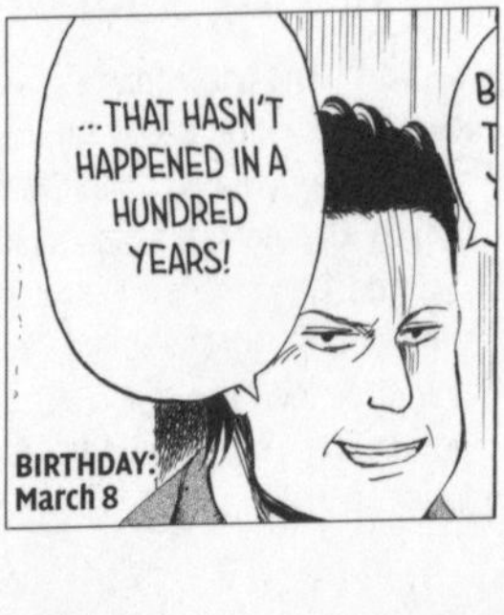
...THAT HASN'T HAPPENED IN A HUNDRED YEARS!

BIRTHDAY: March 8

THE GARRISON

GARRISON OFFICER A

An officer who defends Trost District while leading the Training Corps.

ADVANCE TEAM SOLDIER

A soldier who appears in front of Eren and friends when they encounter the Colossus Titan while servicing the wall-mounted artillery. He orders anyone who came in contact with the Colossus Titan to report to HQ before heading into battle (Volume 1, Episode 4).

GARRISON SOLDIER YELLED AT BY REEVES

This soldier is unable to do anything about Reeves when he gets in the way of the evacuation.

WALL-MOUNTED ARTILLERY OFFICER

YOUR WIFE AND DAUGHTER ARE INSIDE THIS WALL, AREN'T THEY?!

A soldier who doesn't stop attacking the Titans as they enter into Trost District.

GARRISON SOLDIER

THER 'RE E OR THAT TE'S MIN' WN!

I'M GONNA GO SEE MY DAUGHTER!

While this man tries to agitate the Training Corps and abandon his duty, he then has a change of heart.

GARRISON OFFICER B

An officer who reprimands Daz when he tries to abandon his duty.

73

ORVUD DISTRICT GARRISON COMMANDER

BIRTHDAY: June 22
HEIGHT: 176 cm (5'9")
WEIGHT: 80 kg (176 lbs)
AFFILIATION: Orvud District Garrison

A soldier who loves his hometown of Orvud and goes to the front lines to direct the firing of the wall-mounted artillery when Rod Reiss approaches its wall as a Titan (Volume 17, Episode 68).

FEMALE SOLDIER IN SQUAD RICO

Fights valiantly under Rico's command during the battle for Trost District.

MEDIC

BIRTHDAY: January 29

When Jean is shaken by the sight of Marco's dead body, this soldier asks him to identify the corpse.

FEMALE GARRISON SOLDIER

Tells citizens to evacuate when Rod Reiss's Titan approaches, falsely claiming that it is a drill.

SOLDIER IN SQUAD RICO

Responsible for holding the eastern line of defense inside Wall Rose.

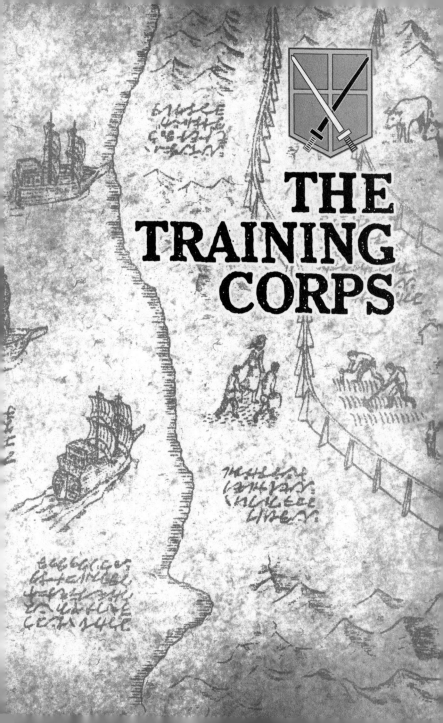

THE
TRAINING
CORPS

I was nothing more than a BYSTANDER...

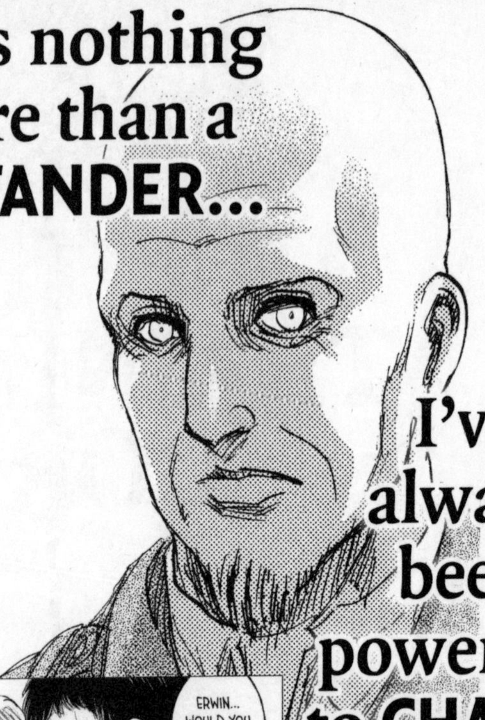

I've always been powerless to CHANGE anything.

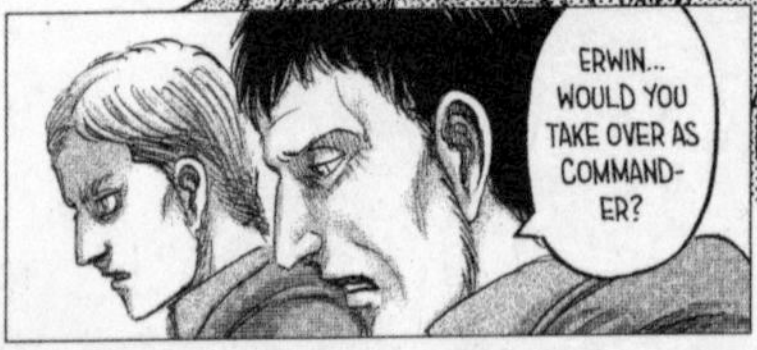
ERWIN... WOULD YOU TAKE OVER AS COMMAND-ER?

KEITH SHADIS

BIRTHDAY: August 18 • **HEIGHT:** 198 cm (6'6") • **WEIGHT:** 107 kg (236 lbs)
AFFILIATION: Training Corps Instructor

A man who witnessed the moment when history changed

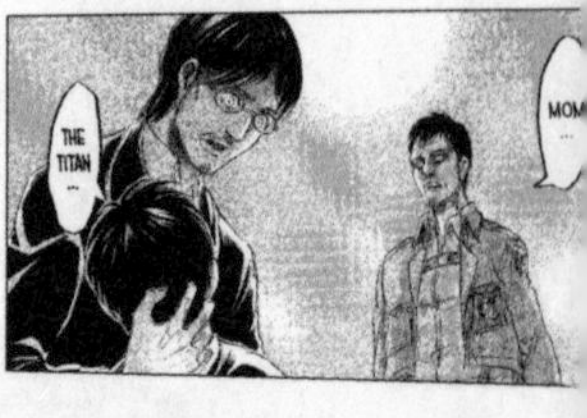
THE TITAN ...

Keith Shadis was the former Commander of the Survey Corps. He gave his position to Erwin because he felt that the many losses the Corps suffered during expeditions was due to his own middling abilities. Keith had known Grisha almost 20 years ago, so he is familiar with how Grisha met Carla and how deeply Grisha loved his family. Keith was the living witness to the Yeager family's secret, when Grisha told Eren to get revenge in his place (Volume 18, Episode 71).

So somewhere there are enemy TITANS... ...hiding in the form of HUMANS...

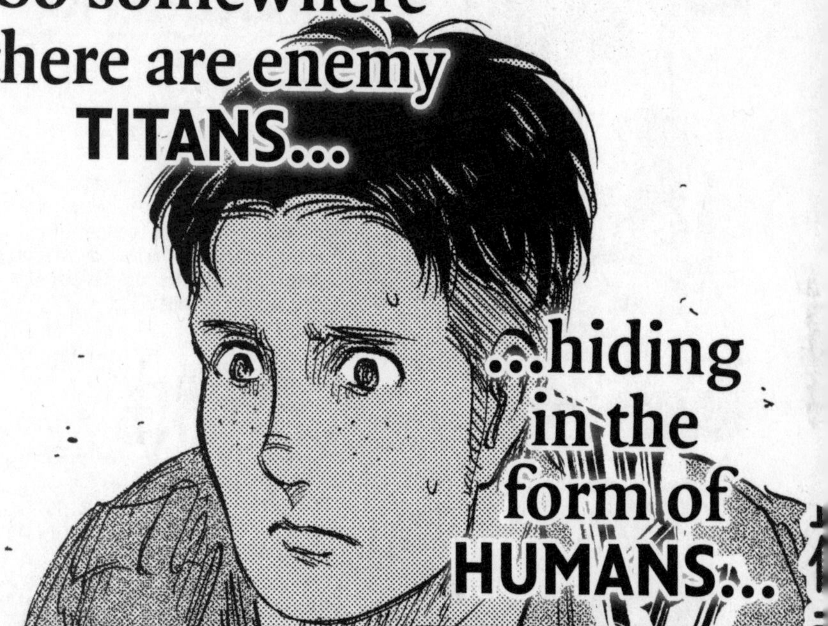

DECEASED

MARCO BOTT

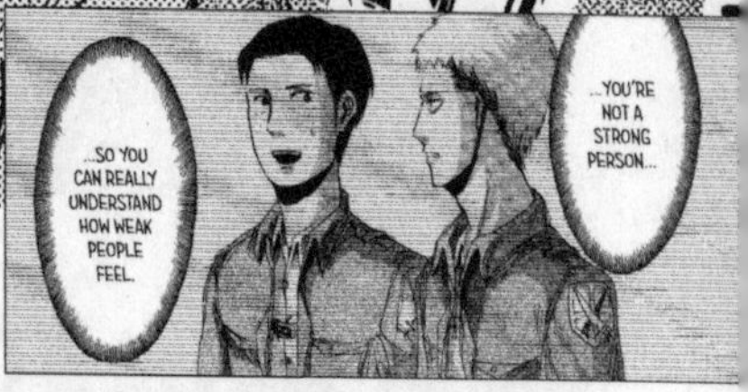
...YOU'RE NOT A STRONG PERSON...
...SO YOU CAN REALLY UNDERSTAND HOW WEAK PEOPLE FEEL.

BIRTHDAY: June 16 • **HEIGHT:** 178 cm (5'10")
WEIGHT: 70 kg (154 lbs)
AFFILIATION: 104th Training Corps

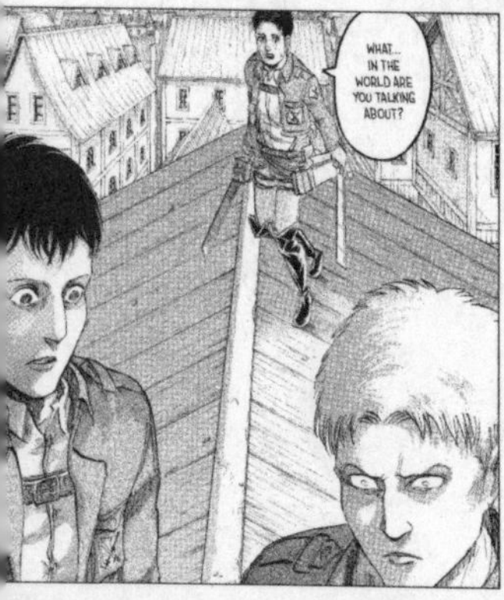
WHAT... IN THE WORLD ARE YOU TALKING ABOUT?

Though he was the first to realize the true identity of Reiner and the others...

Marco was a member of the 104th Training Corps alongside Eren and the others. His strengths included his ability to show consideration to his peers as well as his talent for analyzing situations, earning him a strong degree of trust from Eren and Jean as a leader. However, during the battle for Trost District, he realizes that Reiner and Bertolt are on the side of the Titans, forcing them to silence Marco by feeding him to a Titan (Volume 19, Episode 77).

DECEASED

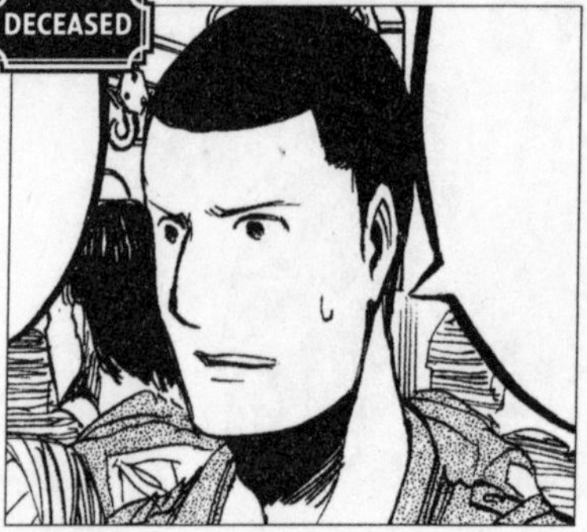

FRANZ KEFKA

BIRTHDAY: November 18
HEIGHT: 188 cm (6'2")
WEIGHT: 74 kg (163 lbs)
AFFILIATION: Training Corps

Like Eren, Franz was a member of the 104th Training Corps. He didn't seem highly concerned about humanity's situation because of his blooming romance with Hannah, causing Eren to scream and say that "Marriage has turned you soft!" (Volume 1, Episode 3).

DECEASED

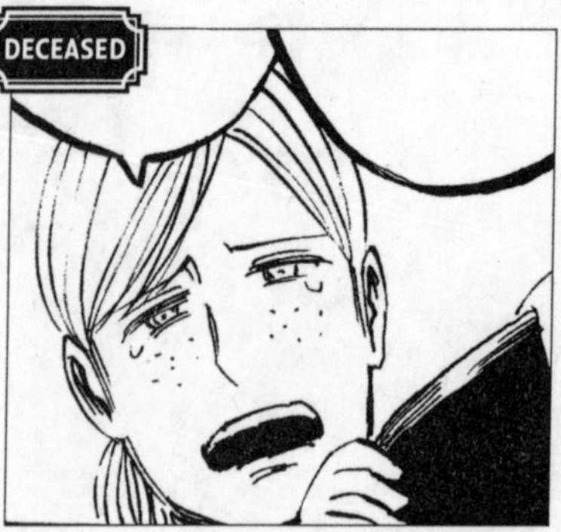

HANNAH DIAMANT

BIRTHDAY: April 12
HEIGHT: 154 cm (5'0")
WEIGHT: 50 kg (110 lbs)
AFFILIATION: Training Corps

Franz swore to Hannah that he would protect her in Trost District, but he died. Unable to accept reality, she continued her attempts to resuscitate him despite the obvious (Volume 2, Episode 5).

DECEASED

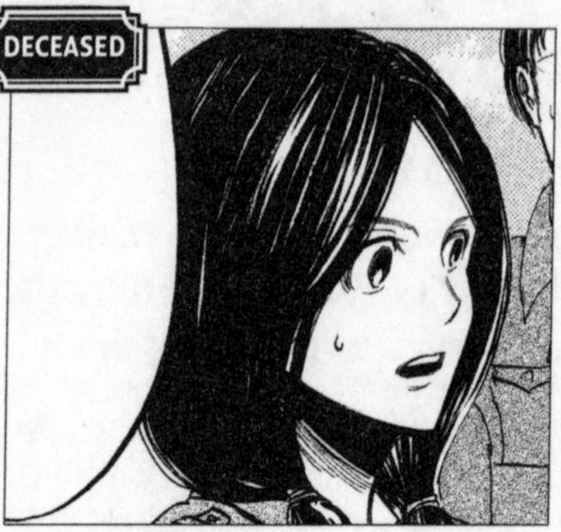

MINA CAROLINA

BIRTHDAY: March 24
HEIGHT: 143 cm (4'8")
WEIGHT: 48 kg (106 lbs)
AFFILIATION: Training Corps

As a member of Training Corps Squad 34 alongside Eren and Armin, Mina fought in Trost District. Though ready to flee when Eren was injured, she was then attacked by Titans and died (Volume 1, Episode 4).

SAMUEL

DECEASED

BIRTHDAY: December 20

Fell from the wall during the Colossus Titan's attack, but saved by Sasha.

THOMAS WAGNER

DECEASED

BIRTHDAY: June.10

Attacked by an Abnormal, Thomas was the first in Training Corps Squad 34 to lose his life.

NAC TIUS

DECEASED

WHAT'S GOING ON?! USUALLY, OUR PEERS IN THE VANGUARD HOG ALL THE ACTION...

BIRTHDAY: June 18

Nack was eaten by a Titan immediately after Eren lost one of his legs.

MYLIUS ZERAMUSKI

DECEASED

BIRTHDAY: November 23

Fought in Trost District as a member of Squad 34.

DAZ

BIRTHDAY: September 22
HEIGHT: 175 cm (5'9")
WEIGHT: 64 kg (141 lbs)
AFFILIATION: Training Corps

Though he survives the Titan attack on Trost District, he later becomes an extreme pessimist. He calls the battle for Trost District "mass suicide," confounding those around him (Volume 3, Episode 12).

CLASSROOM TEACHER

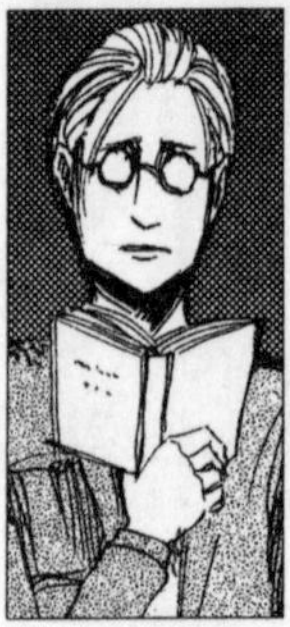

A teacher who watches over Eren's Training Corps induction ceremony and aptitude testing, then later teaches the recruits about history inside the Walls, Titan biology, the Titans' weak point, and more (Volume 1, Episode 4 and Volume 4, Episode 15).

RECRUIT ENVIOUS OF JEAN

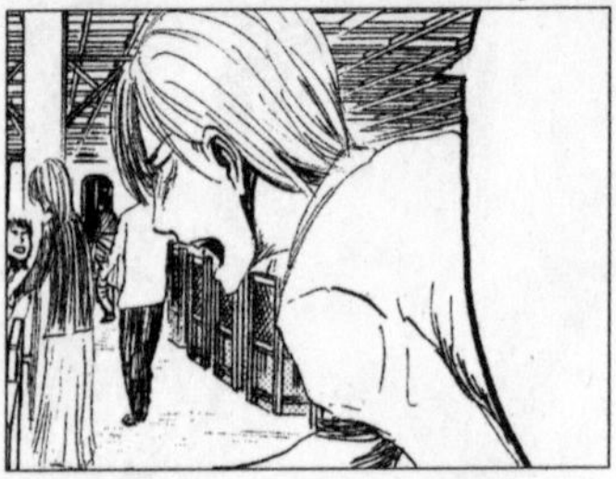

Shows envy for Jean and the other trainees who were at the top of their class during the night of the disbanding ceremony.

MALE RECRUIT WHO TRIES TO SAVE TOM

DECEASED

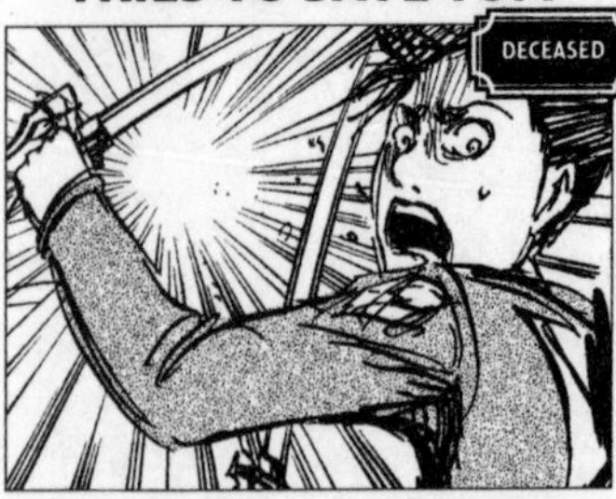

While he attacked the Titans in an attempt to rescue Tom, he falls to their counterattack.

TOM

DECEASED

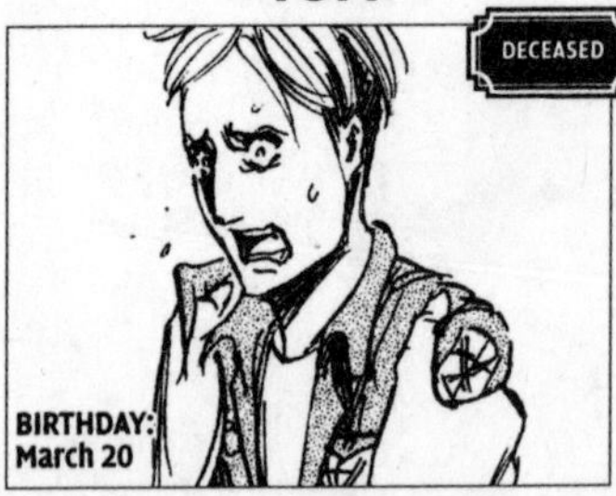

BIRTHDAY:
March 20

Ran out of gas on his way back to headquarters and was eaten by Titans.

TRAINING CORPS INSTRUCTOR

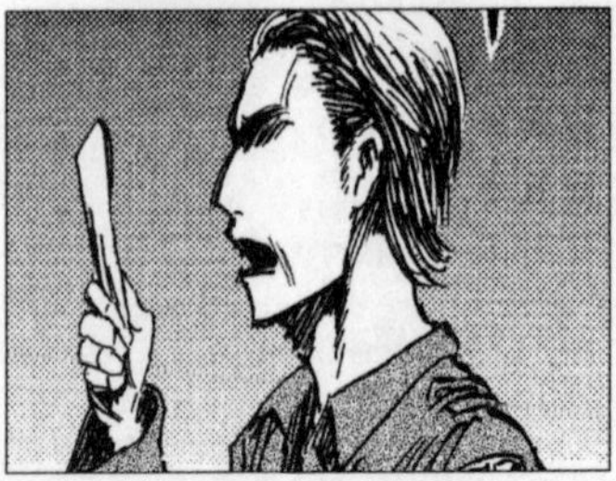

A man who announces the ten members of the 104th with the best marks during their disbanding ceremony.

FEMALE RECRUIT WHO TRIES TO SAVE TOM

DECEASED

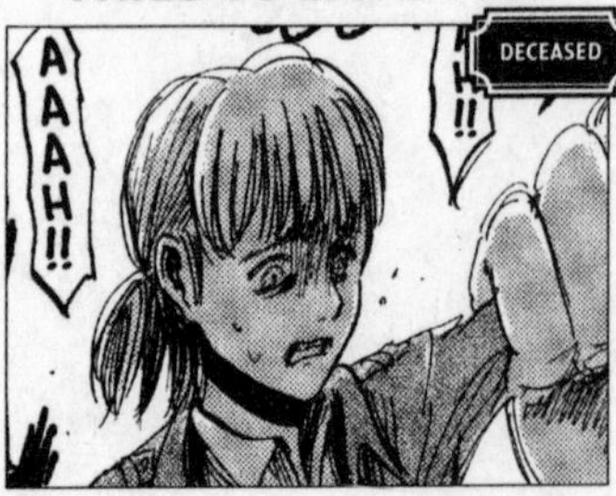
AAAAH!!

While she attempted to rescue Tom, her life is lost to the Titans.

FEMALE RECRUIT WHO TAKES REFUGE INSIDE HQ

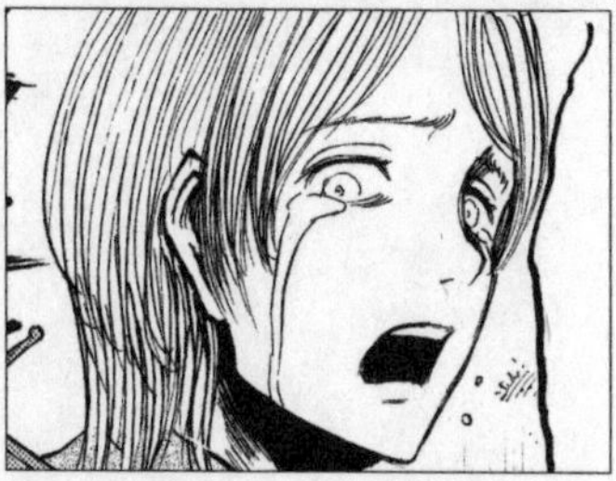

Left terror-stricken when a fellow recruit commits suicide with a pistol in front of her eyes.

MALE RECRUIT WHO TAKES REFUGE INSIDE HQ

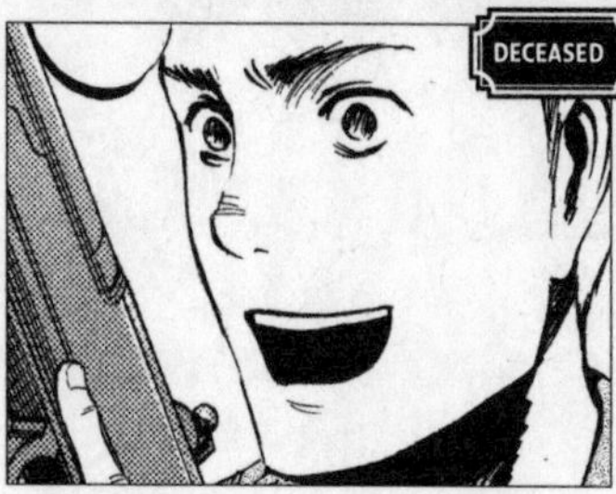
DECEASED

A soldier who took his own life, despairing at his situation when surrounded by Titans.

EATEN SOLDIER

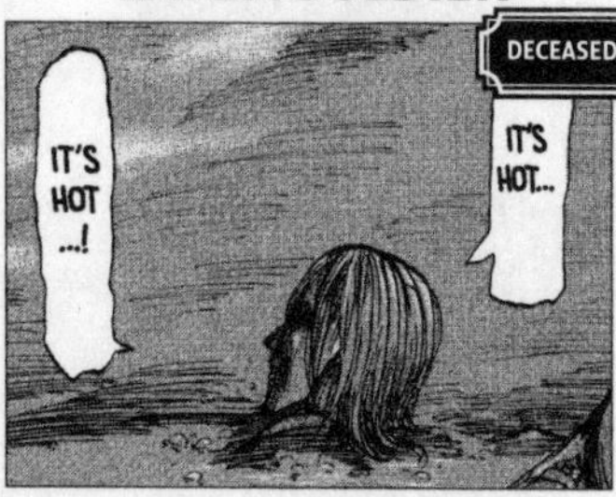
DECEASED
IT'S HOT...
IT'S HOT ...!

A soldier who, like Eren, was eaten. The soldier moaned about the heat.

LOGISTICS SOLDIERS A AND B WHO HIDE UNDER A DESK

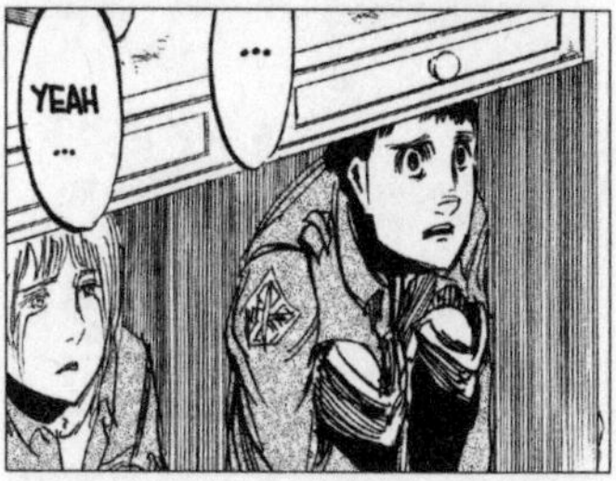
...
YEAH ...

When Titans enter into the supply depot, these two abandon their duty.

RECRUIT INTERESTED IN THE TITANS

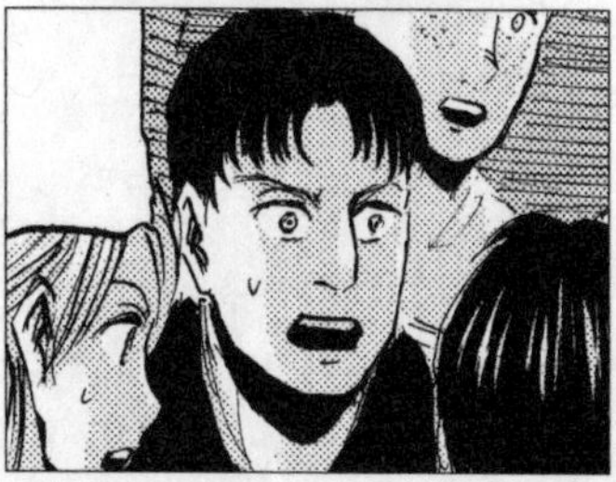

A recruit who asks Eren about the Colossus Titan while they are eating.

UNEASY FEMALE RECRUIT

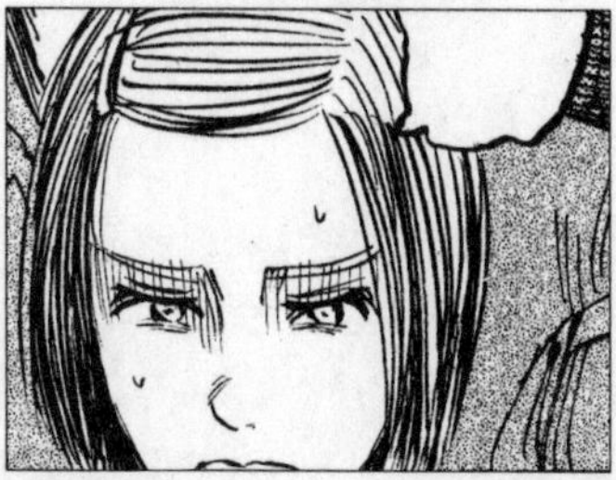

A recruit who begins to fear death when she hears Daz's complaints.

The YEAGER FAMILY and the Survey Corps's PAST as Seen by KEITH SHADIS

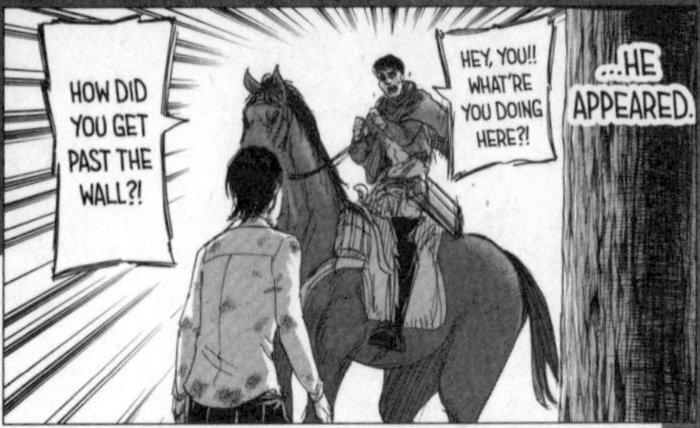
...HE APPEARED.
HEY, YOU!! WHAT'RE YOU DOING HERE?!
HOW DID YOU GET PAST THE WALL?!

Around 830 onward:	• **Keith meets Grisha outside the Walls** • Grisha meets Carla at a pub he visits with Keith • Keith and Grisha work together to deal with an infectious disease that is spreading around Shiganshina District • Keith is made the 12th Commander of the Survey Corps
Around 835:	• Keith despairs after losing many soldiers on an expedition • Keith meets Eren as a baby
845, Shiganshina District Falls:	• **Keith mourns in front of Braun's mother after returning from an expedition** • **Keith decides to retire from the Survey Corps and gives his position to Erwin** • After the fall of Shiganshina District, Keith sees Grisha telling Eren to get revenge for him • Keith finds Eren collapsed in the forest and goes to protect him
847:	• As a Training Corps instructor, Keith meets Eren once more • **Keith sabotages Eren's practice equipment, but Eren still shows talent—which leaves Keith feeling deeply powerless**

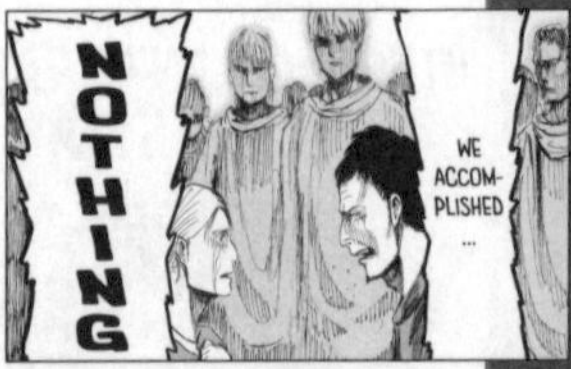
WE ACCOMPLISHED...
NOTHING

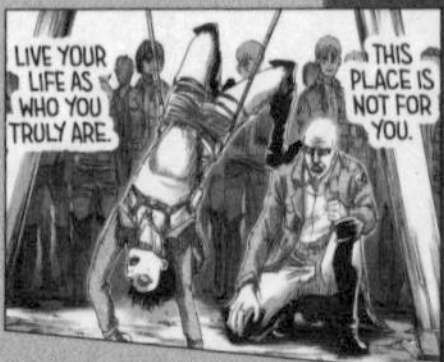
THIS PLACE IS NOT FOR YOU.
LIVE YOUR LIFE AS WHO YOU TRULY ARE.

THE ROYAL GOVERNMENT AND ITS ASSOCIATES

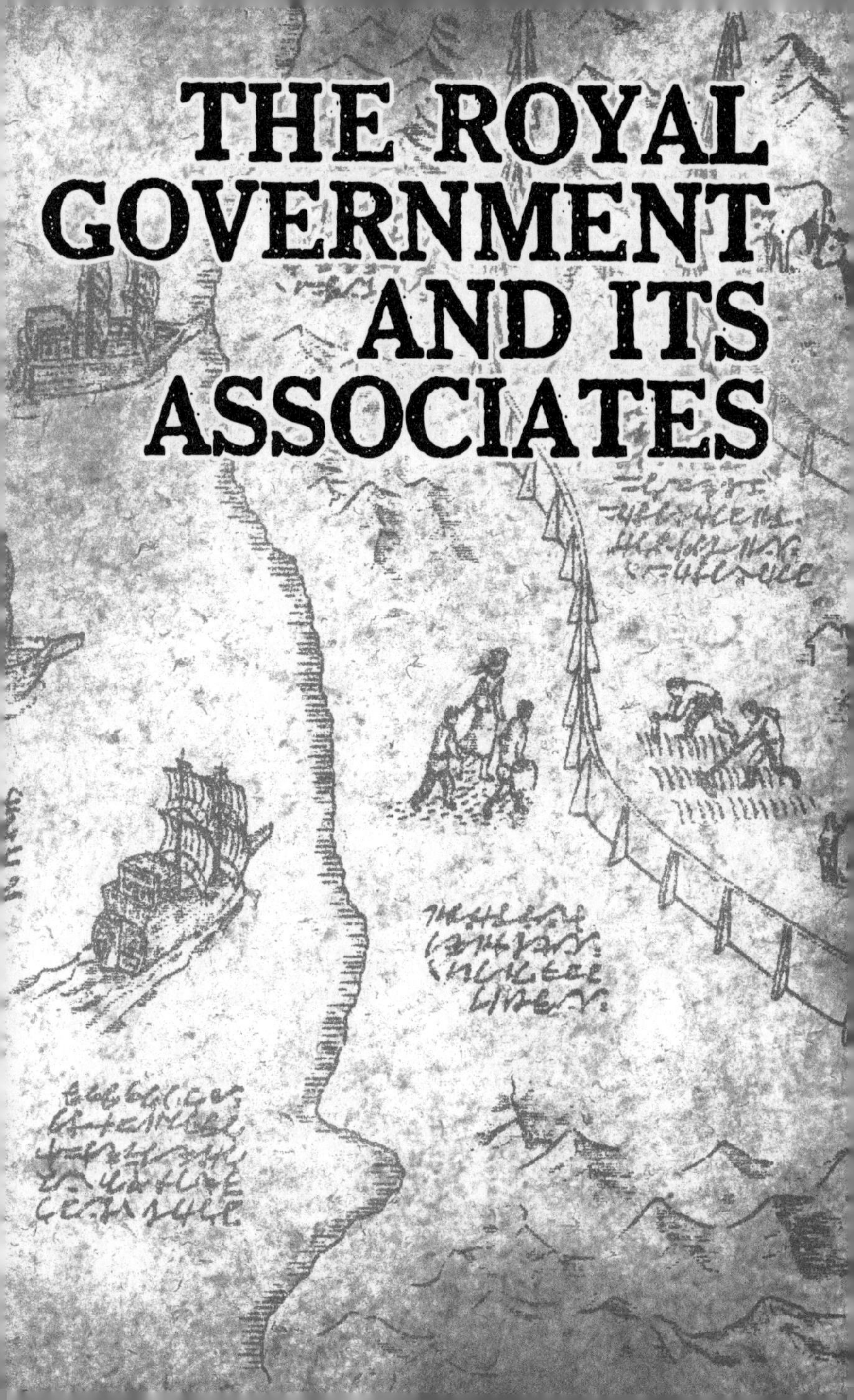

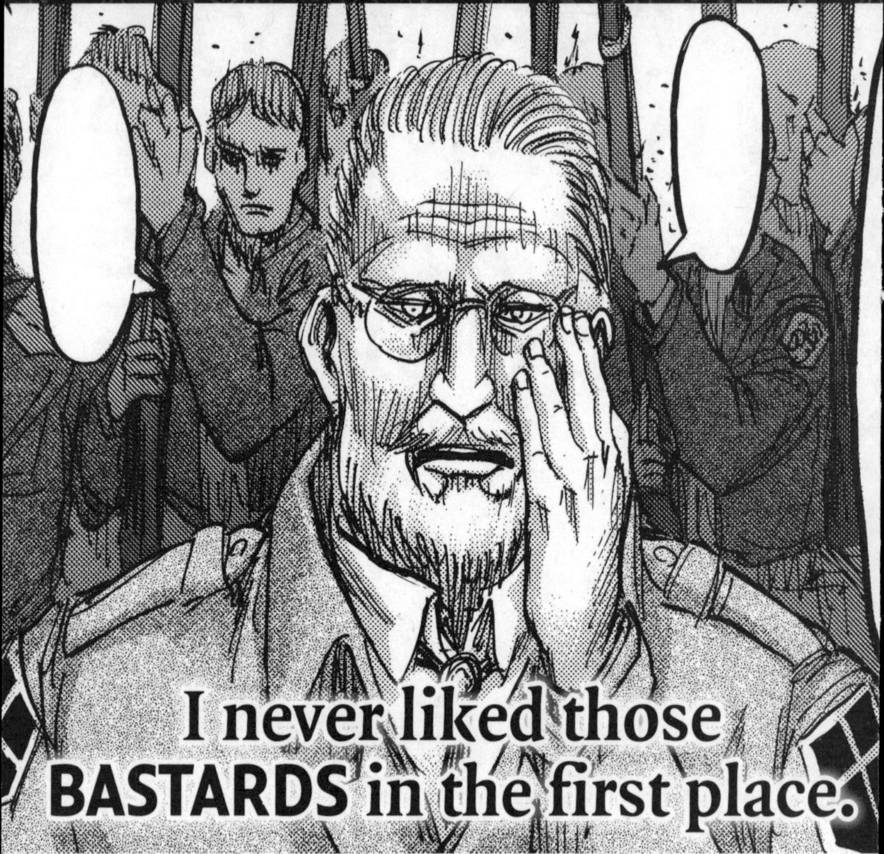
I never liked those
BASTARDS in the first place.

DARIUS ZACKLY

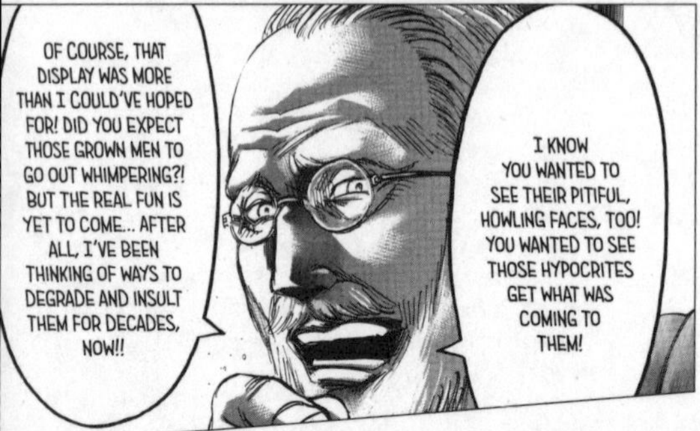
I KNOW YOU WANTED TO SEE THEIR PITIFUL, HOWLING FACES, TOO! YOU WANTED TO SEE THOSE HYPOCRITES GET WHAT WAS COMING TO THEM!
OF COURSE, THAT DISPLAY WAS MORE THAN I COULD'VE HOPED FOR! DID YOU EXPECT THOSE GROWN MEN TO GO OUT WHIMPERING?! BUT THE REAL FUN IS YET TO COME... AFTER ALL, I'VE BEEN THINKING OF WAYS TO DEGRADE AND INSULT THEM FOR DECADES, NOW!!

BIRTHDAY: April 15
HEIGHT: 165 cm (5'5")
WEIGHT: 82 kg (181 lbs)
AFFILIATION: Royal Government, Commander-in-Chief of the three branches of the military

EVEN OVER YOUR LIFE.
NOW, I WILL ASK YOU ONLY ONCE.

The man at the top of all three military branches; he once swore his loyalty to the King

Commander-in-Chief Darius Zackly swore his allegiance to the Royal Government and is responsible for the Garrison, the Survey Corps, and the Military Police Brigade. Though he does not stand on the front lines, he does have the authority to make decisions for the three branches of the military. He was also the one to decide how to deal with Eren at the military court after he shows that he has the power of the Titans (Volume 5, Episode 19). However, he does seem to place distance between himself and the central members of the Royal Government.

YOU WON'T EVEN KNOW HOW TO SHI—
GAA HA HA HA!
TRYING TO INTIMIDATE ME WITH THAT AGAIN?
DON'T YOU HAVE SOMETHING NEW?!

Sneers at the hypocrites from the Royal Government as he tortures them after the successful coup

Zackly devoted his life to rising to his current position so that one day he could look down at the members of the Royal Government. Dreaming of this day, he helps prepare for the coup, something he calls a "lifelong hobby" of his. He takes advantage of Erwin's coup to make his dream of destroying the Royal Government come true and begins torturing nobles (Volume 15, Episode 62 and more).

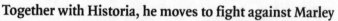

Together with Historia, he moves to fight against Marley

...THAT THE ONLY POSSIBLE WAY TO RESIST SUCH A POWERFUL ENEMY...
...WOULD BE TO USE THE TRUE POWER OF THE FOUNDING TITAN TO ACTIVATE THE WALL TITANS.

After the fall of the Royal Government, he collaborates with the new government that has Historia as its Queen and acts as the Commander-in-Chief of the three branches of the military. He proposes that the only way to drive away their enemies past the Walls is to use the true power of the Founding Titan inside of Eren to activate the Titans lying dormant inside the Walls. Now that Zackly is loyal to Historia in the newly structured monarchy, he will surely make use of his exceptional talents as he acts as Commander-in-Chief both in name and in reality (Volume 22, Episode 89).

My **MISSION** is to summon God back into this world and to **DEVOTE** my prayers to it.

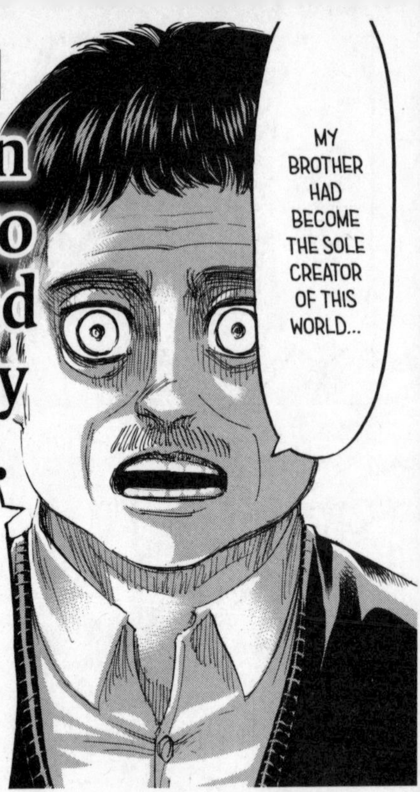
MY BROTHER HAD BECOME THE SOLE CREATOR OF THIS WORLD...

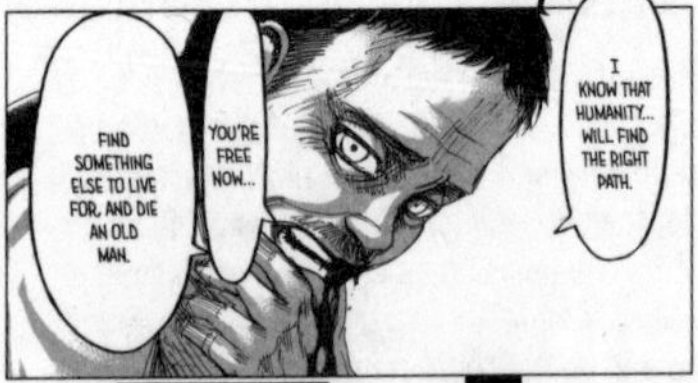
I KNOW THAT HUMANITY... WILL FIND THE RIGHT PATH.
YOU'RE FREE NOW...
FIND SOMETHING ELSE TO LIVE FOR, AND DIE AN OLD MAN.

DECEASED

ROD REISS

BIRTHDAY: September 15 • HEIGHT: 158 cm (5'2") • WEIGHT: 68 kg (150 lbs)

Head of the Reiss Family

The man who controlled the Royal Government from the shadows and plotted to retake the Founding Titan

Rod, a member of the Reiss family (the true royal bloodline), was the most powerful man inside the Walls, controlling the Royal Government from the shadows. He planned to take back the Founding Titan that had been stolen from his younger brother Uri, to give to Historia (Volume 16, Episode 65 and more).

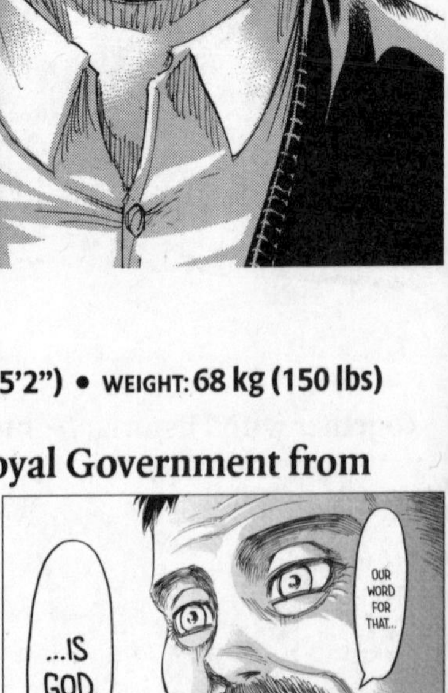
OUR WORD FOR THAT...
...IS GOD.

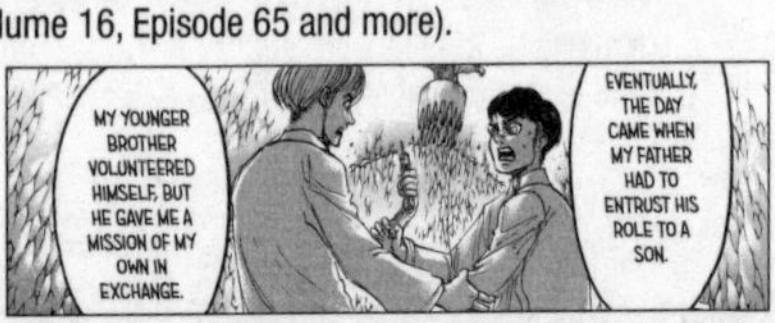
EVENTUALLY, THE DAY CAME WHEN MY FATHER HAD TO ENTRUST HIS ROLE TO A SON.
MY YOUNGER BROTHER VOLUNTEERED HIMSELF, BUT HE GAVE ME A MISSION OF MY OWN IN EXCHANGE.

I want to create a PARADISE for the surviving, waning remnants of humanity.

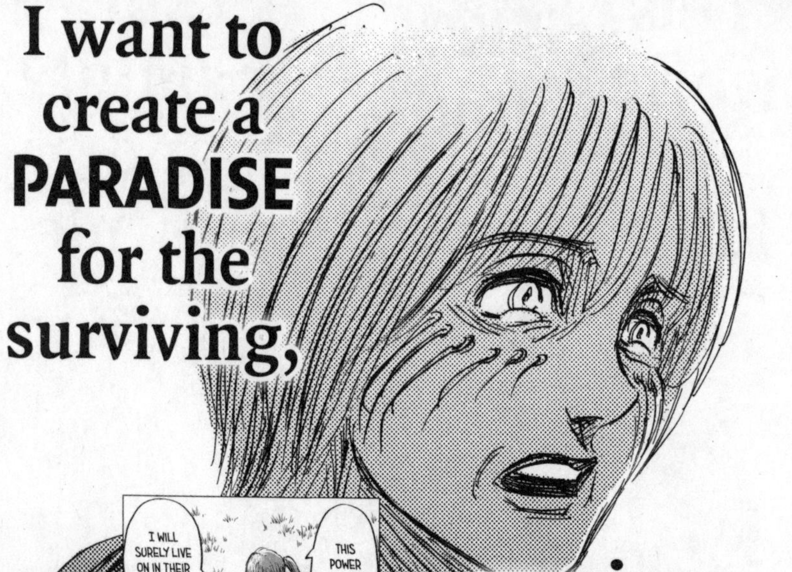

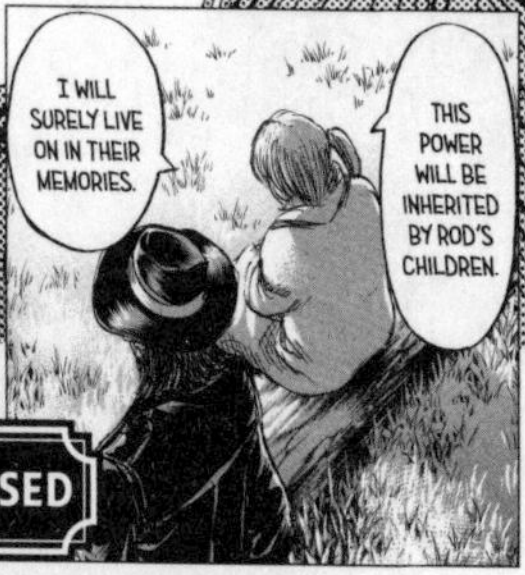
THIS POWER WILL BE INHERITED BY ROD'S CHILDREN.
I WILL SURELY LIVE ON IN THEIR MEMORIES.

DECEASED

URI REISS

BIRTHDAY: December 31 • **HEIGHT:** 155 cm (5'1") • **WEIGHT:** 54 kg (119 lbs)
LOCATION: The Reiss territory

Though he tries to create a paradise inside the Walls using the miracle between himself and Kenny...

Uri, the former inheritor of the Founding Titan, called the friendship that blossomed between Kenny and himself a "miracle" and used it in an effort to create paradise inside the Walls. He was eaten by his niece Frieda after she transformed into a Titan (Volume 16, Episode 64 and more).

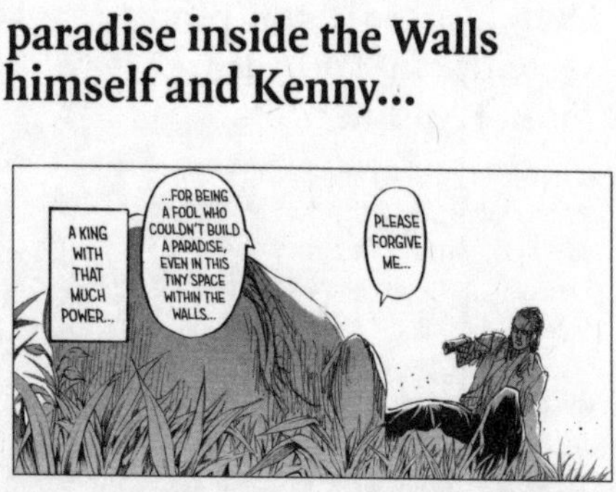
PLEASE FORGIVE ME...
...FOR BEING A FOOL WHO COULDN'T BUILD A PARADISE, EVEN IN THIS TINY SPACE WITHIN THE WALLS...
A KING WITH THAT MUCH POWER...

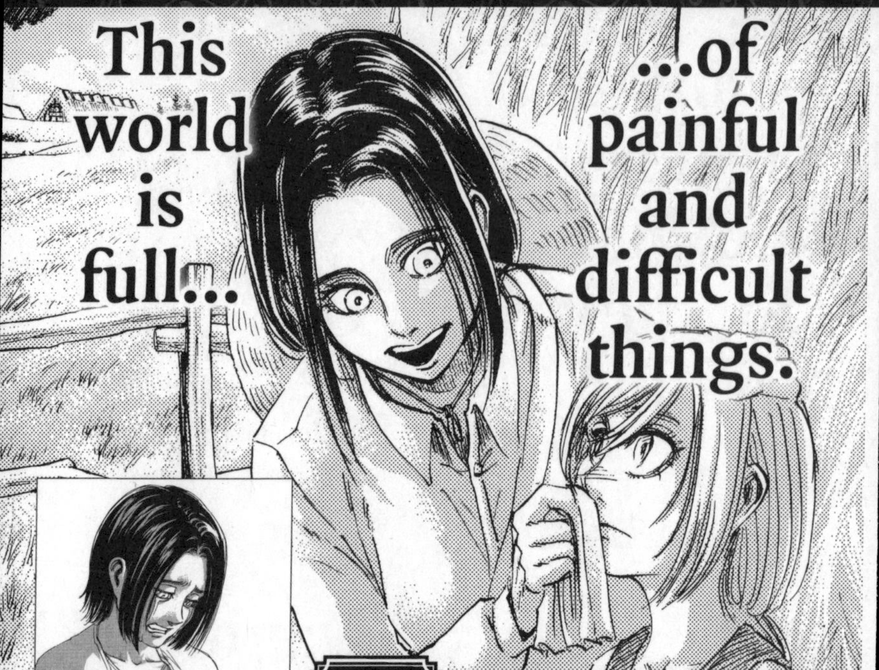
This world is full...
...of painful and difficult things.

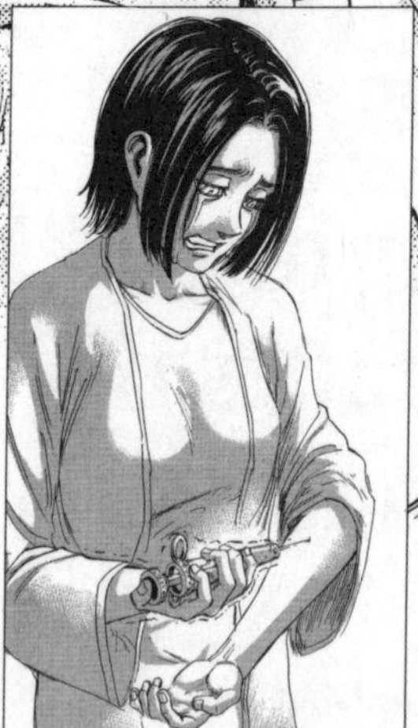

DECEASED

FRIEDA REISS

BIRTHDAY: February 2 • **HEIGHT:** 171 cm (5'7")
WEIGHT: 57 kg (126 lbs)
LOCATION: The Reiss territory

Died after Grisha stole the Founding Titan from her

As a member of the Reiss family, Frieda looked after Historia, the child of Rod and Alma Reiss. Around the time she was 15 years old, she turned into a Titan and ate her uncle Uri, inheriting the ideology of the first king. However, she was then eaten by Grisha, who possessed the Attack Titan, losing the power of the Founding Titan (Volume 16, Episode 63 and more).

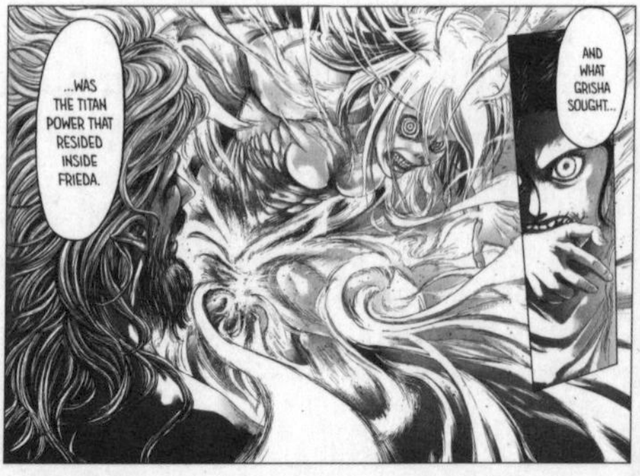
AND WHAT GRISHA SOUGHT...
...WAS THE TITAN POWER THAT RESIDED INSIDE FRIEDA.

ABEL REISS

DECEASED

BIRTHDAY:
August 7

The second daughter of the Reiss family, Abel was squashed by Grisha when she was 12.

ULKLIN REISS

DECEASED

BIRTHDAY:
May 19

The oldest son of the Reiss family, Ulklin was crushed to death by Grisha when he was 17.

FLORIAN REISS

DECEASED

BIRTHDAY:
January 14

The third daughter of the Reiss family, she was stomped on by Grisha when she was 10.

DIRK REISS

DECEASED

BIRTHDAY:
October 12

The second son of the Reiss family, Dirk was squashed by Grisha when he was 14.

ROD AND URI'S FATHER

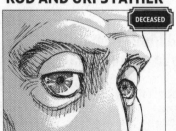

DECEASED

Turned down the request from Rod to free humanity from the Titans.

ROD'S WIFE

DECEASED

BIRTHDAY:
May 17

Died when she was stomped on by Grisha with Florian in her arms.

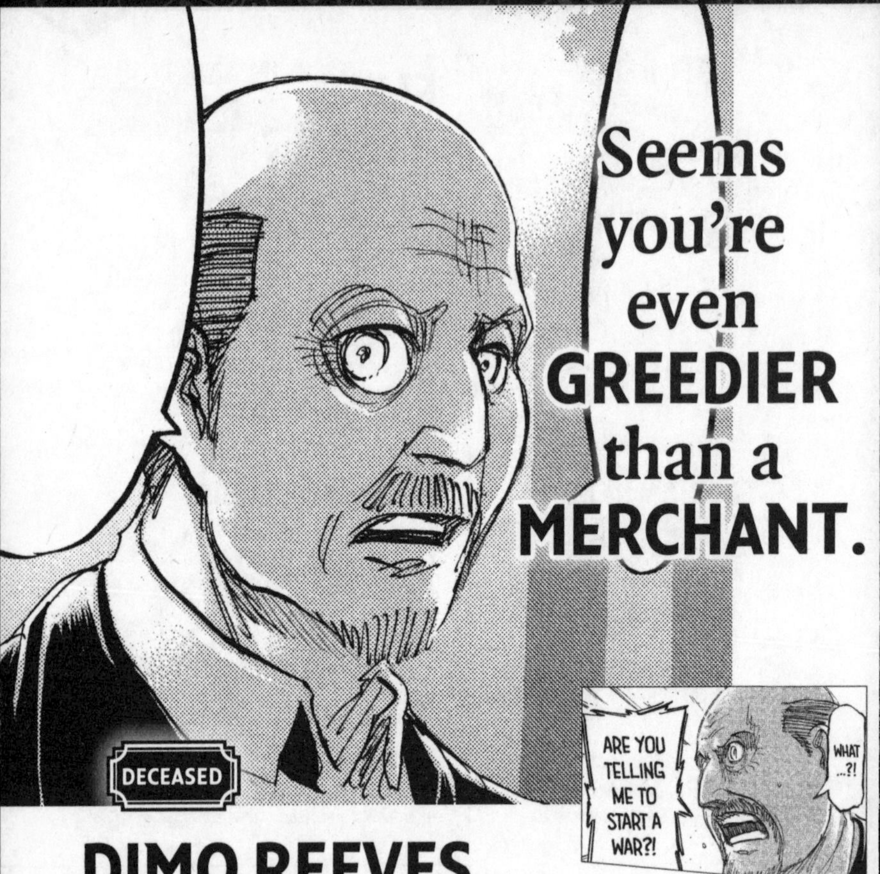
Seems you're even GREEDIER than a MERCHANT.
DECEASED
WHAT ...?!
ARE YOU TELLING ME TO START A WAR?!

DIMO REEVES

BIRTHDAY: **November 27** • **HEIGHT:** **162 cm (5'4")** • **WEIGHT:** **76 kg (168 lbs)**
AFFILIATION: **Reeves Company**

An influential man who allied himself with the Survey Corps for the sake of the people of Shiganshina District

Dimo was the chairman of Reeves Company, which organized the merchants of Trost District. He initially tried to use his power so that he could be the first to escape during the fall of Trost (Volume 2, Episode 5). But then he then saw Levi's resolve when it came to war with the Royal Government, so he decided to cooperate with the Survey Corps. He was eventually killed by Kenny (Volume 14, Episode 56).

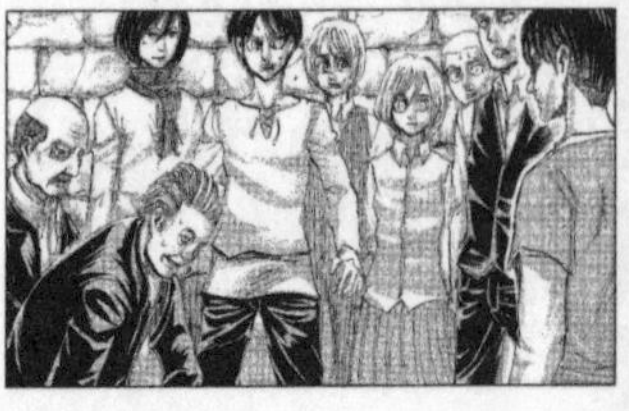

FLEGEL REEVES

BIRTHDAY: September 11
HEIGHT: 165 cm (5'5")
WEIGHT: 74 kg (163 lbs)
AFFILIATION: Reeves Company

Though Flegel was once such an amateur that he dared to ask Levi for snacks, he changes suddenly after his father is killed before his eyes. He does everything he can to expose the atrocities committed by the Interior Squad (Volume 15, Episode 60 and more).

DIMO REEVES'S WIFE AND DAUGHTER

They mistakenly take their anger over Dimo's murder out on Erwin.

REEVES COMPANY UNDERLING A

After abducting Jean and the others, he is attacked by Mikasa, and she knees him.

REEVES COMPANY UNDERLING B

Chokeslammed by Levi after abducting Jean and the others.

REEVES COMPANY UNDERLING C

YOU... YOU'RE REALLY A BOY...

Finds his eyes opened to a new world after abducting Armin.

Now...! RELEASE this HAND from me now!!

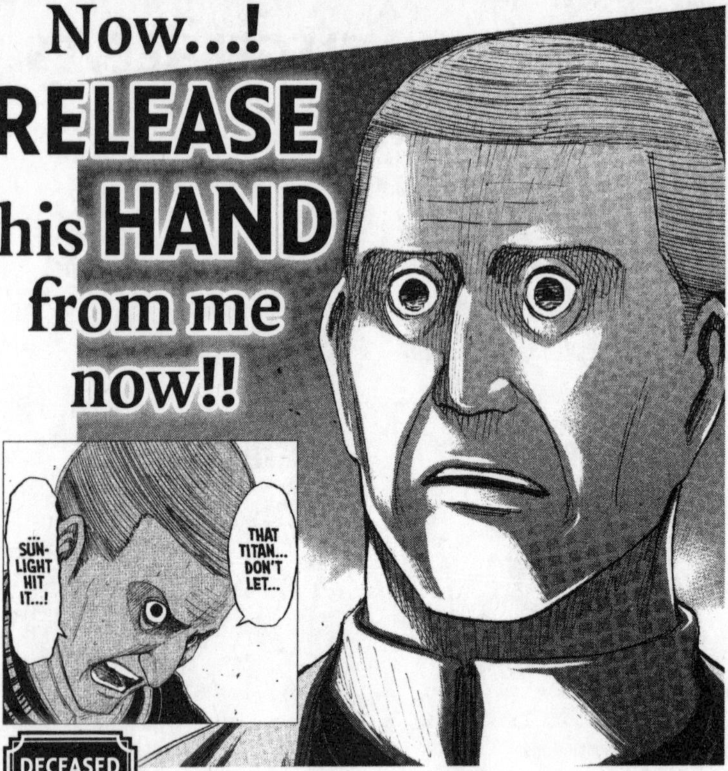
THAT TITAN... DON'T LET...
...SUN-LIGHT HIT IT...!

DECEASED

NICK

BIRTHDAY: November 9 • **HEIGHT:** 192 cm (6'4") • **WEIGHT:** 72 kg (159 lbs)
LOCATION: Trost District barracks

A minister who always kept his mouth shut despite knowing the secret of the Walls.

The minister of the Wall Religion (also known as the Wallists), who worship the Walls as gods. Though he knew about how the Walls were created, he continued to hide this information in accordance with the Wall Religion's vows that had been passed down for generations, staying silent even when his own life was threatened. He was eventually tortured and killed by the Military Police Brigade's Interior Squad (Volume 13, Episode 52).

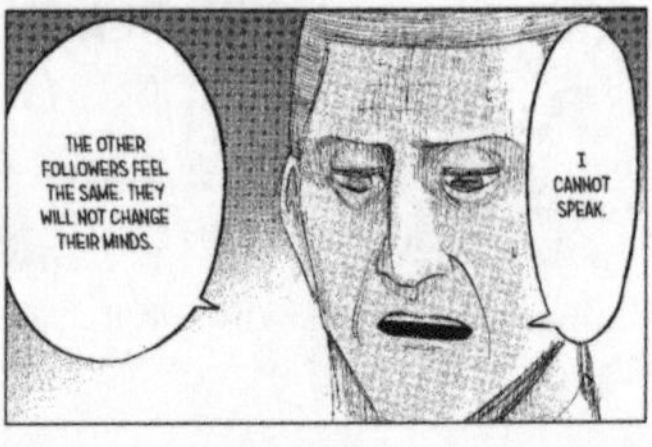
I CANNOT SPEAK.
THE OTHER FOLLOWERS FEEL THE SAME. THEY WILL NOT CHANGE THEIR MINDS.

HIGH-RANKING MILITARY OFFICIAL

BIRTHDAY: May 27

One of the nobles who led the Royal Government and stood at the top of the military structure.

CHUBBY ROYAL GOVERNMENT MINISTER

BIRTHDAY: September 9

An aristocrat who stood at the top of the Royal Government's administration.

HIGH-RANKING MAN FROM THE WALL RELIGION

BIRTHDAY: October 5

A man who knows the secret of the Walls and stood at the top of the Wall Religion.

HIGH-RANKING MERCHANT

BIRTHDAY: November 17

One of the nobles who knows the secrets of the world inside the Walls and brought together all of its companies.

KING FRITZ

BIRTHDAY: October 23
HEIGHT: 177 cm (5'10")
WEIGHT: 62 kg (137 lbs)
AFFILIATION: Royal Government

A puppet king meant to distract the populace inside the Walls from the true crown, the Reiss family. While he was thought to be a quiet, thoughtful man, even that turns out to not be the case about him.

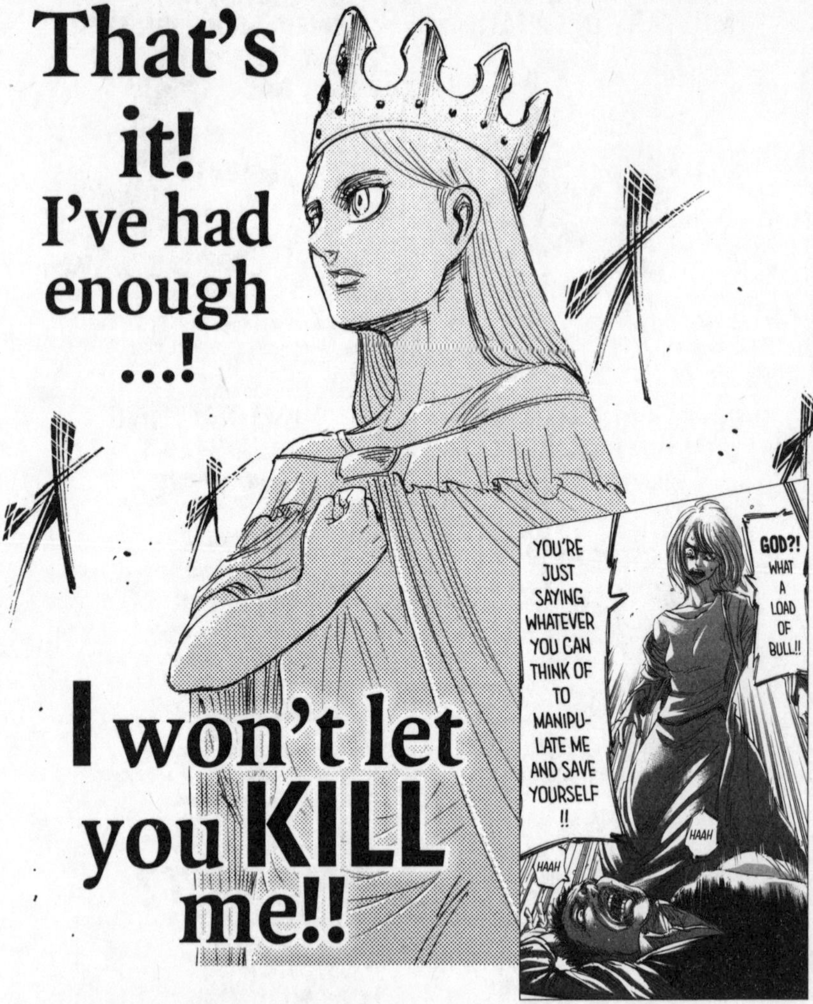
That's it! I've had enough ...!
I won't let you KILL me!!
YOU'RE JUST SAYING WHATEVER YOU CAN THINK OF TO MANIPU-LATE ME AND SAVE YOURSELF !!
GOD?! WHAT A LOAD OF BULL!!
HAAH
HAAH

HISTORIA REISS
(Krista Lenz)

BIRTHDAY: January 15 • HEIGHT: 145 cm (4'9") • WEIGHT: 42 kg (93 lbs)
LOCATION: Mitras, the Royal Capital

I...
I WANTED TO DO THIS...
...BE-CAUSE I WANT TO BE THOUGHT OF AS HELPFUL.

I MET MY FATHER FOR THE FIRST TIME.

Sick of the Royal Government, she changes her name and joins the military

Historia was born to Rod Reiss and his mistress Alma. Around the time she was ten years old, the Royal Government attempts to kill her in order to eliminate the stain on the Royal Family that she represents. However, she is then forced by Rod's words to change her name from Historia to Krista and to live in the settlements. She later goes on to join the Training Corps (Volume 13, Episode 52 and more).

I CAN'T BE A GOOD GIRL...
...AND I DON'T WANT TO BE A GOD.
BUT...
...WHEN I SEE SOMEONE CRYING, SAYING...
...NO ONE NEEDS THEM...

Stops killing the person she is and decides to live a life true to herself

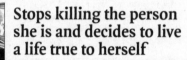

After becoming Krista, Historia pretends to be a "good girl" like the ones she read about in picture books together with Frieda. But when Ymir, who knows the truth about the Reiss family, tells Krista to "Live your life with pride in your heart," Historia is encouraged and decides to be true to herself. She now acts for the sake of those who cry about how they're not needed in the world (Volume 16, Episode 66).

Reveals the secrets of the Walls as Queen, encouraging its people to come together

WE WILL BE RETURNING THE MEMORIES KING REISS TOOK FROM THE PEOPLE A CENTURY AGO...
...BACK TO THE PEOPLE, A CENTURY LATER. THAT'S ALL.

Taking the name Historia Reiss once more, Historia wishes for the people inside the Walls to come together now that she is at the core of the new order set up after the fall of the Royal Government. She encourages this by revealing the secrets of the Walls and the Titans that had been hidden by the Reiss family and the Royal Government, preparing for battle against the "world" that sends Titans their way (Volume 22, Episode 90).

HAJIME ISAYAMA Reveals

How His CHARACTERS WERE BORN: Part 3

HISTORIA REISS (KRISTA LENZ)

At first, I only had the vague idea of wanting someone born into a noble family making it into the top 10 of the Training Corps. While Krista was simply a character who looked good at first, I felt like she was becoming too much of a trope, and I couldn't stand that. My thought of "I need to add a *moe** character!" went from being something I wanted to do, to something I felt like I was obligated to do. That is when I added to her character the metafictional element of her wishing that she had not been born the way she is. Ultimately, though, Historia was able to grow to the point of overcoming even that meta element of her character, and she is now one of my favorites.

YMIR

Ymir was a character who appeared in the thumbnails of *Attack on Titan* during its earliest days, but she had a different name then. Even at that time, I had the idea that there would be a meddling character who wanted to get Krista into the top 10.

I drew Ymir with freckles because I thought that would make her seem more like a commoner, contrasting with Krista. I wanted to make a story where a regular person like her is put into an important position by chance, though even I don't know if you could call her luck good or bad.

As with Jean, it's fun to be able to draw a heelish character who says exactly what's on her mind, unconcerned about what others think.

SASHA BLOUSE

Sasha started as a character with 8:20 eyebrows** and droopy eyes. I also designed her so that her hair was only long on the right, making it look like she has short hair if seen from the left.

Because I wanted to make her a comic relief character, her name comes from the comedian Sacha Baron Cohen. I also liked the way the name sounds.

**Moe: Moe* originally described a person or character who is undeniably cute, endearing, and attractive. The Japanese character for "*moe*" means "to bud" or "to sprout," perhaps because these objects of affection are often youthful.

**8:20 eyebrows: When eyebrows have an angle like the arms of a clock—the minute hand resting at 20 minutes and the hour hand at 8 o'clock.

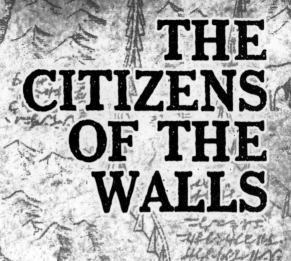

THE
CITIZENS
OF THE
WALLS

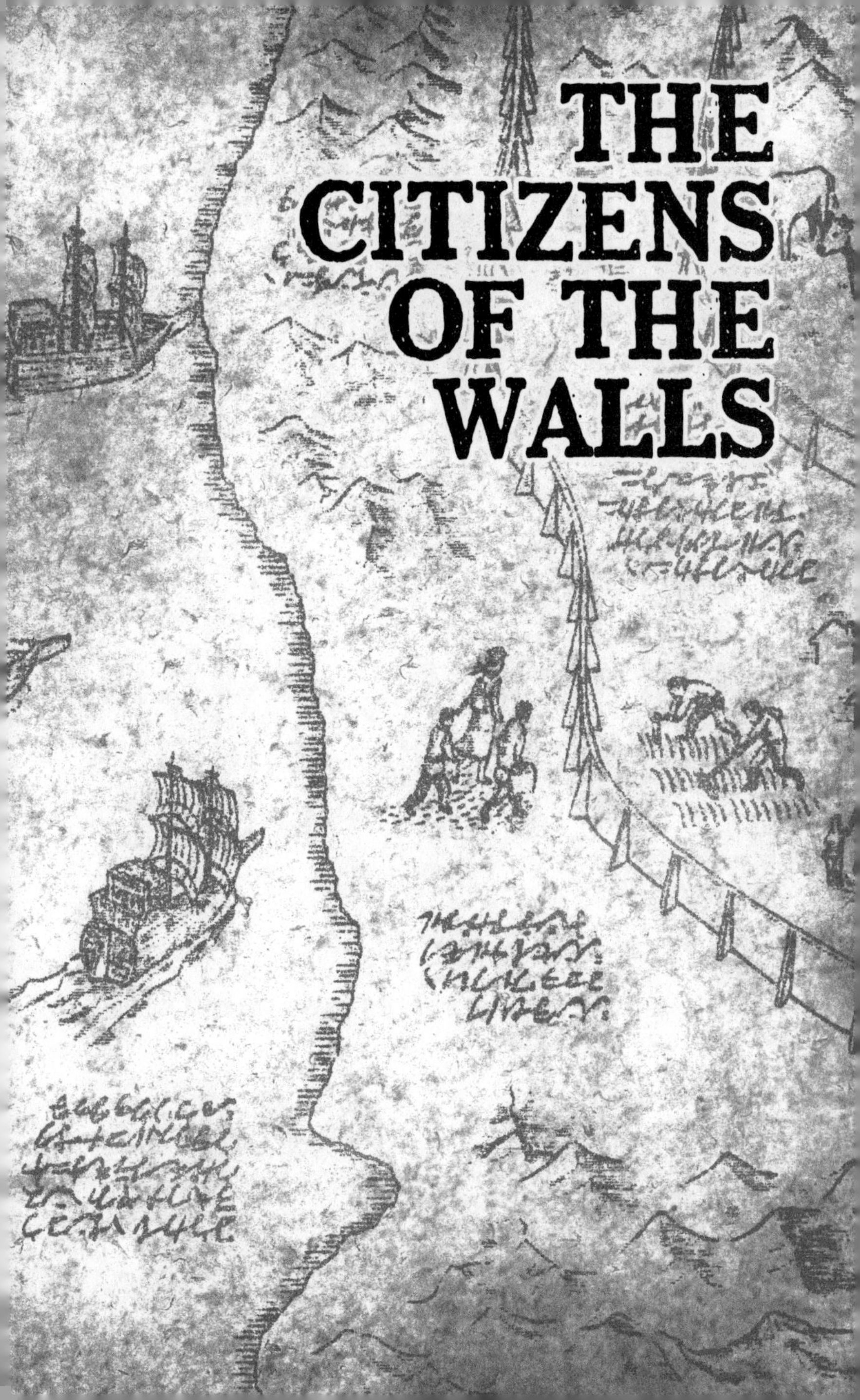

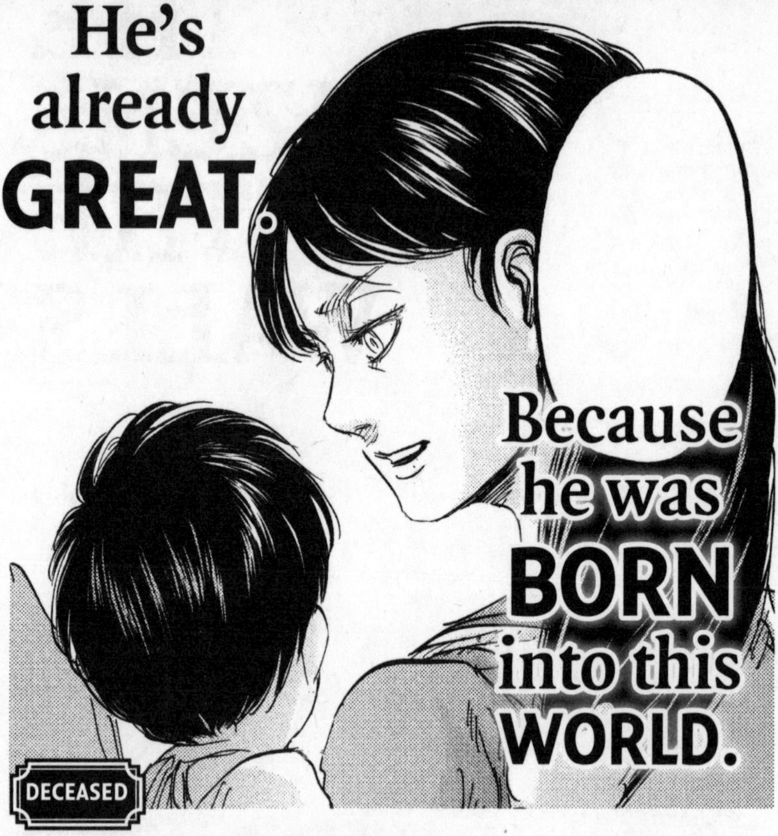
He's already GREAT.
Because he was BORN into this WORLD.
DECEASED

CARLA YEAGER

BIRTHDAY: January 29 • **HEIGHT:** 165 cm (5'5") • **WEIGHT:** 58 kg (128 lbs)
LOCATION: Shiganshina District

Gave unconditional love to her child

Eren's mother created a happy family inside Shiganshina District. She met Grisha 20 years earlier at a pub where she worked, eventually marrying him. She then gave birth to Eren and showed him unconditional love. She was eaten by a Pure Titan during the fall of Shiganshina District (Volume 1, Episode 1 and more).

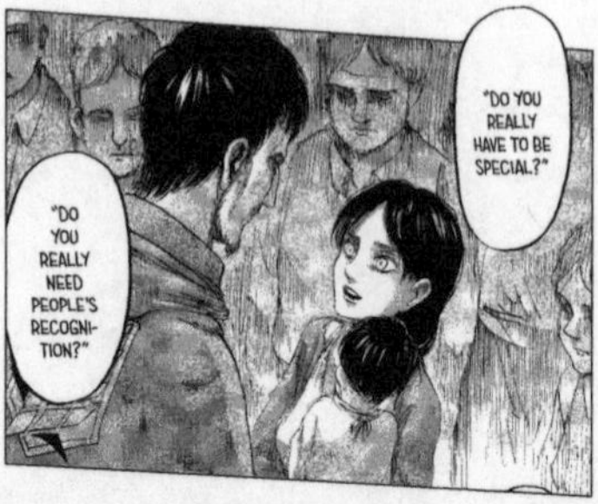
"DO YOU REALLY HAVE TO BE SPECIAL?"
"DO YOU REALLY NEED PEOPLE'S RECOGNITION?"

ALMA

BIRTHDAY: July 14
HEIGHT: 168 cm (5'6")
WEIGHT: 54 kg (119 lbs)
LOCATION: A small farm in northern Wall Sheena

A woman who offered up her daughter and begged for her life

Historia's mother. She developed a relationship with Rod when she worked for the Reiss Family and eventually gave birth to Historia, but she abandoned raising Historia and left the home. When she was captured by Kenny, who had accepted the mission of cleaning stains on the Royal Family, she offered Historia to him and begged for her life, but to no avail (Volume 13, Episode 52).

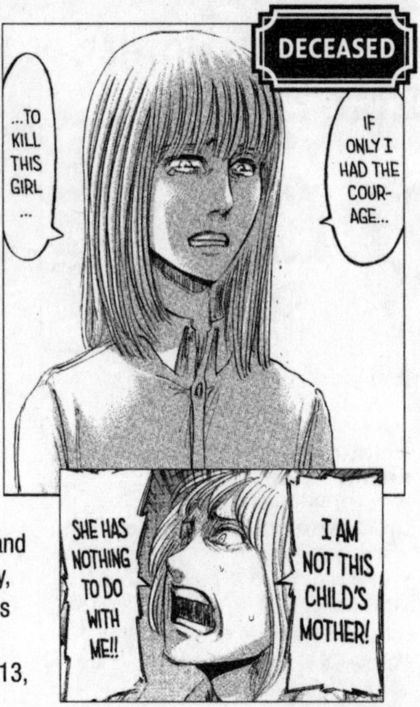
DECEASED
IF ONLY I HAD THE COURAGE...
...TO KILL THIS GIRL...
I AM NOT THIS CHILD'S MOTHER!
SHE HAS NOTHING TO DO WITH ME!!

ERWIN'S FATHER

BIRTHDAY: February 28
HEIGHT: 180 cm (5'11")
WEIGHT: 86 kg (190 lbs)
LOCATION: ???

When he told his son Erwin about the discrepancies in their history...

A teacher of children, Erwin's father told his son about the history of humanity that was no longer even spoken about. He also taught Erwin the inconsistencies in the history promoted by the Royal Government. Immediately after, he was captured by MPs and punished, dying in what was made to look like an accident (Volume 14, Episode 55).

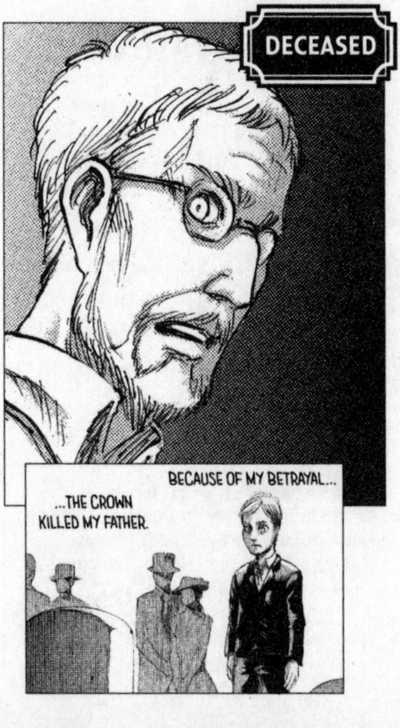
DECEASED
BECAUSE OF MY BETRAYAL...
...THE CROWN KILLED MY FATHER.

MIKASA'S MOTHER

DECEASED

THIS BRAND MUST BE PASSED DOWN FROM GENERATION TO GENERATION IN OUR FAMILY.

BIRTHDAY: November 8
HEIGHT: 158 cm (5'2")
WEIGHT: 45 kg (99 lbs)
LOCATION: Shiganshina District outskirts

A member of the Asian bloodline, who are unaffected by the King's powers. While she lived a modest life so as not to draw the attention of others, she loses her life in a robbery (Volume 2, Episode 6).

MIKASA'S FATHER

DECEASED

BIRTHDAY: January 21
HEIGHT: 183 cm (6'0")
WEIGHT: 68 kg (150 lbs)
LOCATION: Shiganshina District outskirts

Threatened as a member of the Ackerman family, he married Mikasa's mother, who was in a similar situation. He was blessed with one daughter, Mikasa (Volume 2, Episode 6).

PETRA'S FATHER

BIRTHDAY: November 6
HEIGHT: 174 cm (5'9")
WEIGHT: 78 kg (172 lbs)
LOCATION: Karanes District

Ignorant of his daughter's death, he tells Levi of the letter he received from her after the Survey Corps returns from the 57th expedition outside the Walls (Volume 7, Episode 30).

CONNIE'S FAMILY (PARENTS)

DECEASED

BIRTHDAY: July 30 (Father) / December 1 (Mother)
LOCATION: Ragako Village

Both of Connie's parents were turned into Titans by Zeke, along with his little sister Sunny and his younger brother Martin. Of them, Connie's mother was the only one he found still alive (Volume 9, Episode 37).

KENNY'S GRANDFATHER

DECEASED

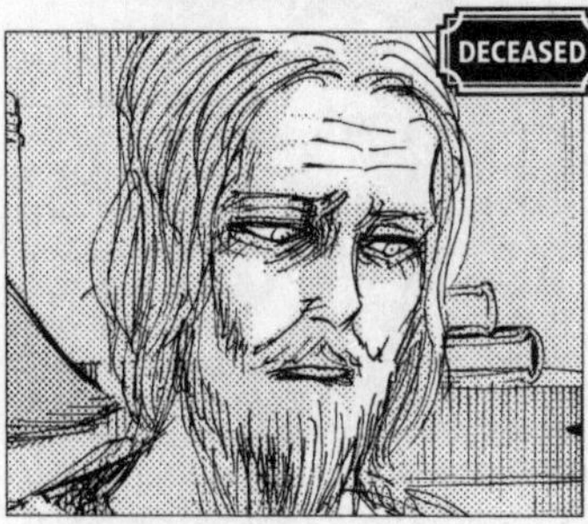

BIRTHDAY: January 22
HEIGHT: 182 cm (6'0")
WEIGHT: 58 kg (128 lbs)
LOCATION: The old underground city

Kenny's grandfather told him about the history of humanity under the King's rule, as well as the true nature of the persecution faced by the Ackerman family (Volume 16, Episode 65).

SASHA'S FATHER

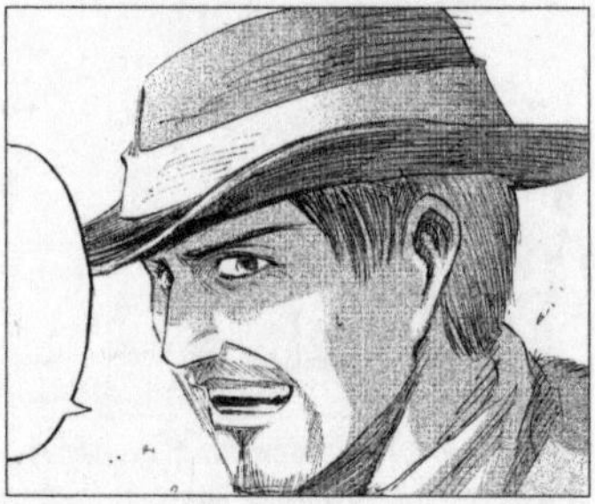

BIRTHDAY: November 9
HEIGHT: 181 cm (5'11")
WEIGHT: 75 kg (165 lbs)
LOCATION: Dauper Village

A member of a family of hunters who live in the forest. He sends Sasha, who avoids interaction with those from outside her village, to the Training Corps (Volume 9, Episode 36).

PEAURE

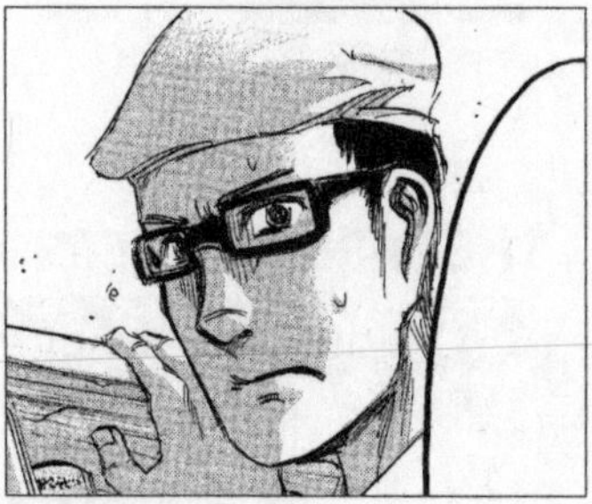

BIRTHDAY: February 28
HEIGHT: 173 cm (5'8")
WEIGHT: 62 kg (137 lbs)
AFFILIATION: Berg Newspapers

A young and enthusiastic reporter for Berg Newspapers, Peaure is fed up because he can't report the truth. Together with Hange, he tries to convince Roy to see things their way (Volume 15, Episode 60).

ROY

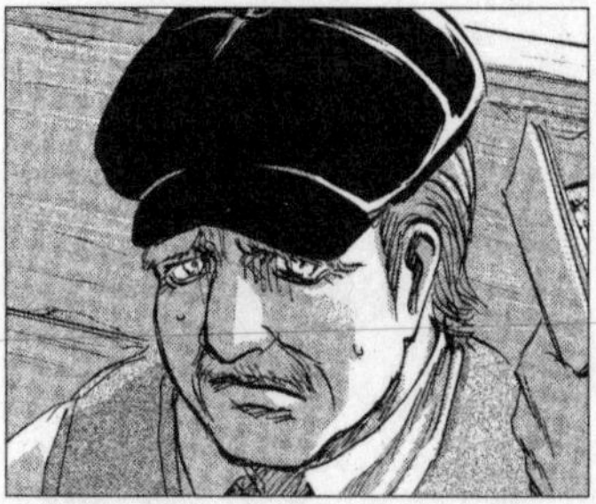

BIRTHDAY: April 29
HEIGHT: 163 cm (5'4")
WEIGHT: 60 kg (132 lbs)
AFFILIATION: Berg Newspapers

A veteran reporter for Berg Newspapers, Roy works with Hange and exposes the crimes of the Interior Squad (Volume 15, Episode 61).

CHUBBY MAN

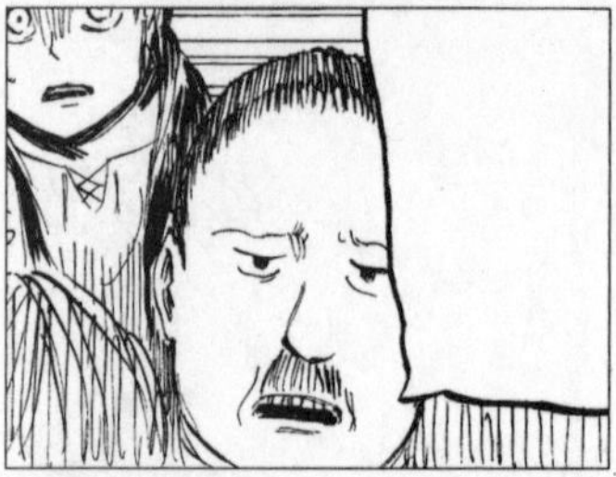

Calls the Survey Corps a waste of tax money as they return from outside the Walls.

SURVEY CORPSMAN BRAUN'S MOTHER

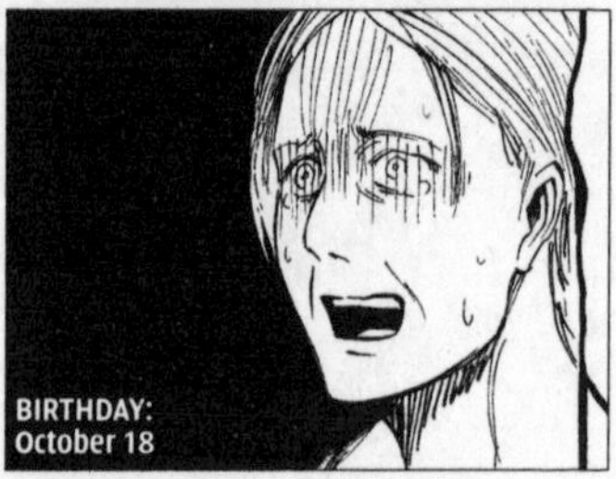
BIRTHDAY:
October 18

Asks Keith what her deceased son accomplished during the expedition.

MOTHER AND DAUGHTER WHO NOTICE THE CHARGING ABNORMAL

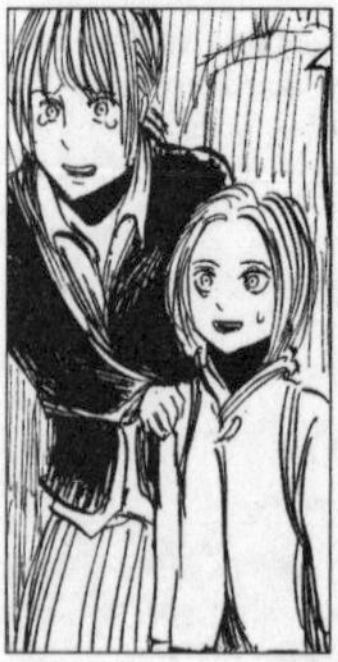

Though they are attacked by an Abnormal when Dimo Reeves delays the evacuation, Mikasa swoops in and saves them (Volume 2, Episode 5).

THE THREE BULLIES

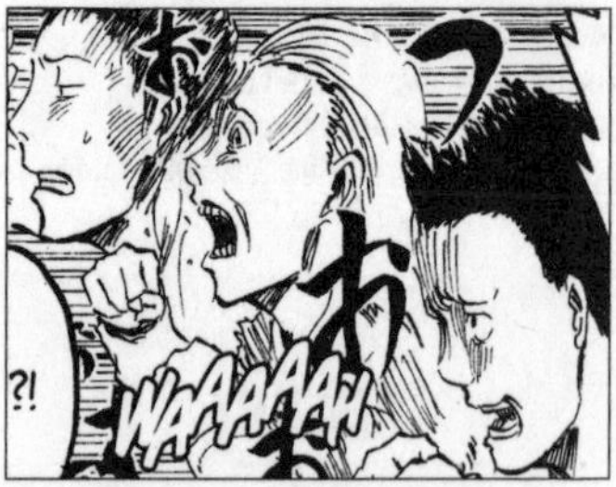
?!
WAAAAAH

Eren, Armin, and Mikasa's fated rivals.

ELDERLY SETTLEMENT DWELLERS

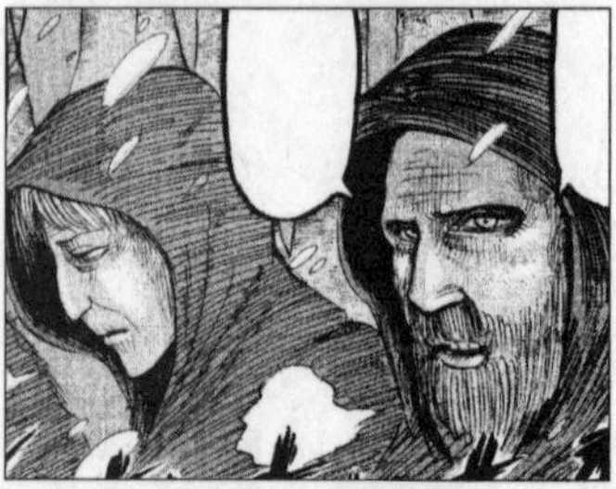

Before Eren joins the Training Corps, he cleared the land with these elderly individuals.

THE THREE ROBBERS

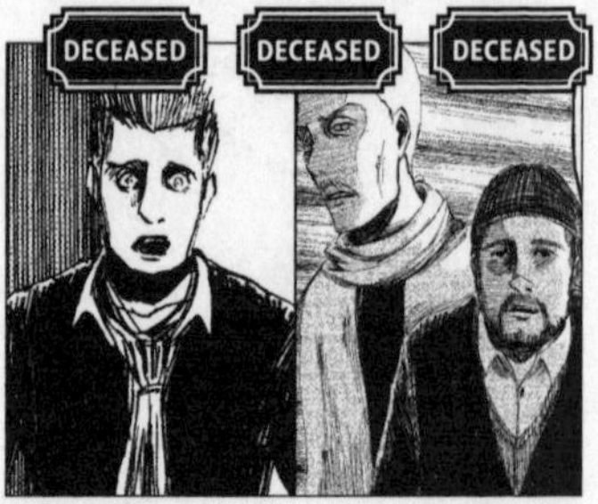
DECEASED
DECEASED
DECEASED

The trio who attacked Mikasa's home in order to capture people and sell them as slaves.

ELLIE AND THE BOY WITH A MISSING TOOTH

After the Survey Corps returns having taken major losses at the hands of the Female Titan, two kids look to Eren with adoration—which haunts him (volume 7, Episode 30).

MERCHANT

Advocates for the closing of the gates during the military trial held to judge Eren.

FERVENT MALE WALLIST

OH...

Draws close to the citizen who flippantly mentions the closing of the gates.

CITIZEN WHO HOPES FOR THE GATES TO CLOSE

He mentions the closing of the gates while on the street, earning the ire of a Wall Religion believer.

STOHESS DISTRICT MAYOR

Asks Erwin about the pros and cons of the plan to capture the Female Titan.

FEMALE WALLIST

DECEASED

BIRTHDAY:
April 16

Crushed by the Female Titan while worshipping at church.

GIRL SAVED BY SASHA

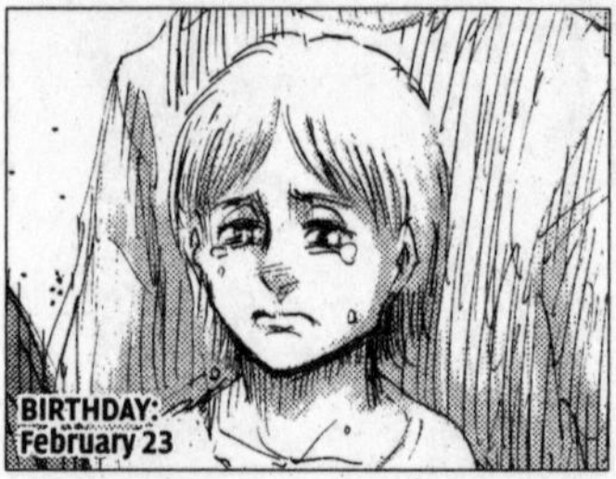
BIRTHDAY: February 23

Left stunned when her mother is attacked by Titans in front of her eyes.

MOTHER ATTACKED BY TITANS IN FRONT OF HER DAUGHTER

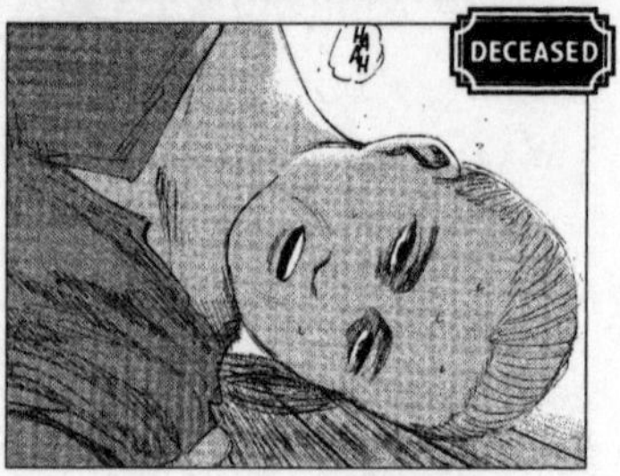
DECEASED

Lost her life when she was unable to run from the Titans because of her leg condition.

WOMAN AND CHILD WHO WATCH THE TURMOIL

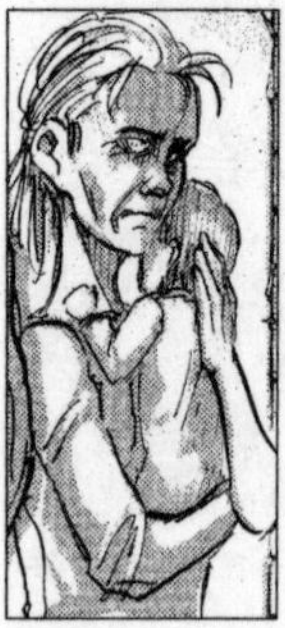

Watches from afar when uneasy citizens argue with Levi and the others (Volume 13, Episode 53). She later sees the Survey Corps off with a smile as they go off to retake Wall Maria (Volume 18, Episode 72).

OLD UNDERGROUND CITY EVACUEE

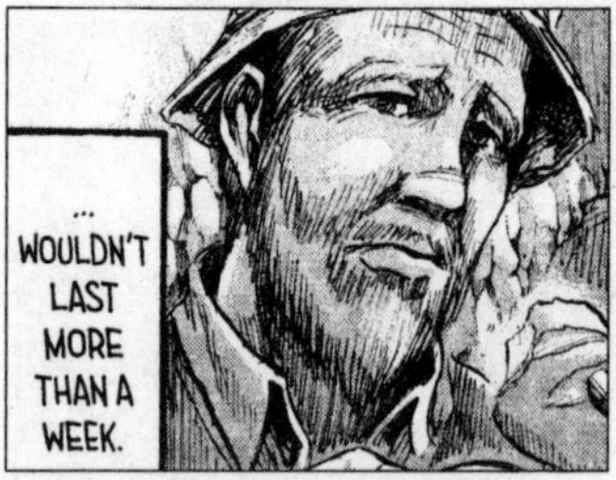
...WOULDN'T LAST MORE THAN A WEEK.

Forced to evacuate when he hears of Wall Rose being breached.

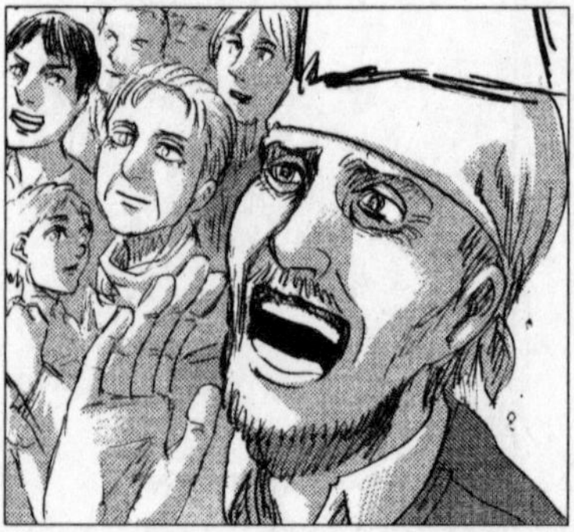

TROST DISTRICT CITIZEN

BIRTHDAY: August 12
HEIGHT: 180 cm (5'11")
WEIGHT: 72 kg (159 lbs)
LOCATION: Trost District

Believing that the Survey Corps are to blame for his miserable circumstances, he confronts Levi and the others with his displeasure (Volume 13, Episode 53). He changes his mind after the coup succeeds and says that his town was saved by the Survey Corps (Volume 18, Episode 72).

CRAFTSMAN WHO MAKES A REVOLUTIONARY WEAPON

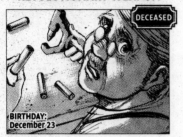

DECEASED

BIRTHDAY:
December 23

Killed by the Royal Government when they felt threatened by the weapon he developed.

ARMIN'S PARENTS

DECEASED

BIRTHDAYS:
November 18 (Father) / June 5 (Mother)

They planned to escape the Walls by way of hot air balloon, but were killed by Sannes and the others.

OWNER OF THE BAR WHERE LEVI ESCAPES

BIRTHDAY:
July 21

Stunned silent when his store suddenly becomes a battlefield.

BAR CUSTOMER

BIRTHDAY:
June 27

A man who eats something that appears to be a sausage in the pub.

THREE CHILDREN FROM ORVUD DISTRICT

These three look up at Eren and friends with adoration as they prepare for a Titan attack.

NEWSPAPER JOURNALIST

Tells Nile of the unease felt by the people about the political change.

MASTER OF THE UNDERGROUND CITY'S BROTHEL

Lets Kuchel, who is ill, stay at the brothel, without kicking her out.

OLD MAN IN ORVUD DISTRICT

Refuses to obey the evacuation order disguised as a drill, saying that he'll open his store instead.

DECEASED

KUCHEL (OLYMPIA)

BIRTHDAY: May 20
HEIGHT: 164 cm (5'5")
WEIGHT: 43 kg (95 lbs)
LOCATION: A brothel in the underground city

Kenny's younger sister and Levi's mother. Though she survived by working as a prostitute as she raised Levi by herself, she had already passed away from disease by the time that Kenny tracked her down (Volume 17, Episode 69).

CHILDREN AT THE ORPHANAGE

Children who live in the orphanage founded by Historia.

COLUMN The Goddess's Orphanage

After ascending to the throne, Historia is lovingly called the "cow-herding goddess" by the people. This is because she conducts a full investigation of the areas inside the Walls, including the old underground city, and comes up with measures to house and protect orphans and the destitute on the grounds of a certain farm (Volume 17, Episode 70).

HAJIME ISAYAMA Reveals

How His CHARACTERS WERE BORN: Part 4

LEVI

Levi's design first came from the idea of a small but mighty character, like Astro Boy or Ushiwakamaru (Minamoto no Yoshitsune). I think that Japanese people like these kinds of characters. I also love the character Rorschach from the movie *Watchmen*, but I thought that while the two characters may be small men, it would be better if Levi's appearance was the opposite of Rorschach's and made him pretty. This is also where his nature as a clean freak comes from.

I decided on Levi's personality as I was sketching his face. I felt like he would have a sour and difficult personality because of his sharp eyes and pale complexion.

Levi's name comes from a boy who appears in the documentary *Jesus Camp*. Though Levi is Hebrew for "contradiction," I chose it most of all because of how nice it sounds.

ERWIN SMITH

I modeled Erwin after one of the Secret Service members who appears in the music video for Paris Hilton's "Paris for President." With his neatly side-parted hair, I tried to make him look like the embodiment of American justice. This is because his image of fighting for freedom and fairness, the way that Superman or Captain America might, seemed appropriate for the head of the Survey Corps.

It took a while for me to settle on Erwin as a character even after he first appeared in the series. There's a scene in Volume 13 where it becomes known that the Titans are in fact, humans, causing everyone to feel depressed except for Erwin, who is laughing. That's around the time when it becomes clear that even Erwin, who was thought to be someone who is always right, was not right about everything, making his character come alive.

HANGE ZOË

When I was thinking about how to differentiate characters, a thought came to me, "That's right, glasses!" Regular glasses would be dangerous to use in combat, though, and so I decided that Hange would wear goggles with corrective lenses. Hange is a character who starts with glasses and goes from there.

Hange is made Commander of the Survey Corps because the organization needs someone to stand at its top, be its face, and take responsibility for it so that its members can move about freely. That's why it couldn't put Levi, who in soccer terms is the Survey Corps's libero, or sweeper, at the top of its organization.

I decided on the name Hange Zoë because I liked the way it sounded a little odd. A majority of the characters who appear in *Titan* have been given actual German names.

TRACKING YMIR'S
Tumultuous FATE
Until She Gained Her
FREEDOM

Around 780 onward	• An unknown man picks her up and names her Ymir when she is a beggar in Marley • Ymir is captured by the Marley Public Security Authorities and persecuted • Ymir is turned into a Pure Titan and expelled from Marley

Wandered around for about 60 years

845, Shiganshina District falls	• Near Wall Maria on the island of Paradis, Ymir eats one of Marley's Warriors named Marcel, gains the power of the Jaw Titan, and returns to human form • Vows to stop pretending to be "Ymir" and to live her life as she sees fit

Around ???	• At a church inside the Walls, Ymir hears rumors of Historia, a young girl pursued by the Royal Family, and joins the Survey Corps in search of her • Ymir meets Historia in the 104th Training Corps

850	• Ymir uses the power of the Jaw and transforms into a Titan to save Historia during the battle inside Wall Rose • Ymir decides to join forces with Reiner and the others, fearing that Historia may fall into Marley's hands • Ymir writes a farewell letter to Historia...

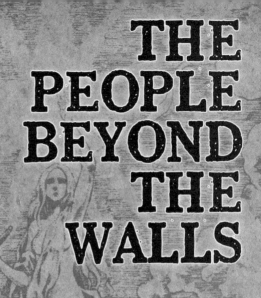

THE
PEOPLE
BEYOND
THE
WALLS

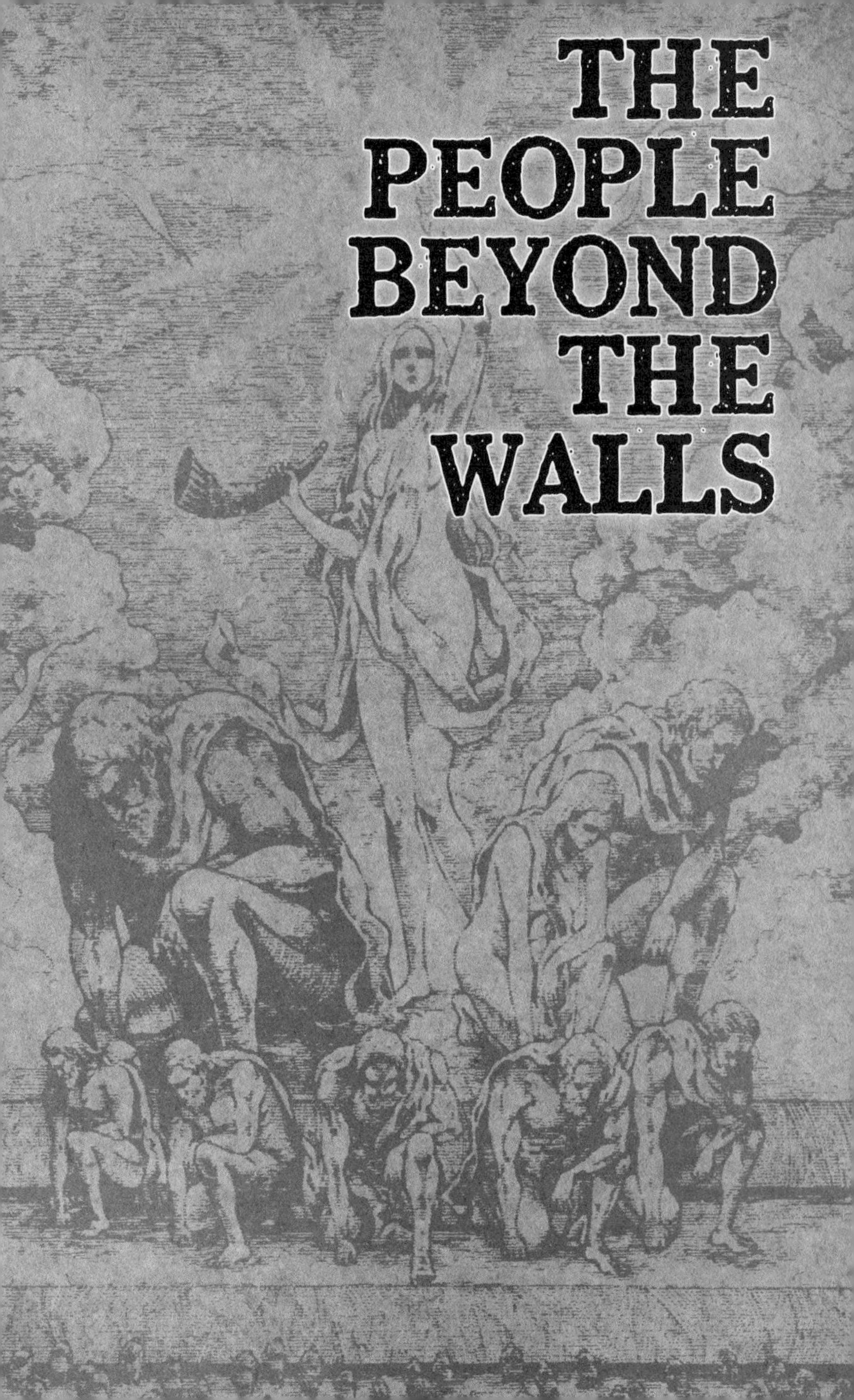

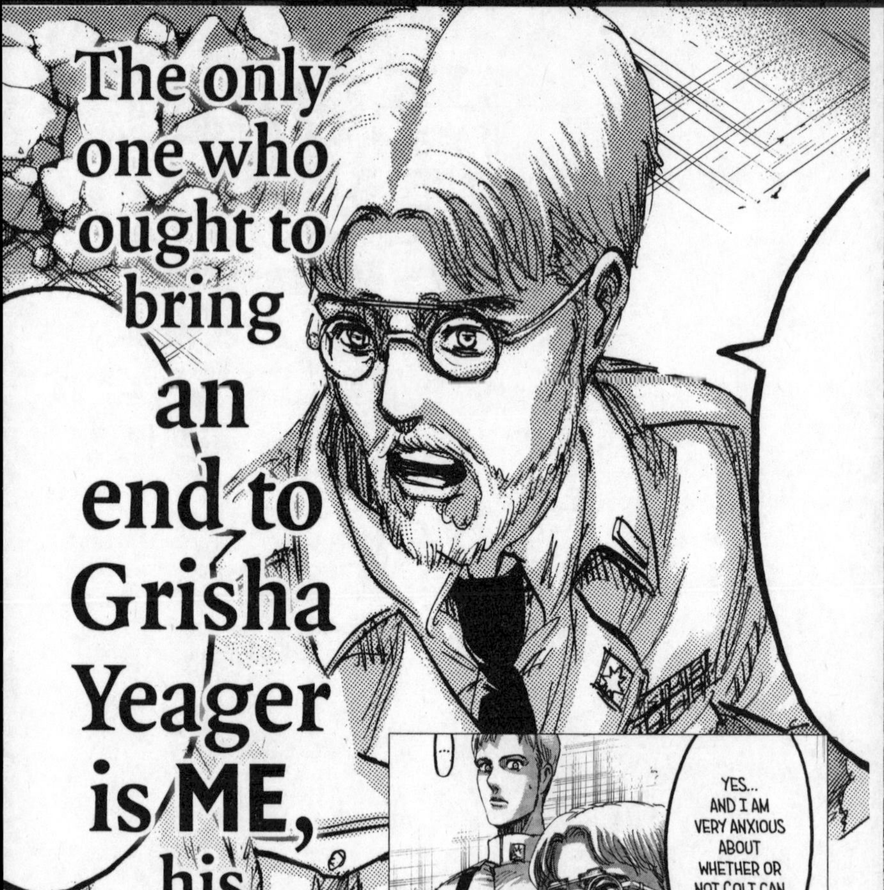
The only one who ought to bring an end to Grisha Yeager is ME, his former son.
...
YES... AND I AM VERY ANXIOUS ABOUT WHETHER OR NOT COLT CAN INHERIT...
...THE FULL POWERS OF MY BEAST.

ZEKE YEAGER

BIRTHDAY: August 1 • **HEIGHT:** 183 cm (6'0") • **WEIGHT:** 92 kg (203 lbs)
AFFILIATION: Marley, Captain of the Warriors

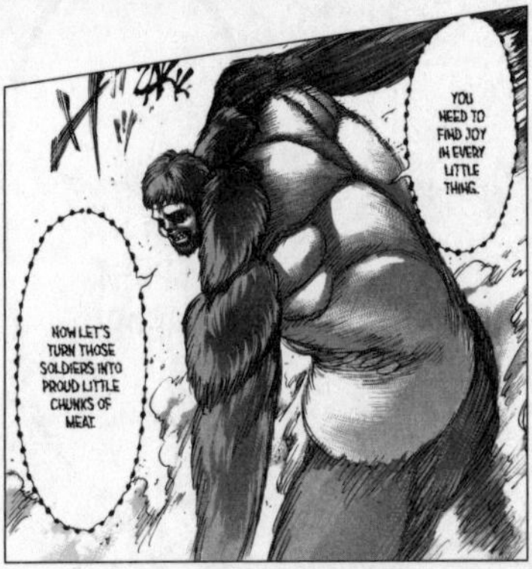
YOU NEED TO FIND JOY IN EVERY LITTLE THING.
NOW LET'S TURN THOSE SOLDIERS INTO PROUD LITTLE CHUNKS OF MEAT.

Marley's Captain of the Warriors who leads their Titans using the power of the Beast

Captain of Marley's Warrior Unit, Zeke uses the Beast Titan, one of the Nine Titans, to attack those who live inside the Walls. His goal is to retake the Founding Titan, which he and others call the "Coordinate." It was once stolen from Marley (Volume 19, Episode 77 and more).

Born as Grisha's son, he sells out his parents for his and his grandparents' safety

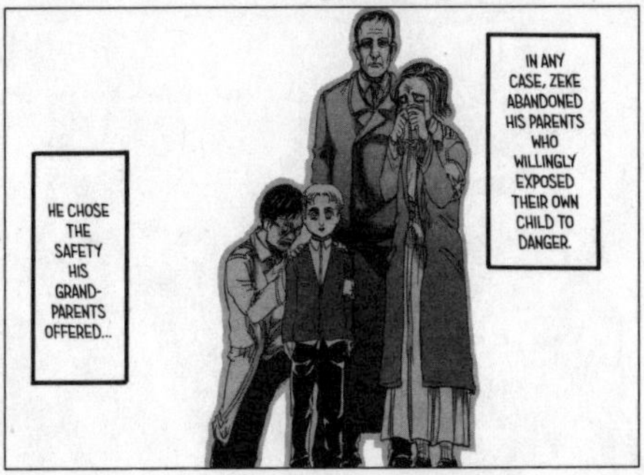
IN ANY CASE, ZEKE ABANDONED HIS PARENTS WHO WILLINGLY EXPOSED THEIR OWN CHILD TO DANGER.
HE CHOSE THE SAFETY HIS GRAND-PARENTS OFFERED...

Zeke was born to Dina Fritz and Grisha Yeager before Grisha came to the Walls. Zeke grows to hate the extreme ideology his parents try to force upon him and sells them out, informing the Marleyan Government about them in order to protect himself and his grandparents (Volume 22, Episode 87).

While he plans to retake the Founding Titan once more as a Marleyan warrior...

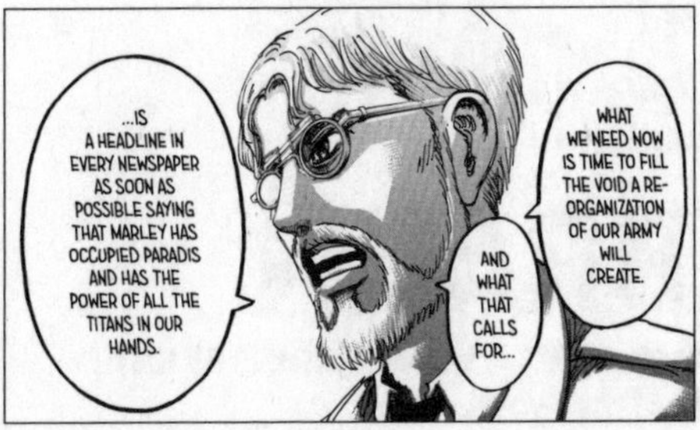
WHAT WE NEED NOW IS TIME TO FILL THE VOID A RE-ORGANIZATION OF OUR ARMY WILL CREATE.
AND WHAT THAT CALLS FOR...
...IS A HEADLINE IN EVERY NEWSPAPER AS SOON AS POSSIBLE SAYING THAT MARLEY HAS OCCUPIED PARADIS AND HAS THE POWER OF ALL THE TITANS IN OUR HANDS.

Zeke is defeated by the Survey Corps in Shiganshina and returns to Marley. He then begins to plan once more to retake the Founding Titan in order to secure the future of his country, which finds itself at war with other nations. Anyone who inherits one of the Nine Titans will die in 13 years—and Zeke has just one year left (Volume 23, Episode 93).

I infiltrated the army on that island.

It was true **HELL.**

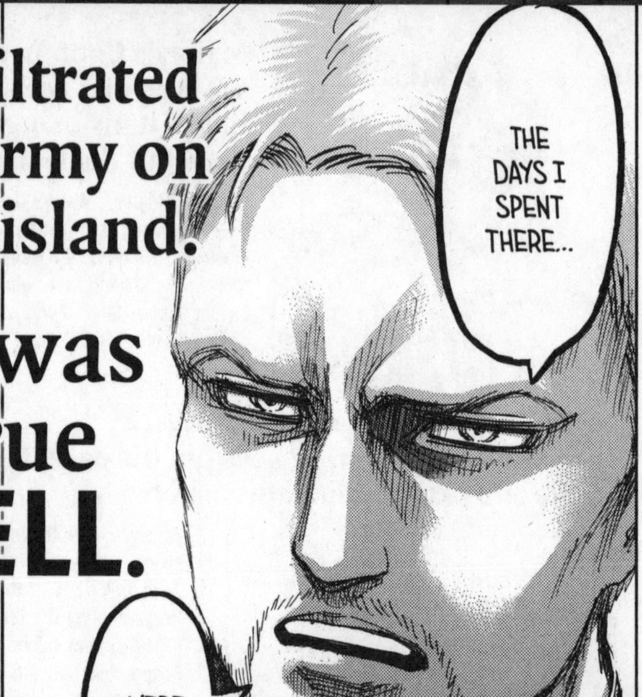
THE DAYS I SPENT THERE...
...WERE TRUE HELL.

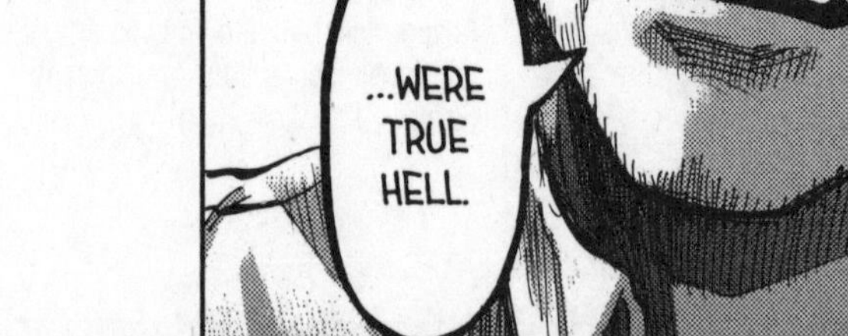
YOU ONLY HAVE TWO YEARS LEFT IN YOUR TERM.
... THAT'S RIGHT.

REINER BRAUN

BIRTHDAY: August 1 • **HEIGHT:** 188 cm (6'2") • **WEIGHT:** 83 kg (183 lbs)
AFFILIATION: Marley, Vice Captain of the Warrior Unit

A Marleyan warrior who snuck inside the Walls, but something happens after spending time with Eren and the others...

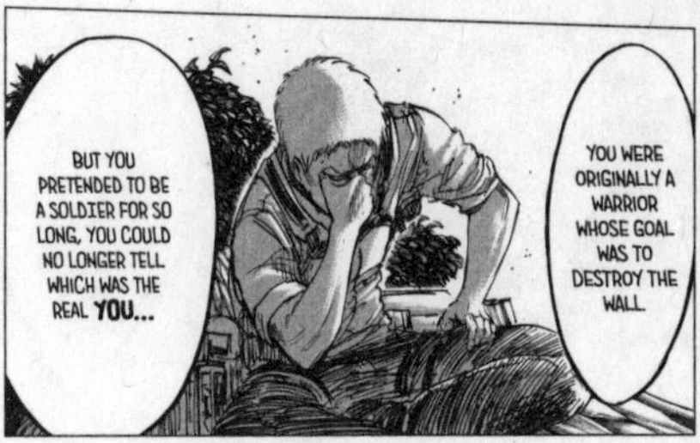
YOU WERE ORIGINALLY A WARRIOR WHOSE GOAL WAS TO DESTROY THE WALL.
BUT YOU PRETENDED TO BE A SOLDIER FOR SO LONG, YOU COULD NO LONGER TELL WHICH WAS THE REAL YOU...

Reiner is a Marleyan Warrior who once snuck inside the Walls in order to take back the Founding Titan. After joining the Survey Corps and meeting Eren and the soldiers, his guilt causes him to lose sight of what he truly is—a Marleyan Warrior or a soldier for humanity. He cannot seem to balance his mind anymore (Volume 11, Episode 46 and more).

Transforms into the Armored Titan to fight Eren and the others to carry out his mission as a Warrior

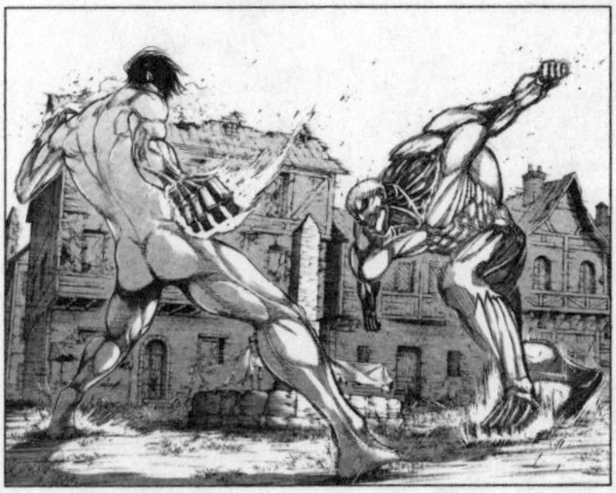

Of the Nine Titans, Reiner possesses the power of the Armor. As the Armored Titan, he teams with Bertolt's Colossus Titan and attacks Shiganshina District (Volume 1, Episode 2). After he regains his nearly lost sense of self, he goes head-to-head with Eren's Titan twice in order to retake the Founding Titan (Volume 19, Episode 75 and more).

Though he fights as the Armored Titan after returning to Marley...

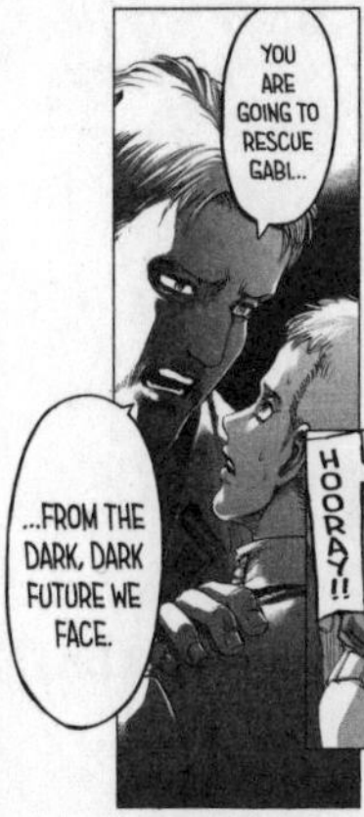
YOU ARE GOING TO RESCUE GABI...
...FROM THE DARK, DARK FUTURE WE FACE.

Reiner is defeated in the decisive battle in Shiganshina District and his severe wounds force him to retreat. After returning to Marley, he participates in a four-year war with the Mid-East Allied Forces as a Warrior who possesses the Armor. Now that he is nearly down to two years remaining in his 13-year term, he waits for the Armor's inheritor to be fostered from among the Warrior candidates... While he seems to be concerned for Falco and Gabi, both Warrior candidates, what are Reiner's true motives...? (Volume 23, Episode 93).

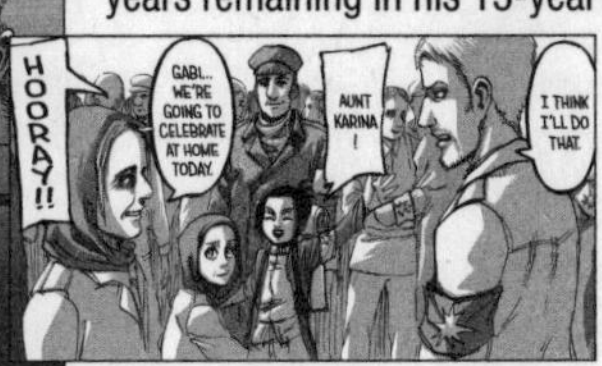
I THINK I'LL DO THAT.
AUNT KARINA!
GABI... WE'RE GOING TO CELEBRATE AT HOME TODAY.
HOORAY!!

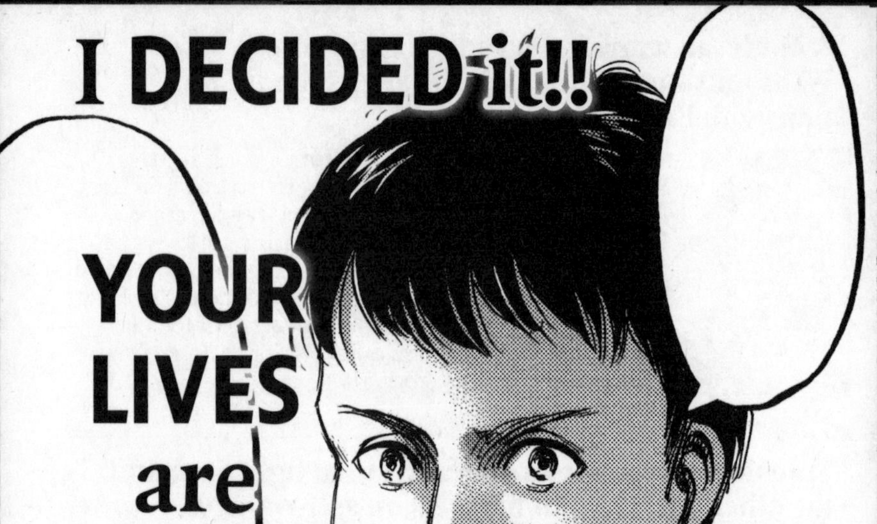
I DECIDED it!!
YOUR LIVES are coming to an END right here!!

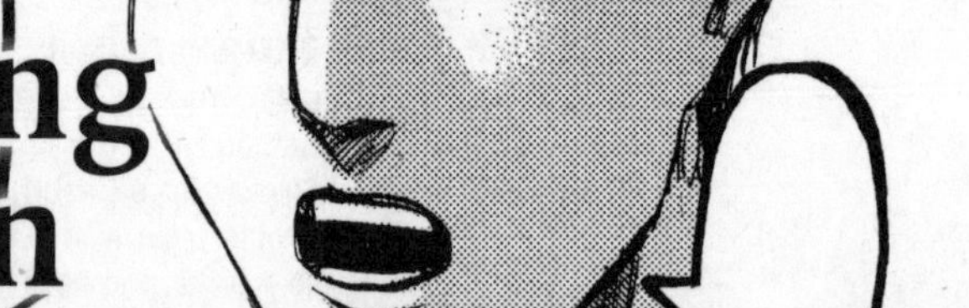
WHAT'RE YOU GOING TO DO...
...
BERTOLT?

DECEASED

BERTOLT HOOVER

BIRTHDAY: December 30 • **HEIGHT:** 192 cm (6'4") • **WEIGHT:** 81 kg (179 lbs)
AFFILIATION: Marley, Warrior Unit

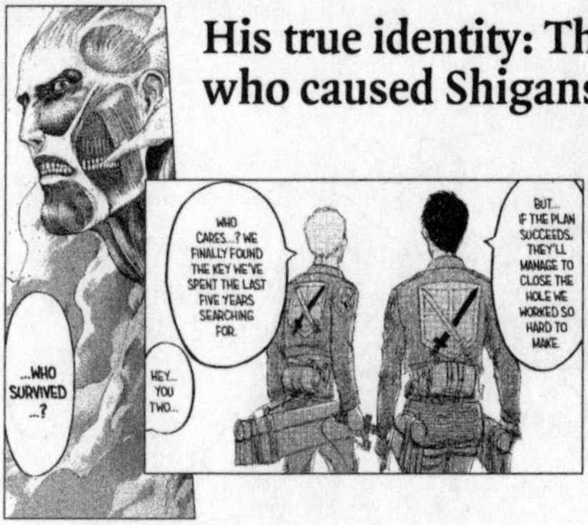
BUT... IF THE PLAN SUCCEEDS, THEY'LL MANAGE TO CLOSE THE HOLE WE WORKED SO HARD TO MAKE.
WHO CARES...? WE FINALLY FOUND THE KEY WE'VE SPENT THE LAST FIVE YEARS SEARCHING FOR.
HEY... YOU TWO...
...WHO SURVIVED ...?

His true identity: The Colossus Titan, the one who caused Shiganshina District's destruction

Bertolt was a Marleyan Warrior who held the power of a Titan, and he was none other than the Colossus Titan who appeared in Shiganshina District in 845 (Volume 1, Episode 1). This attack was carried out as part of the Marleyan Army's plan to retake the Founder. Afterwards, he, Reiner, and Annie infiltrated the Corps as soldiers and waited for their opportunity (Volume 19, Episode 77 and more).

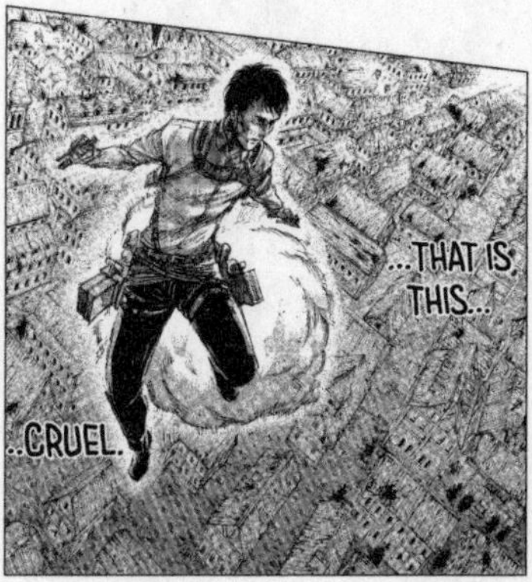
...THAT IS THIS...
...CRUEL.

Tossed out his emotions for his peers and bared his fangs at humanity

Though his personality caused him to leave important decisions up to others, Bertolt awakened when he saw that Eren and the others were his enemy during the decisive battle in Shiganshina District. He threw out everything he felt for his fellow trainees that he slept and ate alongside and attempted to end humanity inside the Walls in order to retake the Founding Titan for Marley. It was only possible because Bertolt had accepted the cruelty of the world (Volume 19, Episode 78).

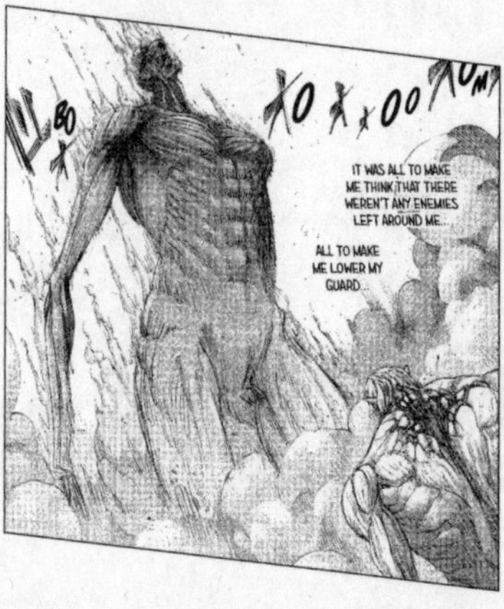
IT WAS ALL TO MAKE ME THINK THAT THERE WEREN'T ANY ENEMIES LEFT AROUND ME...
ALL TO MAKE ME LOWER MY GUARD...

Fell to Eren during the decisive battle in Shiganshina District

Though he nearly drove the Survey Corps to destruction in the decisive battle in Shiganshina District, he was defeated by the plan that put Eren and Armin's lives at risk. Though he sought help from Reiner while fatally wounded, his cries went unanswered and he was eaten by Armin, who had been turned into a Pure Titan. Now Armin possesses the power of the Colossus Titan (Volume 21, Episode 84).

Even if I'm the kind of **WEAK** person who gets swept along with the flow...

I just want you to think of me as **HUMAN...**

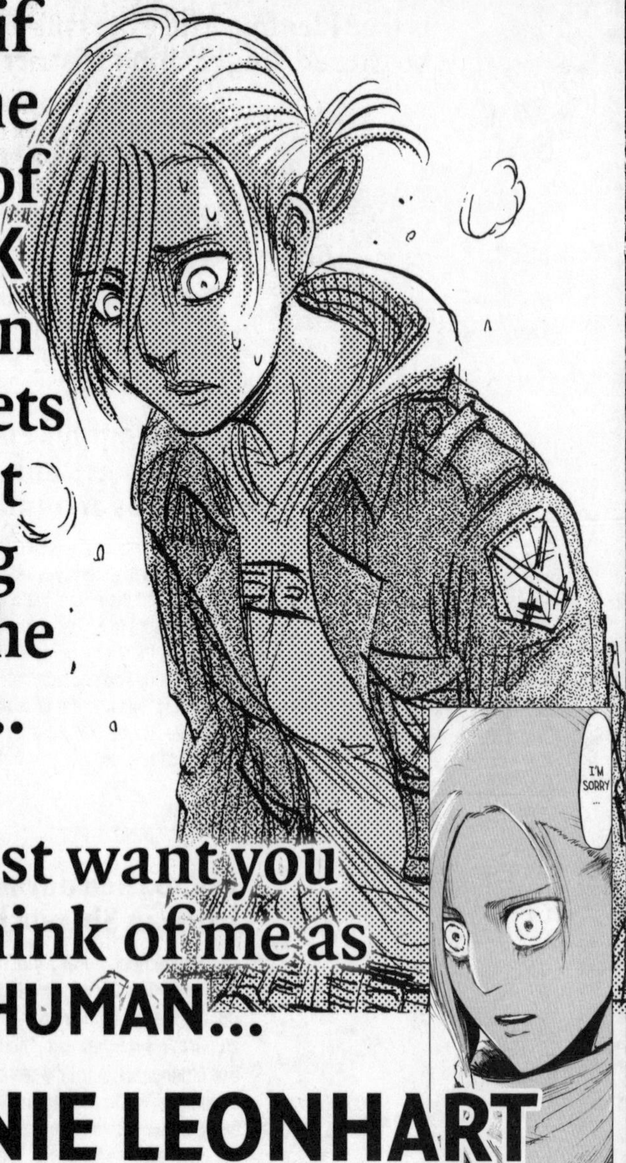
I'M SORRY...

ANNIE LEONHART

BIRTHDAY: March 22 • **HEIGHT:** 153 cm (5'0") • **WEIGHT:** 54 kg (119 lbs)
AFFILIATION: Marley, Warrior Unit

WHY IS IT THAT IN THIS WORLD THE PEOPLE WITH THE BEST ABILITY TO OPPOSE THE TITANS GET THE PRIVILEGE OF STAYING FAR AWAY FROM THEM?

A hidden Warrior who points out the farce taking place inside the Walls

Annie is another one of the Marleyan Warriors who infiltrates the Corps. While in the Training Corps, she points out the contradiction in the way the organizations inside the Walls operate, saying, "Why is it that in this world, the people with the best ability to oppose the Titans get the privilege of staying far away from them?" (Volume 4, Episode 17). Annie has a cool personality, avoiding contact with friends and allies.

FOSSSSHH
BOTH TITANS HAVE BEEN KILLED !!

Works with Reiner and Bertolt as the Female Titan

As a Warrior who has inherited the Female Titan, she works in secret with Reiner and Bertolt toward their goal of retaking the Founding Titan. She faces off against Eren in direct battle in order to also take his Attack Titan (Volume 7, Episode 29 and more), but Annie's feelings toward Eren and the others are complicated...

SHE IS CURRENTLY BEING DETAINED DEEP UNDER-GROUND.
AS HER ENTIRE BODY IS NOW SURROUNDED BY A HARD, CRYSTALLINE SUBSTANCE...
...IT IS IMPOS-SIBLE TO EXTRACT ANY INFORMA-TION FROM HER.
WHAT THE HELL IS THIS...? WHAT'S GOING ON ...?
C'MON ...

Captured by the Survey Corps but covers herself in a sturdy crystal

Annie falls for a Survey Corps plot in Stohess District and is defeated in battle by Eren's Titan, leading to her arrest. But just before they can confine her, Annie covers herself in a hard crystal substance and falls into a deep sleep, the power of the Female Titan still inside of her. She now seems to be kept somewhere deep underground inside the Walls (Volume 8, Episode 34 and more).

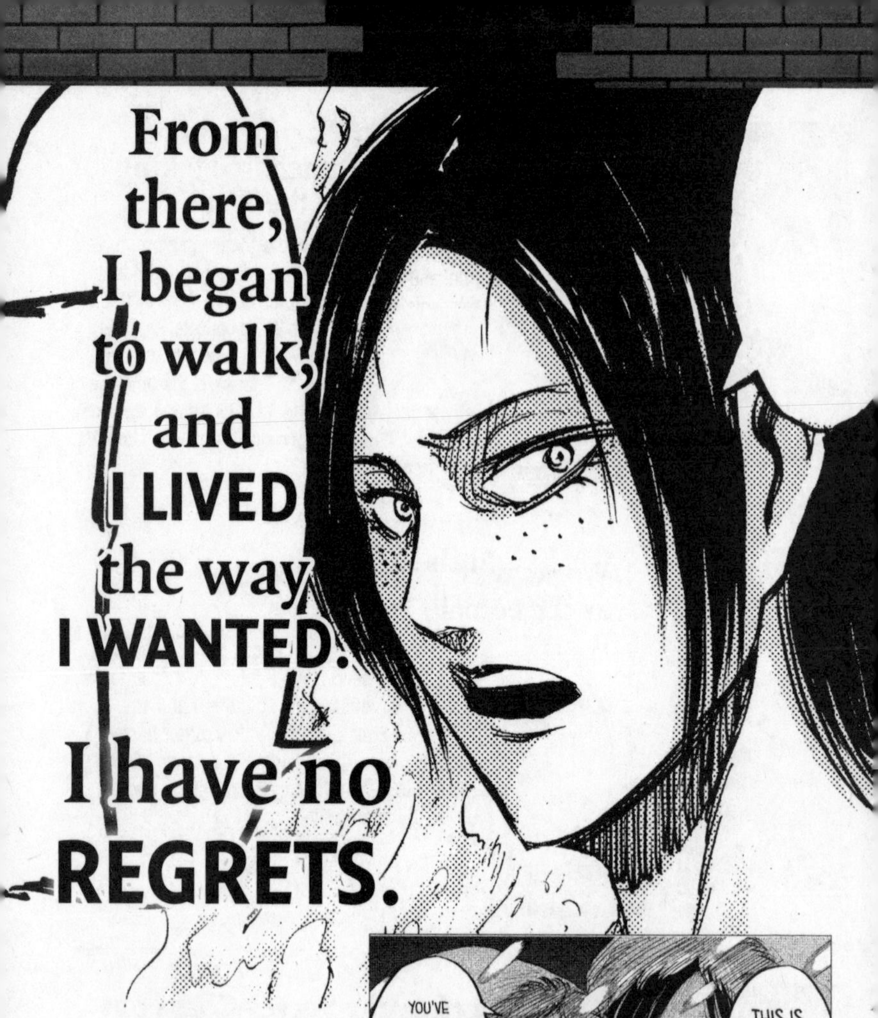

From there, I began to walk, and **I LIVED** the way **I WANTED.**

I have no **REGRETS.**

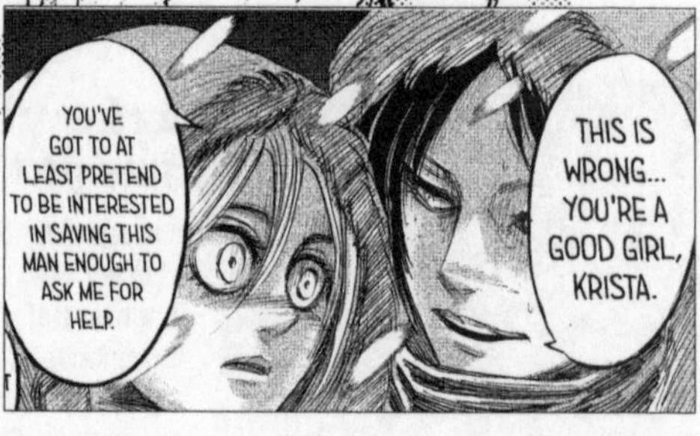
THIS IS WRONG... YOU'RE A GOOD GIRL, KRISTA.
YOU'VE GOT TO AT LEAST PRETEND TO BE INTERESTED IN SAVING THIS MAN ENOUGH TO ASK ME FOR HELP.

DECEASED

YMIR

BIRTHDAY: February 17 • HEIGHT: 172 cm (5'8") • WEIGHT: 63 kg (139 lbs)

An outspoken girl who fussed over Krista

As a member of the 104th Training Corps, Ymir trained alongside Eren and the others. She had a cruel side to her, and she often picked at people's insecurities. For some reason, she had a strong interest in Krista from the time she joined the 104th, and it turned out that it was because Krista's way of living, hiding her history with the Reiss Family, was similar to Ymir's own past (Volume 4, Episode 15 and more).

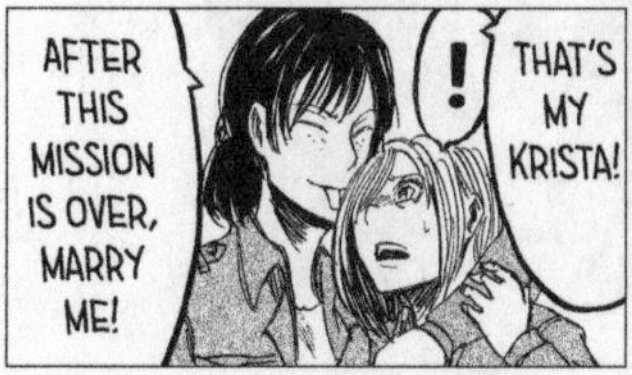
THAT'S MY KRISTA!
!
AFTER THIS MISSION IS OVER, MARRY ME!

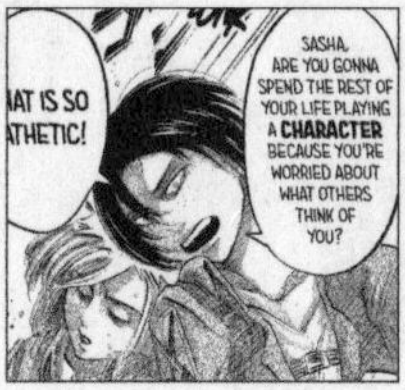
SASHA, ARE YOU GONNA SPEND THE REST OF YOUR LIFE PLAYING A CHARACTER BECAUSE YOU'RE WORRIED ABOUT WHAT OTHERS THINK OF YOU?

Though she used one of the Nine Titans to live a life of freedom...

Though the Jaw Titan dwelled inside of Ymir, she was not a Marleyan Warrior. Certain circumstances in Marley had led to Ymir being turned into a Pure Titan, and she then gained the power of the Jaw while wandering the land (Volume 10, Episode 40). Once she did, she swore to live a life of freedom. Ymir returned to Marley in order to protect Krista, but only punishment awaited her there.

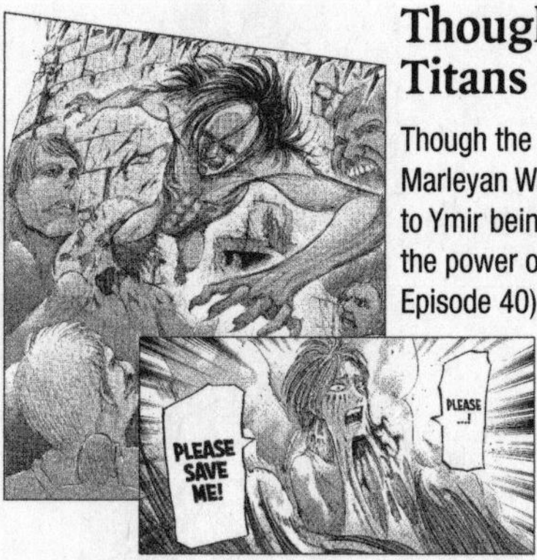
PLEASE ...!
PLEASE SAVE ME!

Hidden in her past were painful experiences in Marley

As a child, Ymir lived in Marley as a beggar. But the appearance of one man led to her being named Ymir and worshipped by many. Even after being raided by the Marley Public Security Authorities, she continued to play the role of Ymir for the sake of others until she was turned into a Pure Titan and expelled from Marley (Volume 22, Episode 89).

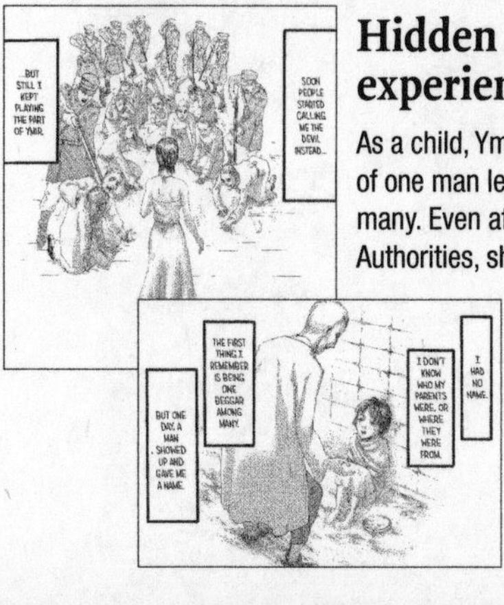
SOON PEOPLE STARTED CALLING ME THE DEVIL INSTEAD...
BUT STILL I KEPT PLAYING THE PART OF YMIR.
I HAD NO NAME.
I DON'T KNOW WHO MY PARENTS WERE, OR WHERE THEY WERE FROM.
THE FIRST THING I REMEMBER IS BEING ONE BEGGAR AMONG MANY.
BUT ONE DAY, A MAN SHOWED UP AND GAVE ME A NAME.

GABI

BIRTHDAY: April 14
HEIGHT: 138 cm (4'6")
WEIGHT: 30 kg (66 lbs)
AFFILIATION: Marley, Warrior candidate

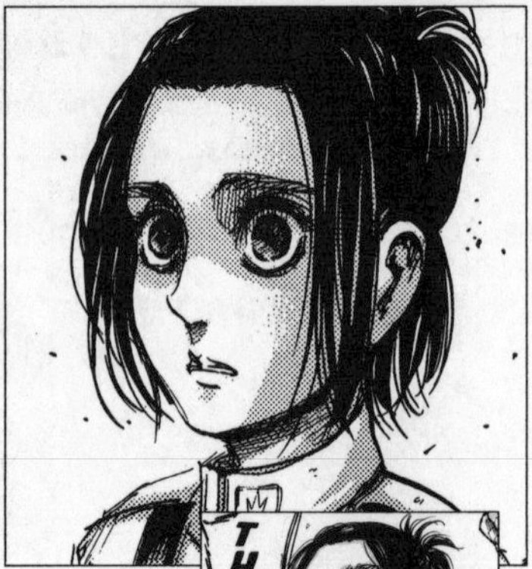

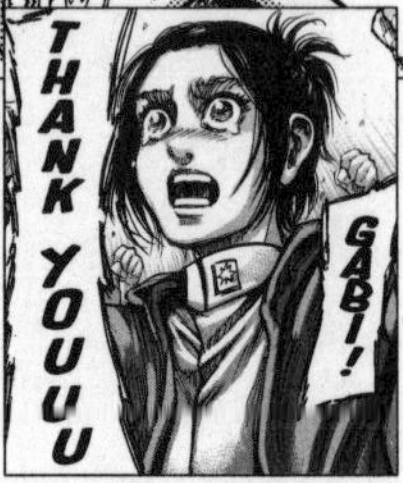
THANK YOUUUU
GABI!

A girl with trusting eyes who throws herself into battle

As Reiner's cousin, Gabi aims to become the next Armored Titan. She believes that if she fights for Marley, she will be able to free Eldians from the wicked Ymir's blood. She has achieved some unprecedented acts of valor, such as pretending to surrender and then destroying an armored train (Volume 23, Episode 91).

FALCO GRICE

BIRTHDAY: February 10
HEIGHT: 140 cm (4'7")
WEIGHT: 34 kg (75 lbs)
AFFILIATION: Marley, Warrior candidate

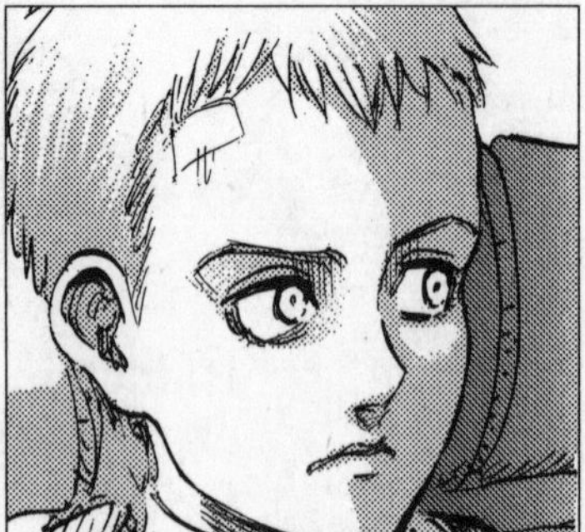

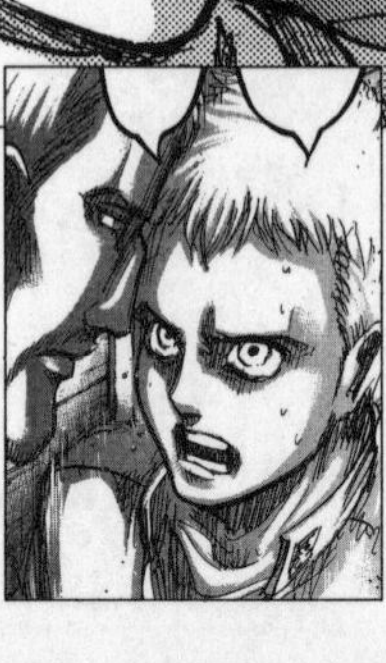

Aims to become the Armored Titan in order to protect Gabi

One of the Marleyan military's Warrior candidates, Falco has a liking for Gabi and swears to Reiner that he will become the next Armored Titan in order to protect her. Unlike the other Warrior candidates, his words and actions sometimes show that he may not think that fighting for Marley will necessarily help the Eldians (Volume 23, Episode 94 and more).

COLT GRICE

BIRTHDAY: August 12
HEIGHT: 180 cm (5'11")
WEIGHT: 65 kg (143 lbs)
AFFILIATION: Marley, Warrior candidate

SHE WENT ALONE IN THE PLACE OF EIGHT HUNDRED OF OUR COMRADES... WITH NOTHING BUT A CLUSTER OF GRENADES!
YOU'RE DRUNK, COLT.
C'MON...
SHE FACED OFF AGAINST THE ARMORED TRAIN AND STOOD HER GROUND!!

The oldest Warrior candidate and their leader

Falco's older brother and the oldest Warrior candidate. Colt braves oncoming enemy fire and rescues an immobile Falco during the battle for Fort Slava (Volume 23, Episode 91). A bad drunk, he loudly makes a fool of himself on the train home from the battlefield, calling Gabi a goddess (Volume 23, Episode 93).

ZOFIA

BIRTHDAY: September 26
HEIGHT: 142 cm (4'8")
WEIGHT: 34 kg (75 lbs)
AFFILIATION: Marley, Warrior candidate

A quiet and unexpressive girl. She sometimes says things that have nothing to do with the conversation (Volume 23, Episode 93).

UDO

BIRTHDAY: October 7
HEIGHT: 146 cm (4'10")
WEIGHT: 39 kg (86 lbs)
AFFILIATION: Marley, Warrior candidate

A boy who battles in order to inherit a Titan. While he may appear to be mild-mannered, he can sometimes go berserk when excited (Volume 23, Episode 91)

PORCO GALLIARD

BIRTHDAY: November 11
HEIGHT: 175 cm (5'9")
WEIGHT: 75 kg (165 lbs)
AFFILIATION: Marley, Warrior Unit

The Warrior who inherited the Jaw Titan from Ymir

The younger brother of Marcel, who participated in the Paradis plan with Reiner and the others. When Marcel saves Reiner from danger during the battle for Fort Slava, he treats Reiner coldly because he blames Reiner for Marcel's death (Volume 23, Episode 92 and more). Pieck sometimes calls him "Pock" (Volume 23, Episode 93).

PIECK

BIRTHDAY: February 10
HEIGHT: 140 cm (4'7")
WEIGHT: 34 kg (75 lbs)
AFFILIATION: Marley, Warrior Unit

A girl with sleepy eyes who inherited the Cart Titan

Pieck supports Zeke and the others during the Paradis plan by carrying supplies and patrolling (Volume 19, Chapter 75 and others). While she is able to maintain Titan form for upwards of two months, she says she forgets how to walk on two legs afterwards (Volume 23, Chapter 93). During their return to Liberio, she hands Colt some liquor and causes a stir (Volume 23, Chapter 94).

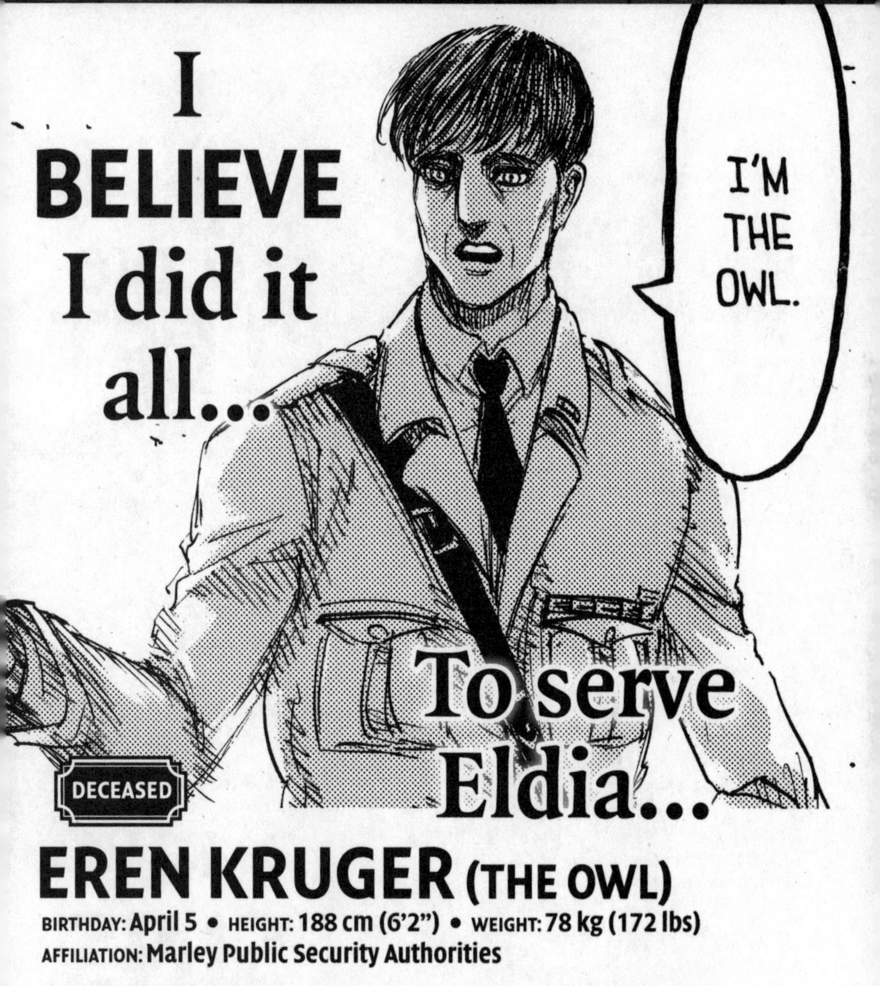
I BELIEVE I did it all...
I'M THE OWL.
To serve Eldia...
DECEASED

EREN KRUGER (THE OWL)

BIRTHDAY: April 5 • **HEIGHT:** 188 cm (6'2") • **WEIGHT:** 78 kg (172 lbs)
AFFILIATION: Marley Public Security Authorities

The man who entrusted Grisha with the Attack Titan

While he appeared to be an officer for the Marley Public Security Authorities, he secretly worked to lead the anti-establishment underground group of Eldian Restorationists as "the Owl." Because of the impending end of his 13-year term, he gave the power of the Attack Titan that was inside of him to Grisha, entrusting him with the mission of taking the Founding Titan to restore Eldia (Volume 22, Episode 88 and more).

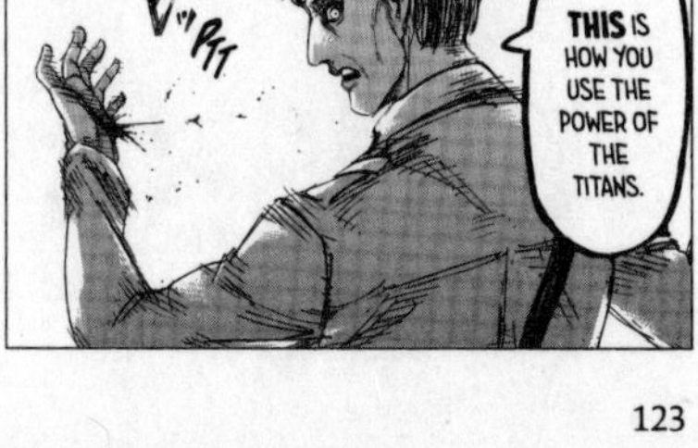
THIS IS HOW YOU USE THE POWER OF THE TITANS.

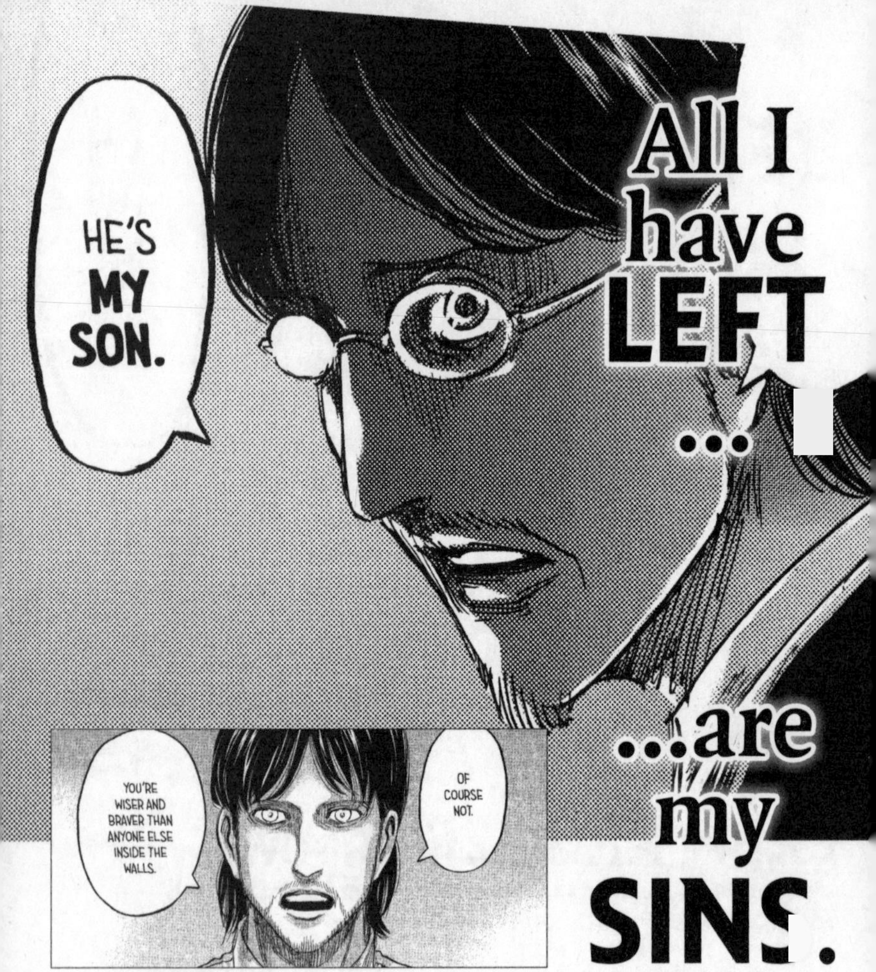
All I have LEFT...
...are my SINS.
HE'S MY SON.
OF COURSE NOT.
YOU'RE WISER AND BRAVER THAN ANYONE ELSE INSIDE THE WALLS.

DECEASED

GRISHA YEAGER

BIRTHDAY: January 26 • **HEIGHT:** 182 cm (6'0") • **WEIGHT:** 78 kg (172 lbs)
AFFILIATION: Eldian

Inherited the Attack Titan from the Owl in order to restore Eldia

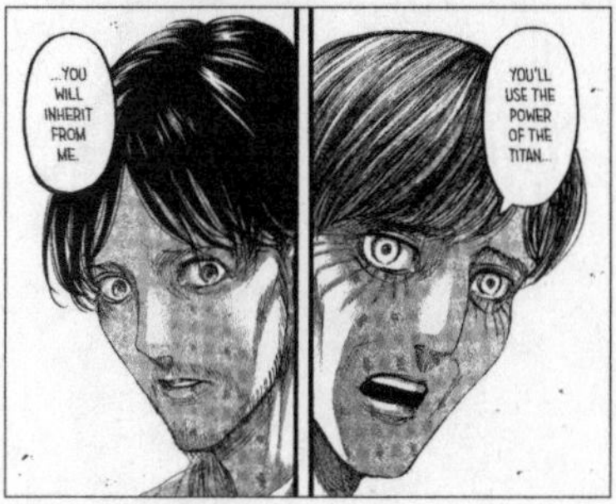
YOU'LL USE THE POWER OF THE TITAN...
...YOU WILL INHERIT FROM ME.

Grisha was born to Eldians in Marley, and the death of his little sister at the hands of the Public Security Authorities drove him to devote himself to the Eldian Restorationists, an underground anti-establishment group. While Grisha lost everything when his son Zeke exposed him, Eren Kruger's betrayal of the government resulted in Grisha inheriting the power of the Attack Titan before moving inside the Walls on the island of Paradis (Volume 22, Episode 88 and more).

Left the Attack and the Founding Titans to Eren before dying

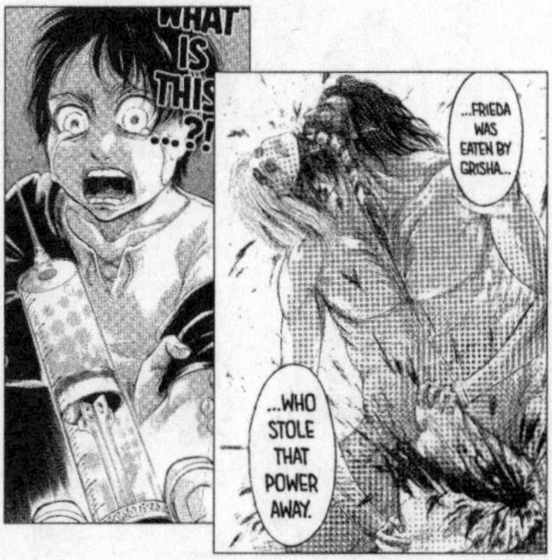
...FRIEDA WAS EATEN BY GRISHA...
...WHO STOLE THAT POWER AWAY.
WHAT IS THIS...?!

Grisha snuck inside the walls in order to retake the Founding Titan, which Marley took from Eldia before losing it once again. Grisha was able to take the Founding Titan from Frieda Reiss before turning Eren—his son with his second wife Carla—into a Titan and feeding himself to him, handing down the powers of the Attack and Founding Titans (Volume 18, Episode 71 and more).

What did he leave in the basement? The truth about the world.

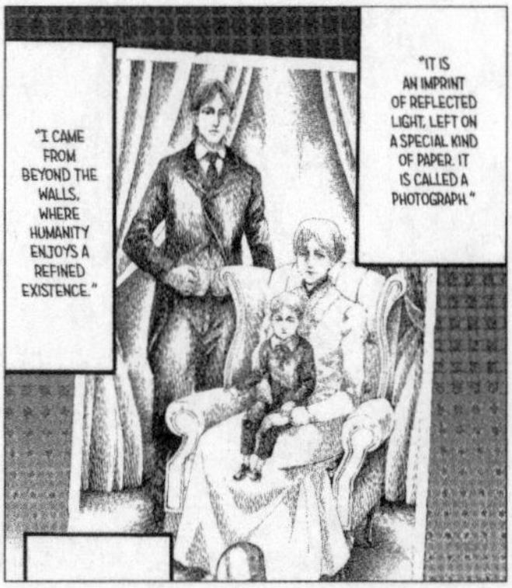
"IT IS AN IMPRINT OF REFLECTED LIGHT, LEFT ON A SPECIAL KIND OF PAPER. IT IS CALLED A PHOTOGRAPH."
"I CAME FROM BEYOND THE WALLS, WHERE HUMANITY ENJOYS A REFINED EXISTENCE."

Grisha once promised to show Eren the basement of his home, where Grisha stored items from his time living in Marley (Volume 21, Episode 85). As Grisha came up on the 13-year time limit since inheriting the Attack Titan, his plan may have been to hand his own mission down to Eren all along. Perhaps this would have happened regardless of whether the Colossus Titan appeared inside of Shiganshina District or not.

DECEASED

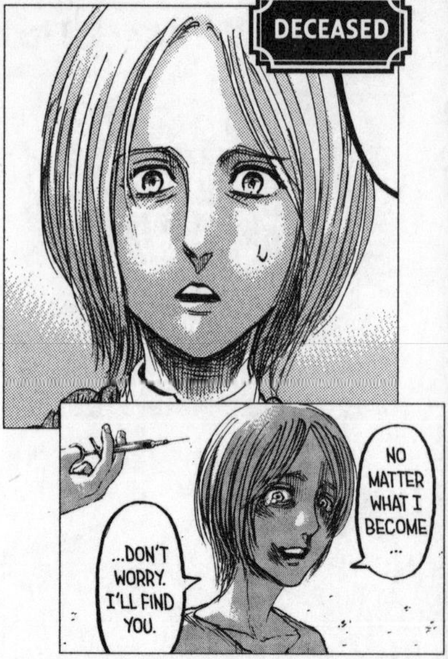
NO MATTER WHAT I BECOME ...
...DON'T WORRY. I'LL FIND YOU.

DINA FRITZ

Birthday: July 26
Height: 168 cm (5'6")
Weight: 45 kg (99 lbs)
Affiliation: Eldian

One of the last members of the Royal Family in the world beyond the Walls

A descendent of the Royal Family who shared the same last name as the "ancestor," Ymir. She joined the Eldian Restorationists and married Grisha before giving birth to a son, Zeke (Volume 21, Episode 86). She was turned into a Titan and sent to Heaven when Zeke betrayed her. She later ate Carla and Hannes (Volume 12, Episode 50 and more).

DECEASED

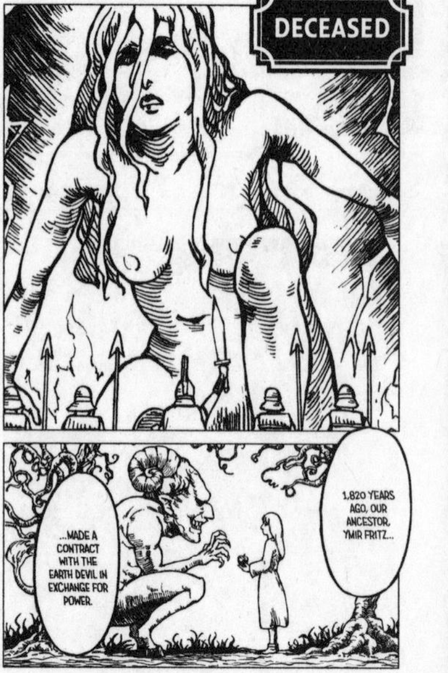
1,820 YEARS AGO, OUR ANCESTOR, YMIR FRITZ...
...MADE A CONTRACT WITH THE EARTH DEVIL IN EXCHANGE FOR POWER.

YMIR FRITZ

Birthday: Unknown
Height: Unknown
Weight: Unknown

The legendary Eldian known also as the "ancestor"

A being who is said to have built the Eldian Empire over 1,800 years ago. Some call her "the girl who came in contact with the source of all organic material." It is said that she gained the power of the Titans by way of a contract with the Devil of All Land, and that her soul was split into the Nine Titans after her death (Volume 21, Episode 86).

GRISHA'S PARENTS

Raised Zeke in place of Grisha and his wife.

FAYE YEAGER

DECEASED

BIRTHDAY:
November 24

Grisha's little sister. Killed by Gross from the Public Security Authorities at the age of 8.

MAN WHO NAMED YMIR

DECEASED

BIRTHDAY:
April 27

Gave the name "Ymir" to a girl with no relatives and used her to make money.

GRICE

DECEASED

BIRTHDAY:
July 31

Invited Grisha, a doctor, to join the Eldian Restorationists.

MARCEL GALLIARD

DECEASED

BIRTHDAY:
August 10

Participated on the Paradis island operation, where he was eaten by Ymir. Porco's older brother.

MYSTERIOUS MAN

Found close to Zeke when he informs the authorities about his parents.

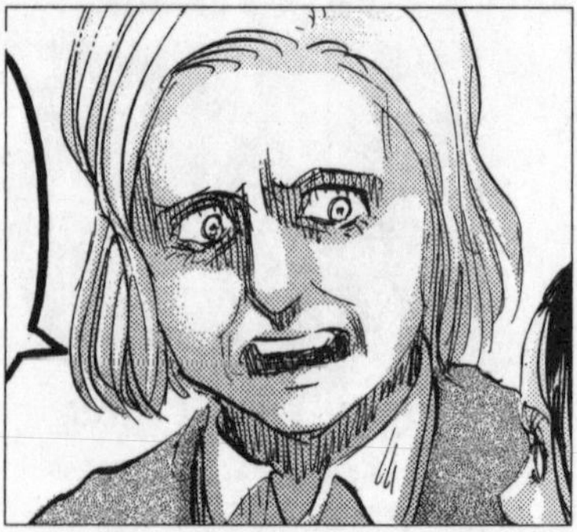

KARINA BRAUN

BIRTHDAY: September 3
HEIGHT: 170 cm (5'7")   WEIGHT: 60 kg (132 lbs)
LOCATION: The Libero Eldian Internment Zone inside of Marley

Reiner's mother. She believes that she must devote her life to Marley and atone for the historical crimes of the Eldians, calling those who live on the island of Paradis devils (Volume 23, Episode 94).

GABI'S PARENTS

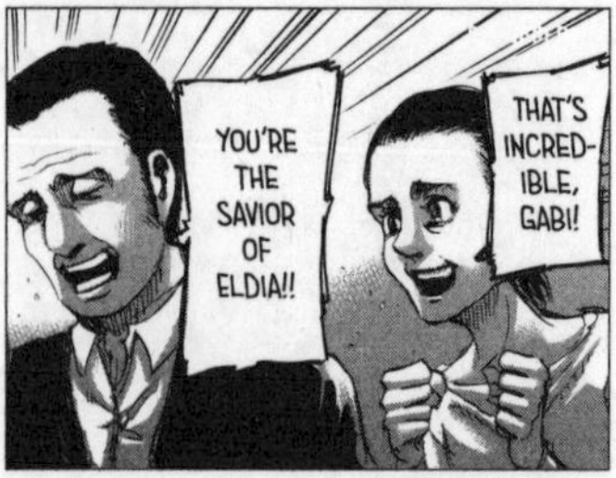
THAT'S INCRED-IBLE, GABI!
YOU'RE THE SAVIOR OF ELDIA!!

Proud of their daughter Gabi for being a talented Warrior candidate.

ANNIE'S FATHER

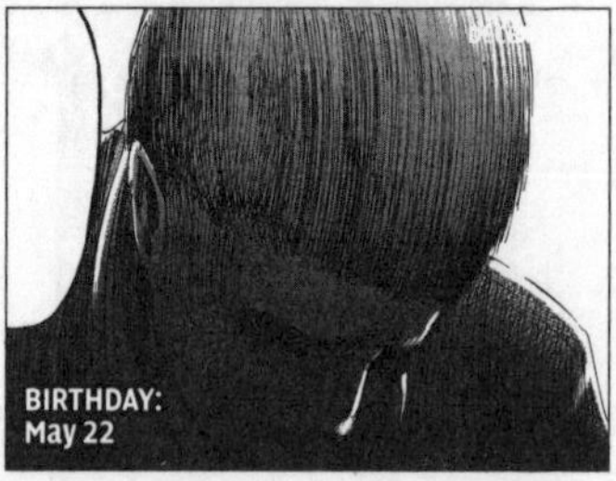

BIRTHDAY:
May 22

Teaches a young Annie hand-to-hand combat skills.

REINER'S UNCLE, AUNT, AND COUSIN

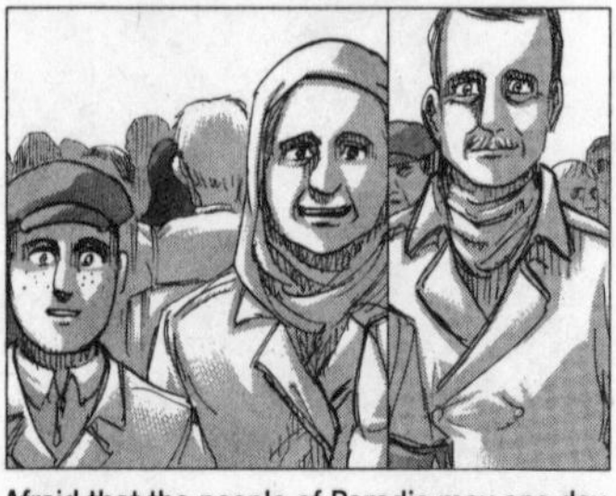

Afraid that the people of Paradis may one day destroy the world.

THE GRICE BROTHERS' PARENTS

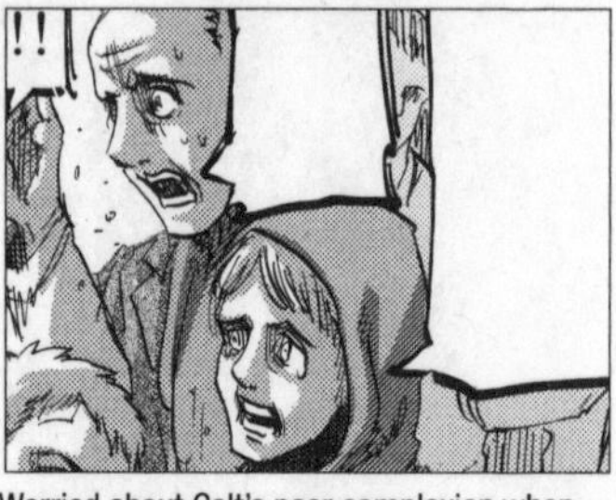
!!

Worried about Colt's poor complexion when greeting him and his brother as they return from the battlefield.

MAGATH

BIRTHDAY: December 21
HEIGHT: 174 cm (5'9")
WEIGHT: 80 kg (176 lbs)
AFFILIATION: Marley Army, Eldian Unit

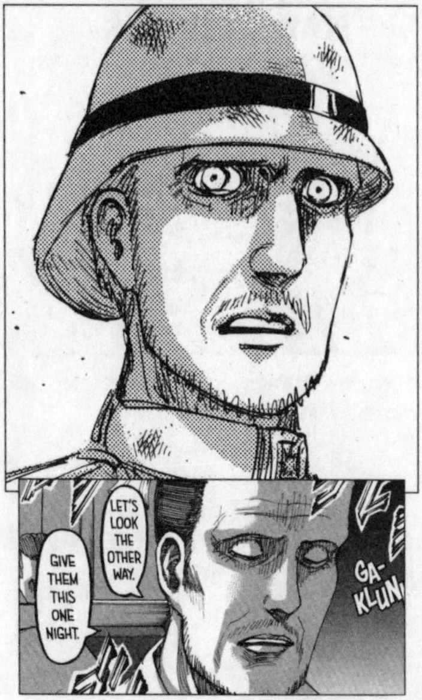
GA-KLUN
LET'S LOOK THE OTHER WAY.
GIVE THEM THIS ONE NIGHT.

A Marleyan soldier who leads the Eldian Unit

As leader of the 800-person Eldian Unit, Magath is an officer in the Marleyan army who works with Titans in a strategic capacity. He is also responsible for watching over the Warrior candidates (Volume 23, Episode 91 and more). He shows tolerance when they cause a commotion on the way home from the battlefield (Volume 23, Episode 93).

GROSS

BIRTHDAY: June 9
HEIGHT: 165 cm (5'5")
WEIGHT: 95 kg (209 lbs)
AFFILIATION: Marley Public Security Authorities

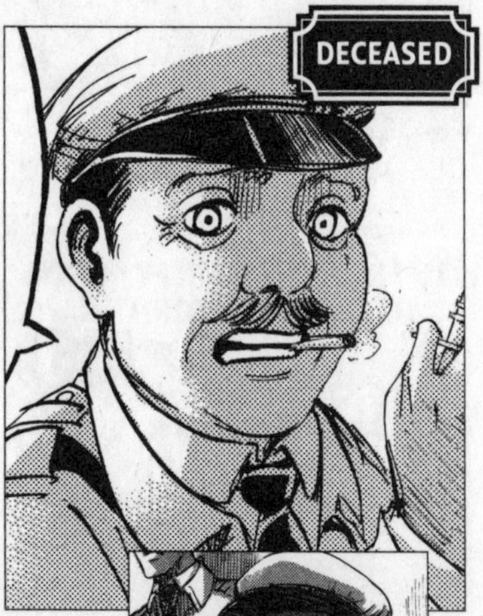
DECEASED

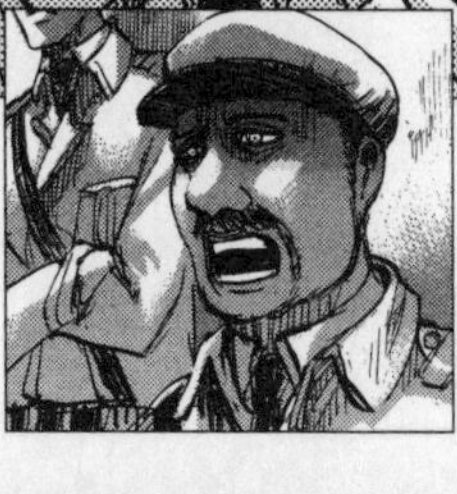

A cruel man who belonged to the Marley Public Security Authorities

Gross killed Faye when she left the Internment Zone without permission by feeding her to dogs. He later was responsible for sending the Eldian Restorationists to the island of Paradis. He committed his cruel actions in order to "face the truth of this cruel world and seek to better understand it," and boasted that he was ready to accept his death no matter when it came (Volume 21, Episode 86 and more).

MARLEYAN NAVAL OFFICER

At odds with the army. Shows his anger toward Magath's words at the war council.

MARLEYAN GENERAL

Laments how Marley's military strength is beginning to fall behind.

COMMANDER OF THE PARATROOPER UNIT ATTACK PLAN

Drops Pure Titans on Fort Slava.

MARLEYAN ARMY OFFICER

The top of the Marleyan Army, which includes the Eldian Unit.

MAN FROM THE MARLEY PUBLIC SECURITY AUTHORITIES

DECEASED

Despite his gentle features, his expression never even changed when torturing Grisha.

KOSLO

Leads the Eldian Unit together with Magath.

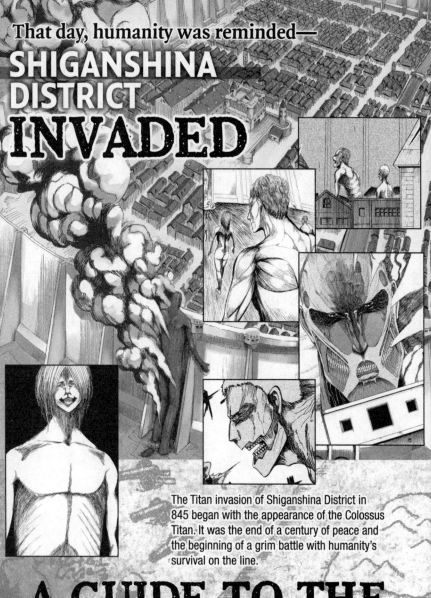

That day, humanity was reminded—

SHIGANSHINA DISTRICT INVADED

The Titan invasion of Shiganshina District in 845 began with the appearance of the Colossus Titan. It was the end of a century of peace and the beginning of a grim battle with humanity's survival on the line.

A GUIDE TO THE TITAN-INHABITED AREAS

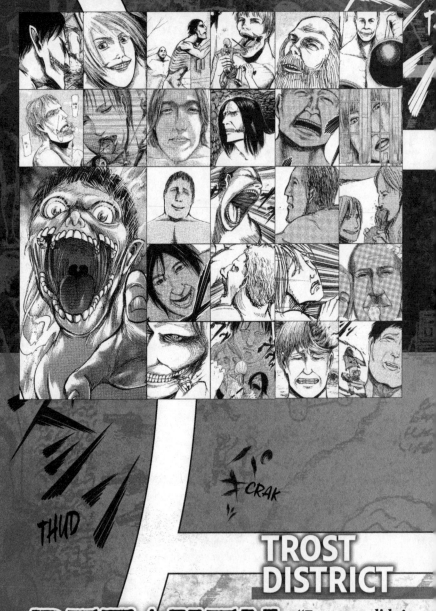

THUD

CRAK

TROST DISTRICT

RETAKEN

"Everyone didn't die in vain... Today the human race won its first victory..."

TROST DISTRICT

INVADED

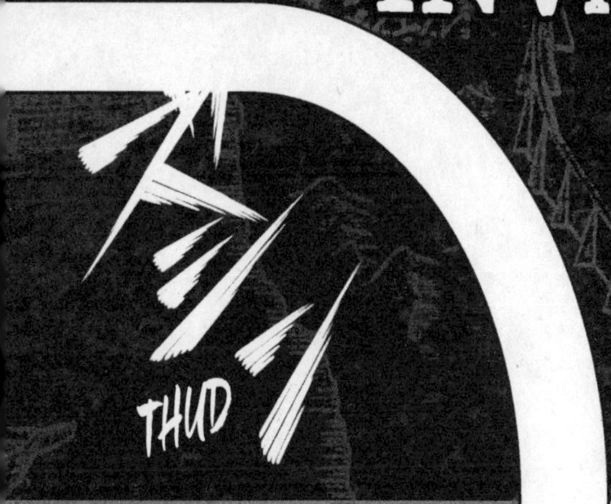
THUD

Following the events of Shiganshina, humanity then lost Trost District in 850. But humanity refused to give up, and together with Eren's Titan, they began their counterattack. After a long struggle against the Titans that cost many soldiers their lives, humanity gained its first victory.

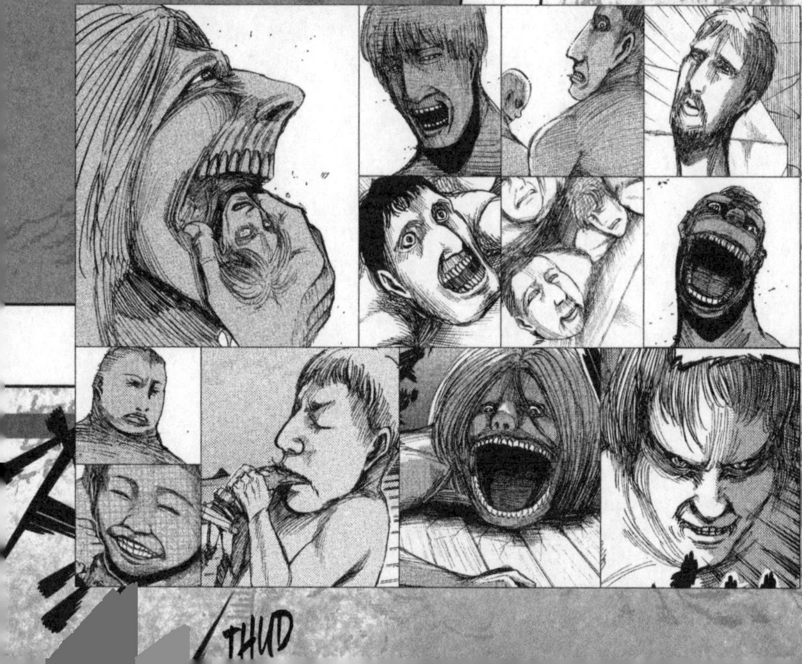
THUD

WALL MARIA: THE INTERIOR

BAM BAM

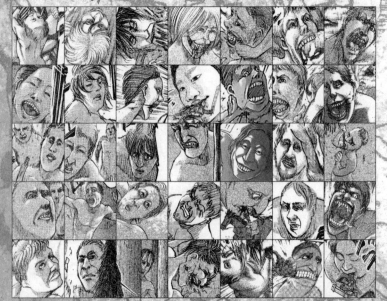

WALL ROSE: SOUTH DISTRICT

Humanity found itself confused when Titans suddenly appeared inside Wall Rose, forcing a new battle with the intelligent Beast Titan, who has the ability to manipulate other Titans.

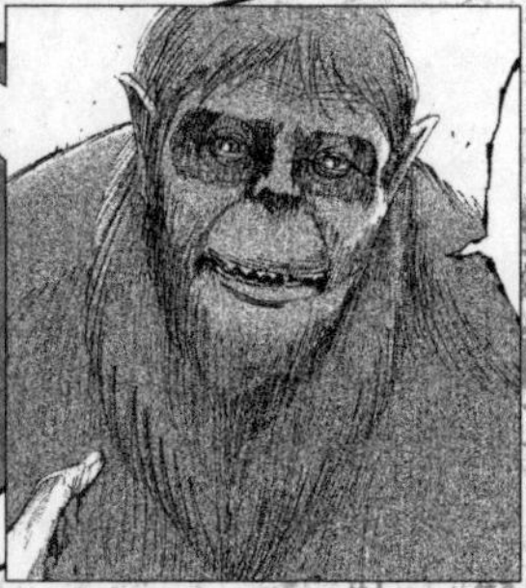

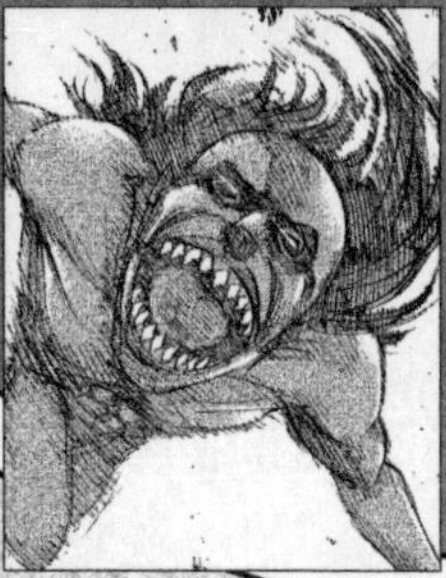

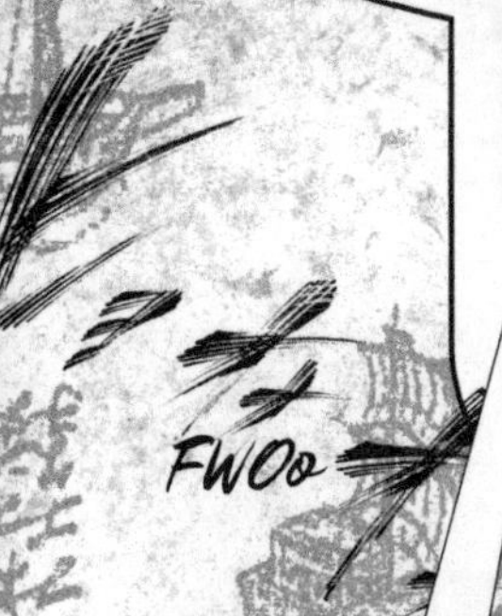
FWOo

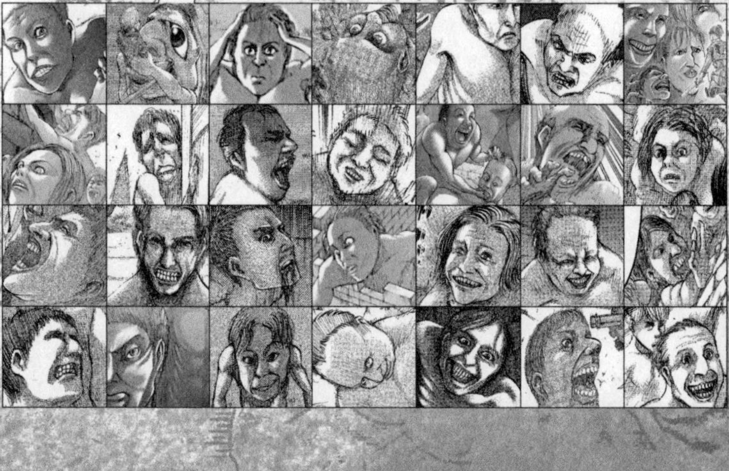

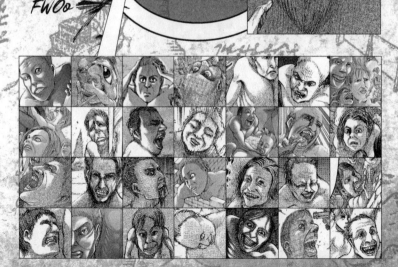

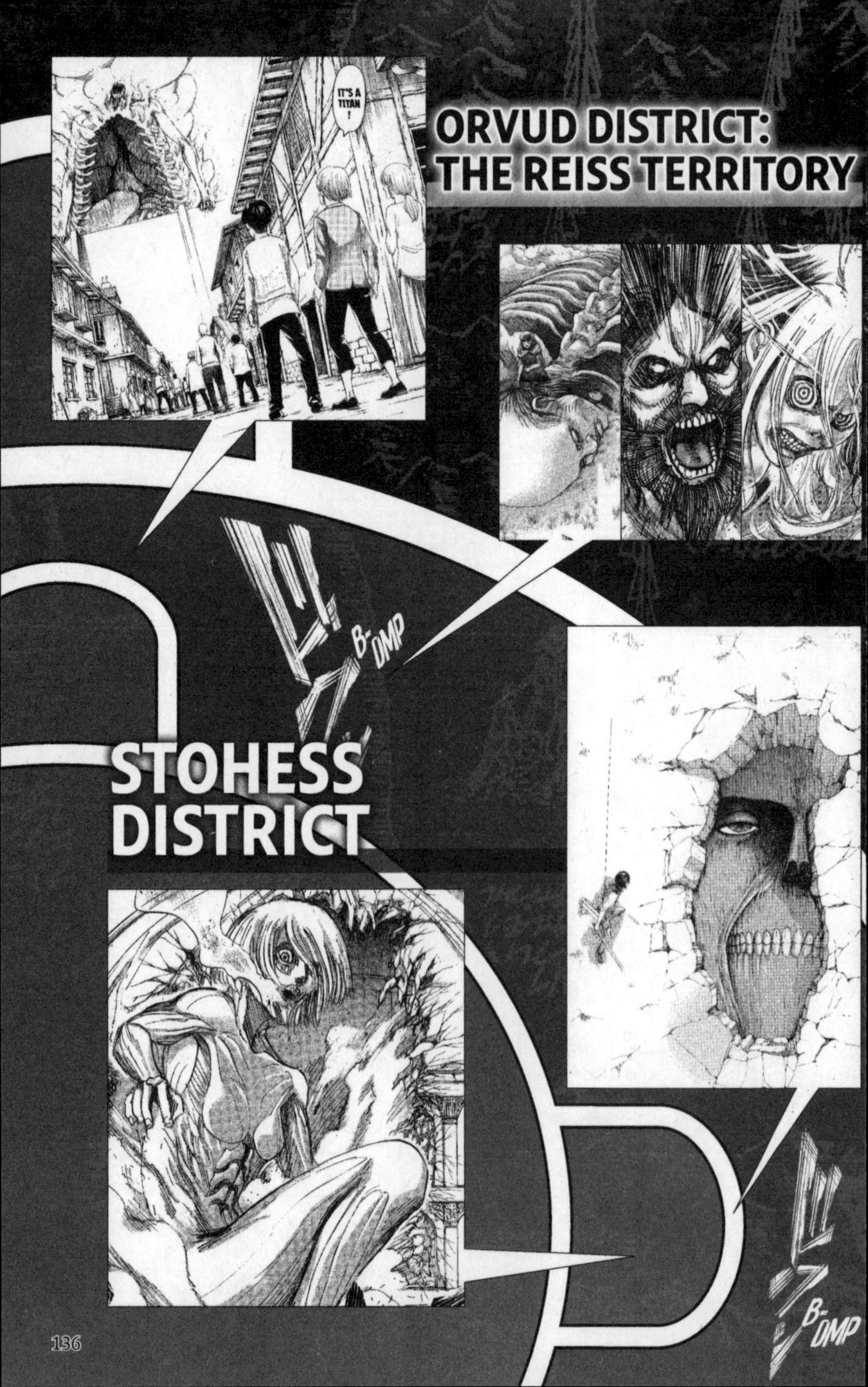
IT'S A TITAN!
ORVUD DISTRICT: THE REISS TERRITORY
B-DOMP
STOHESS DISTRICT
B-DOMP

SHIGANSHINA DISTRICT

THE DECISIVE BATTLE

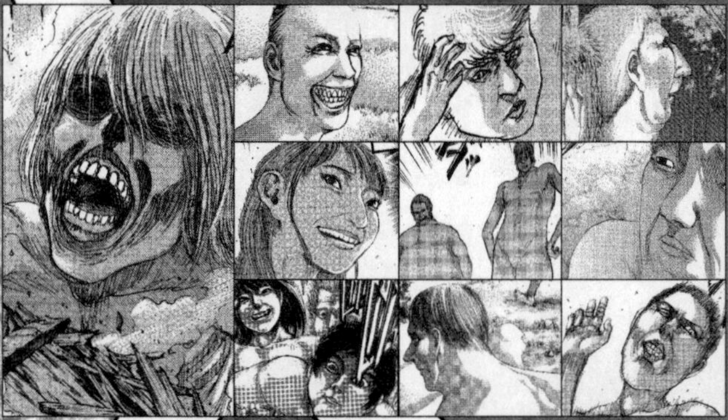

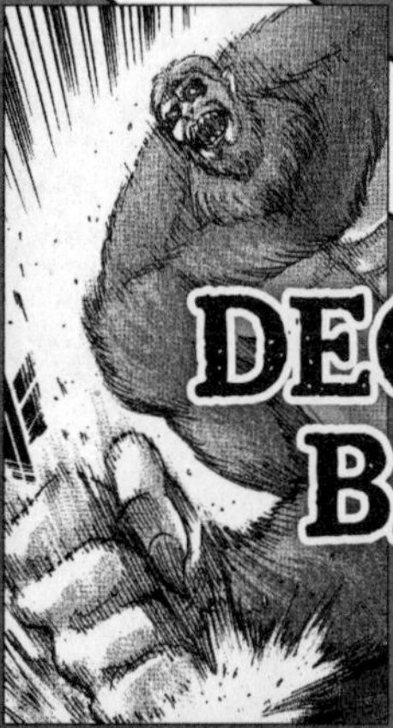

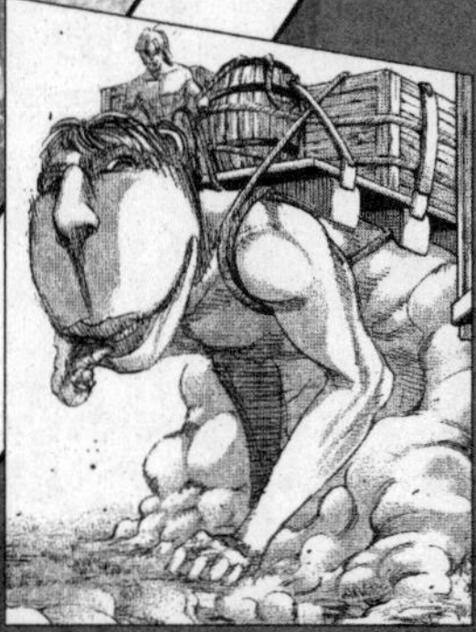

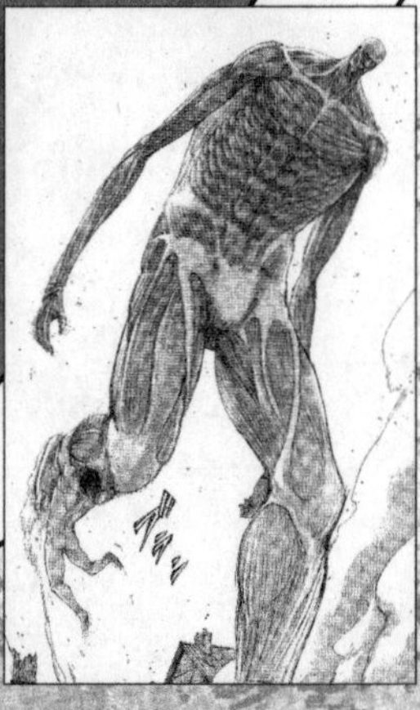

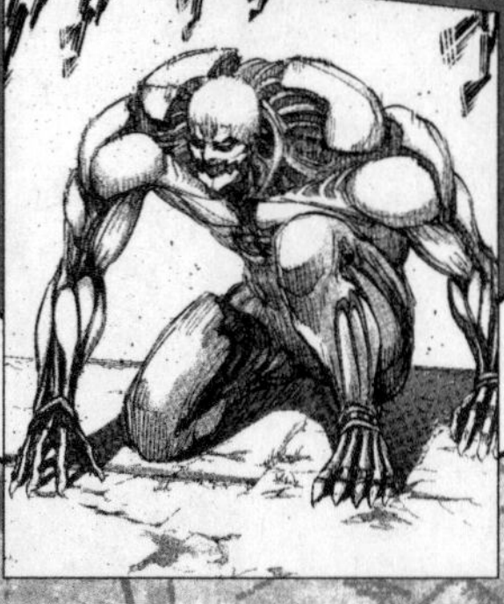

The Beast Titan, Colossus Titan, Armored Titan, and even an unknown Titan who walked on all fours appeared during the decisive battle in Shiganshina District. But what humanity may not have realized at the time was that this was also the prelude to a new battle between them and the Titans...

Expeditions

The Survey Corps took their battles outside the Walls in order to build a base for humanity's future. Soldiers who do not fear death were up against the Pure Titans who moved only by their instincts. Life and death was determined only by power and luck in these melees.

Titans encountered when Keith Shadis was in the Survey Corps

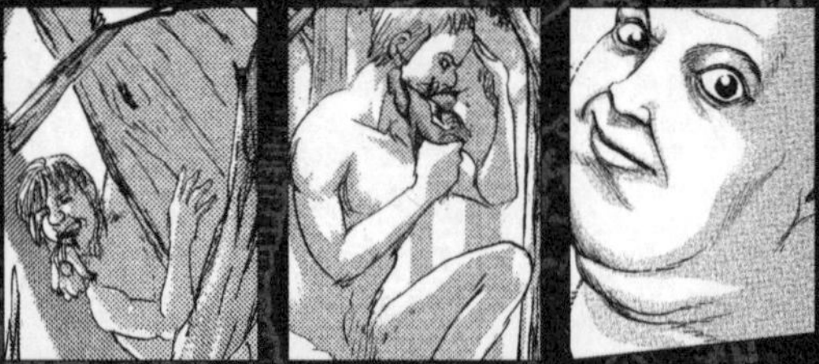

The Titan encountered by Ilse Langnar on the 34th expedition

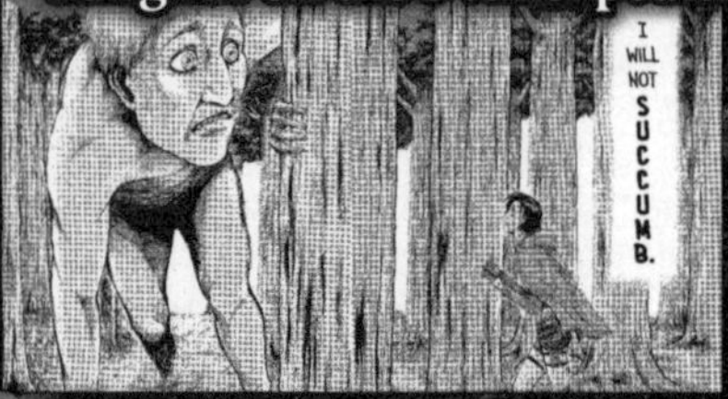
I WILL NOT SUCCUMB.

Titans encountered when Erwin Smith was in the Survey Corps

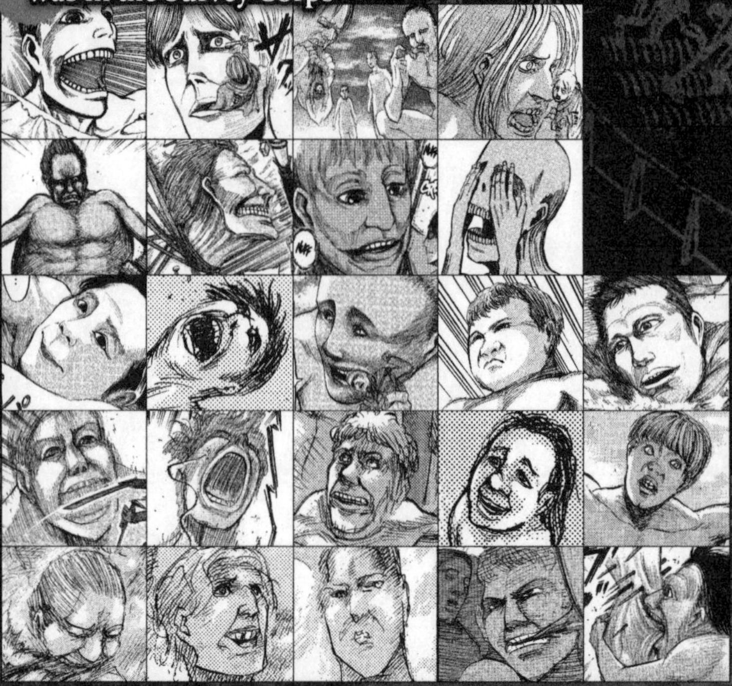

And now they face the SEA...

After countless fights, humanity reaches the wide sea on the other side of the Walls. But this is not the end of their battle. Humanity could never have imagined what was awaiting them beyond the Walls. What does mankind think now that it sees the sea?

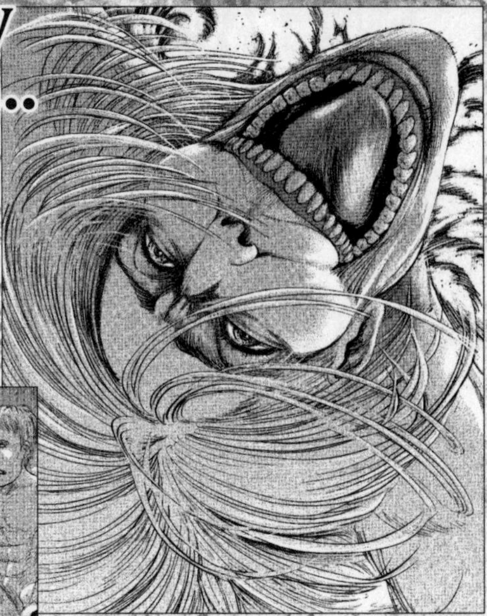

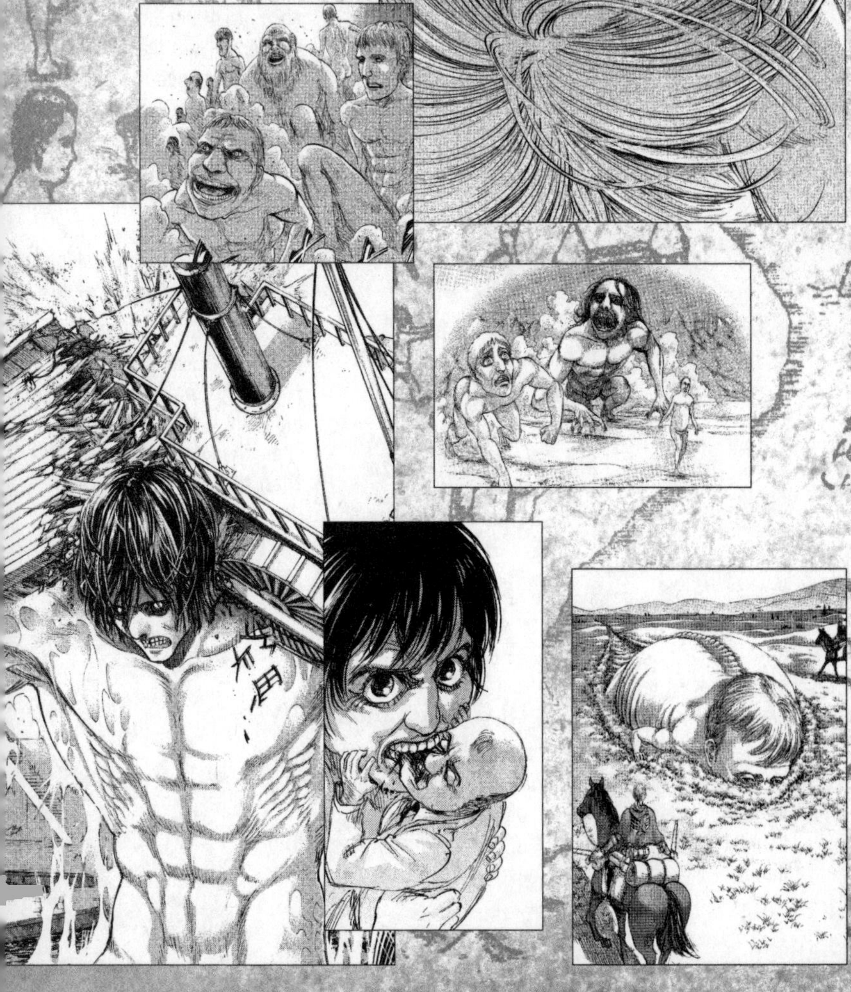

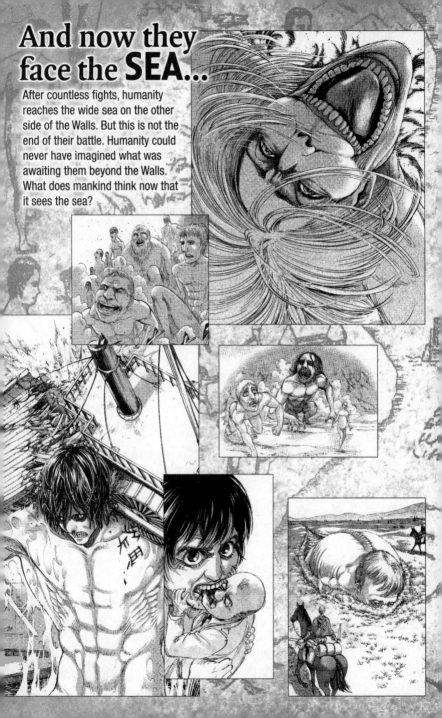

WHAT are the NINE TITANS that gave Eldia power?

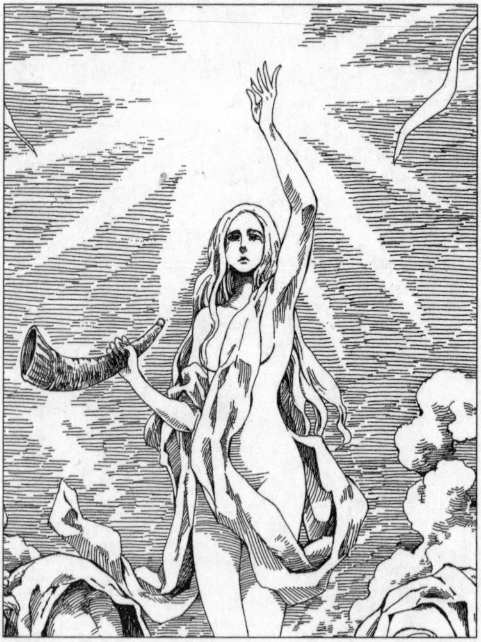

1,820 years ago, Ymir Fritz, the ancestor of the Eldians, made a contract with the Devil of All Land and gained the power of the Titans. She used this power to build the Eldian Empire, and after her death her power was split into the Nine Titans, which are the true identities of the creatures such as the Colossus Titan that Eren and the others call "intelligent Titans."

The Nine Titans include the Founding Titan, the Attack Titan, the Colossus Titan, the Armored Titan, the Female Titan, the Jaw Titan, the Cart Titan, the War Hammer Titan, and the Beast Titan. Of these, the War Hammer Titan is still shrouded in mystery.

THE FATE of the Reiss Family

The Founding Titan, brought inside the Walls by its first king, was passed down through the Reiss family from generation to generation. As a last-ditch effort in order to get the Founding Titan back from Eren, Rod Reiss attempts to turn into a Titan, but fails and is killed by the Survey Corps.

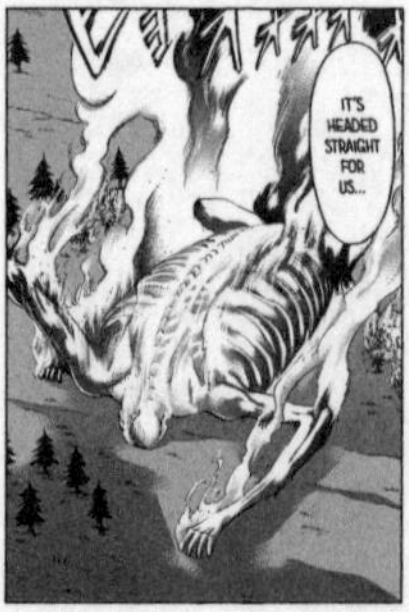
IT'S HEADED STRAIGHT FOR US...

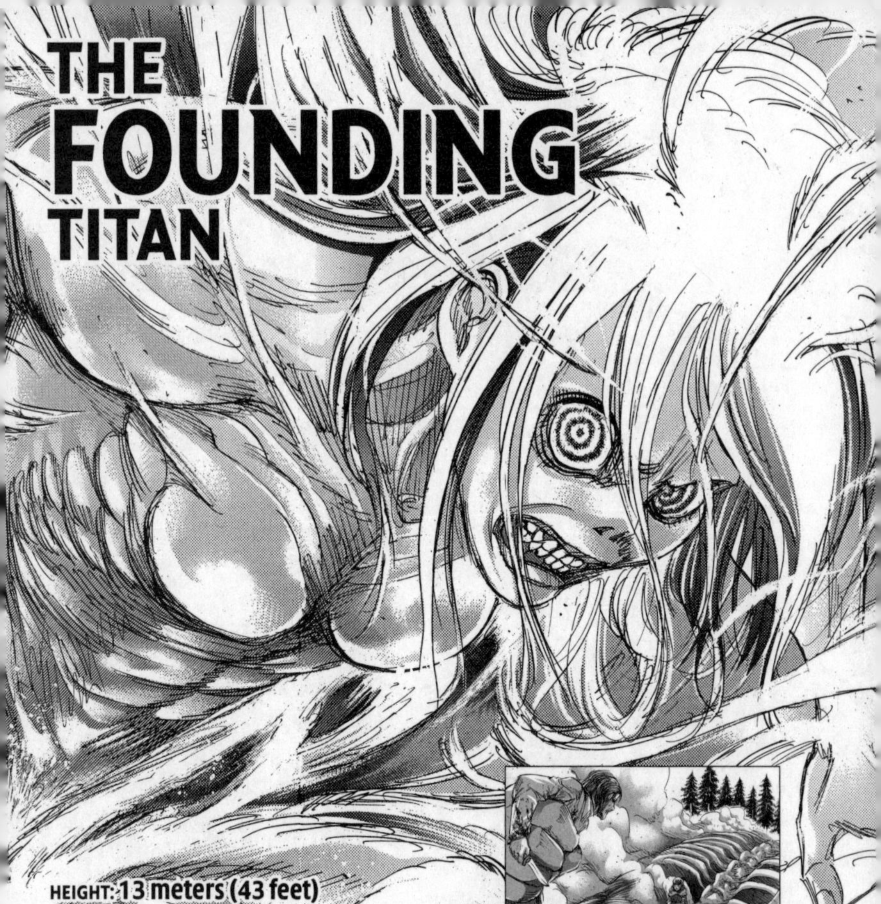

THE FOUNDING TITAN

HEIGHT: 13 meters (43 feet)
INHERITOR: Uri → Frieda → Grisha → Eren?

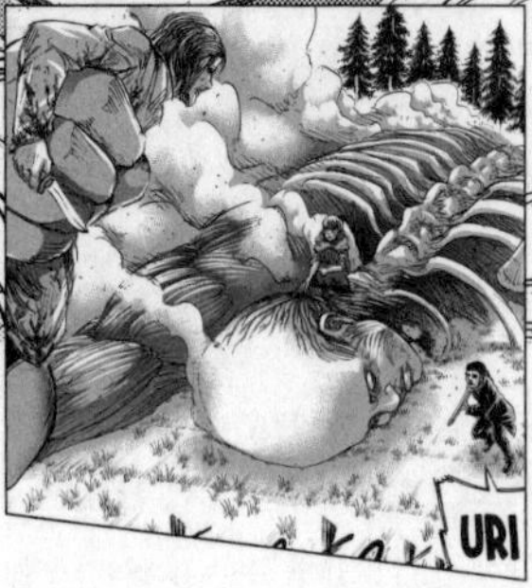
URI

The "Coordinate" that originated from Ymir

If someone who holds one of the Nine Titans within them dies without passing that Titan down, their powers and memories are sent beyond space, through an invisible path, to be inherited by a not-yet-born Subject of Ymir. The Founding Titan is one of the "Coordinates" that connects these paths of the Subjects of Ymir. It has the power to alter the memories of the Subjects of Ymir and to control Titans.

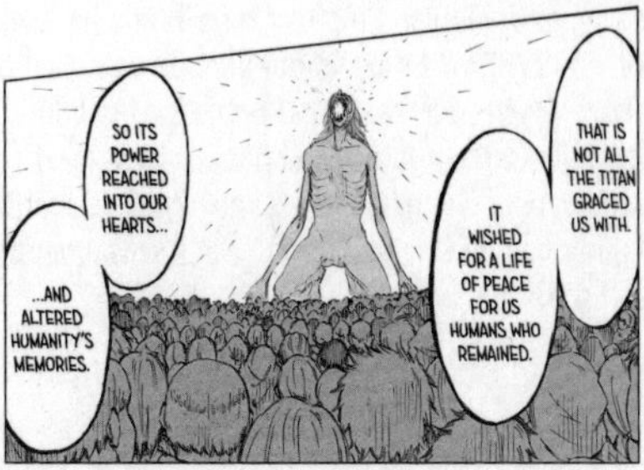
THAT IS NOT ALL THE TITAN GRACED US WITH.
IT WISHED FOR A LIFE OF PEACE FOR US HUMANS WHO REMAINED.
SO ITS POWER REACHED INTO OUR HEARTS...
...AND ALTERED HUMANITY'S MEMORIES.

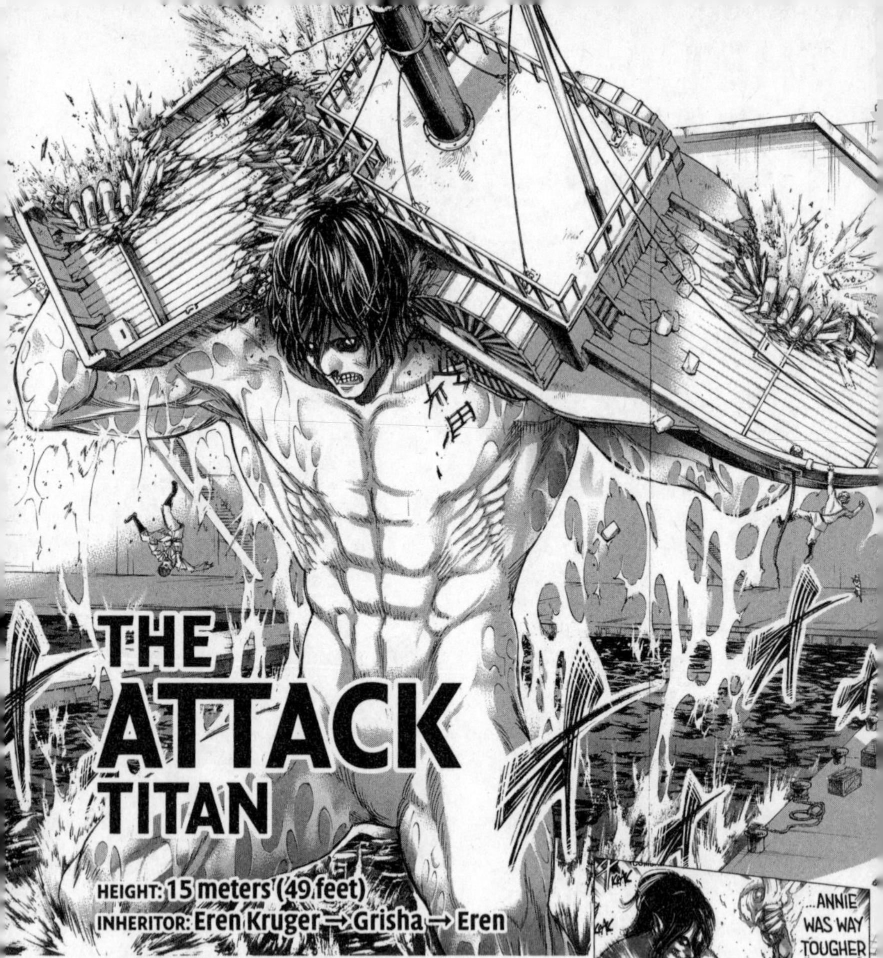

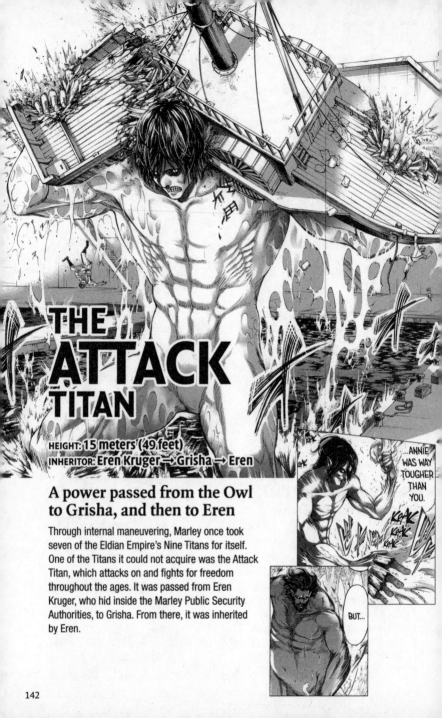

THE ATTACK TITAN

HEIGHT: 15 meters (49 feet)
INHERITOR: Eren Kruger → Grisha → Eren

A power passed from the Owl to Grisha, and then to Eren

Through internal maneuvering, Marley once took seven of the Eldian Empire's Nine Titans for itself. One of the Titans it could not acquire was the Attack Titan, which attacks on and fights for freedom throughout the ages. It was passed from Eren Kruger, who hid inside the Marley Public Security Authorities, to Grisha. From there, it was inherited by Eren.

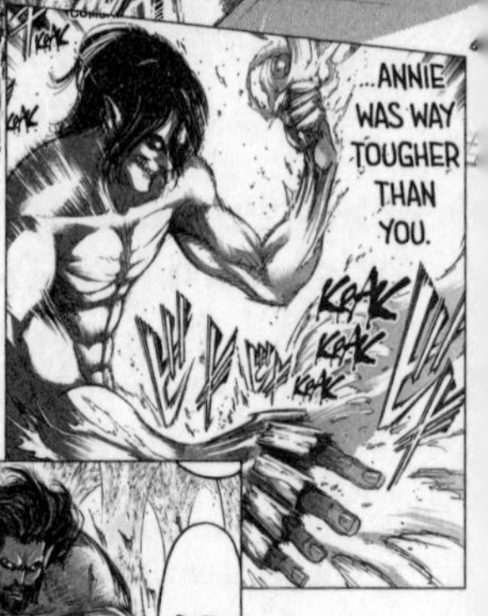
...ANNIE WAS WAY TOUGHER THAN YOU.

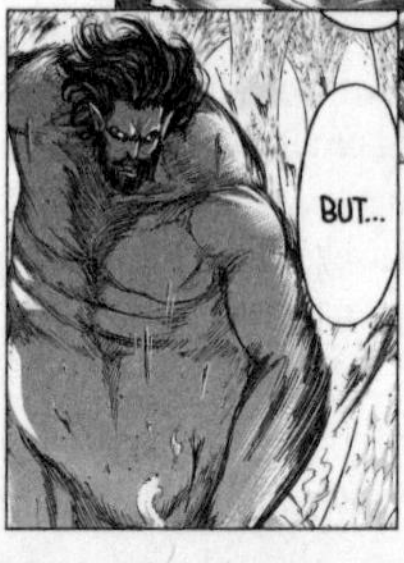
BUT...

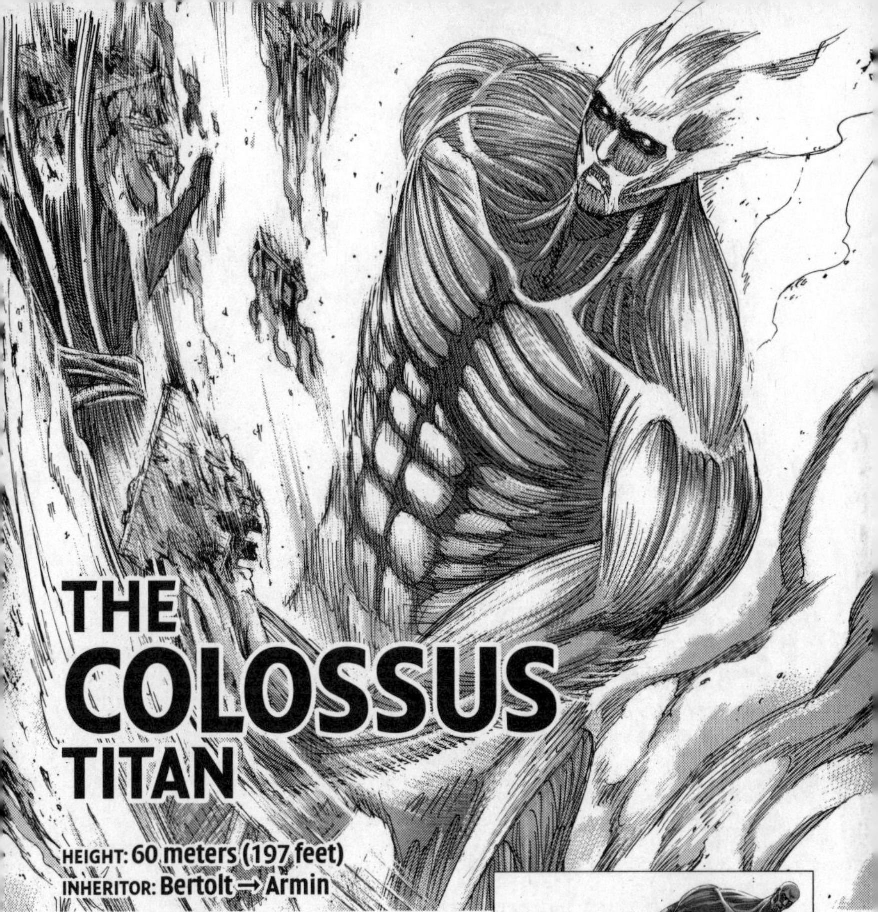

THE COLOSSUS TITAN

HEIGHT: 60 meters (197 feet)
INHERITOR: Bertolt → Armin

A Titan that uses its massive body to create overwhelming destruction

An overwhelmingly massive Titan that stands at over 60 meters tall. Though it is impossible for its body to move quickly, its impressive strength allows it to easily break through the gate on Shiganshina's wall with a single kick. It uses the trait shared by all Titans of emitting hot gusts when transforming to consume the flesh on its gigantic body and generate incredible scalding gusts, dealing the Survey Corps major losses.

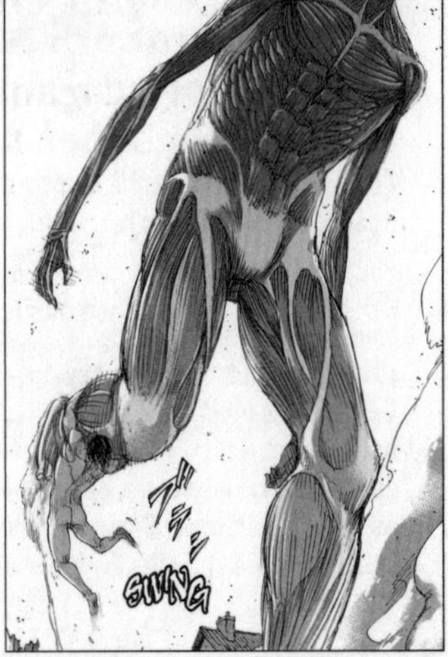
SWING

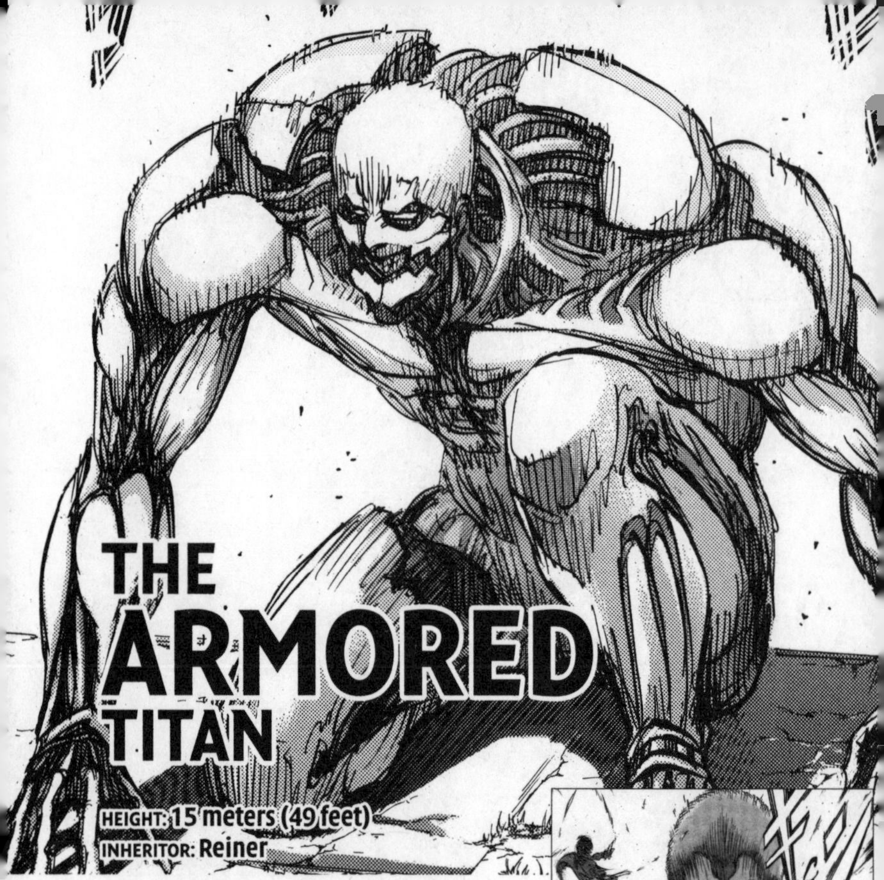

THE ARMORED TITAN

HEIGHT: 15 meters (49 feet)
INHERITOR: Reiner

Marley's Titan Warrior that uses the hard surface of its body to protect against attacks

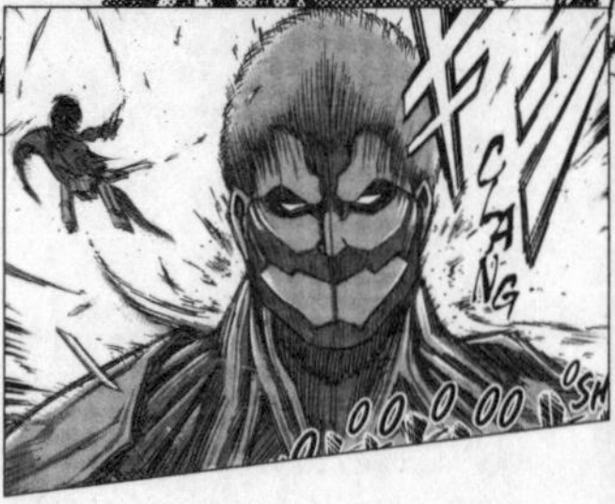

The Armored Titan gets its name from its specialized ability to harden its body. Marley seems to use it to attract enemy fire, essentially acting as a shield. Of course, the blades that are a part of humanity's Vertical Maneuvering Equipment cannot hope to scratch its hard surface, either. Focused attacks such as chokes and joint locks by other Titans, as well as the Survey Corps's Thunder Spears, seem to be effective against it.

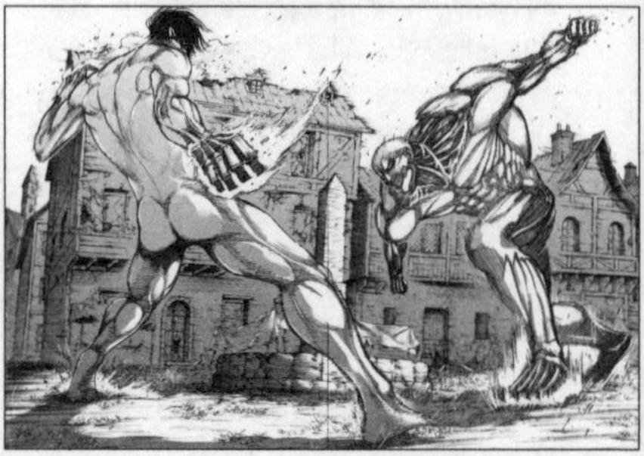

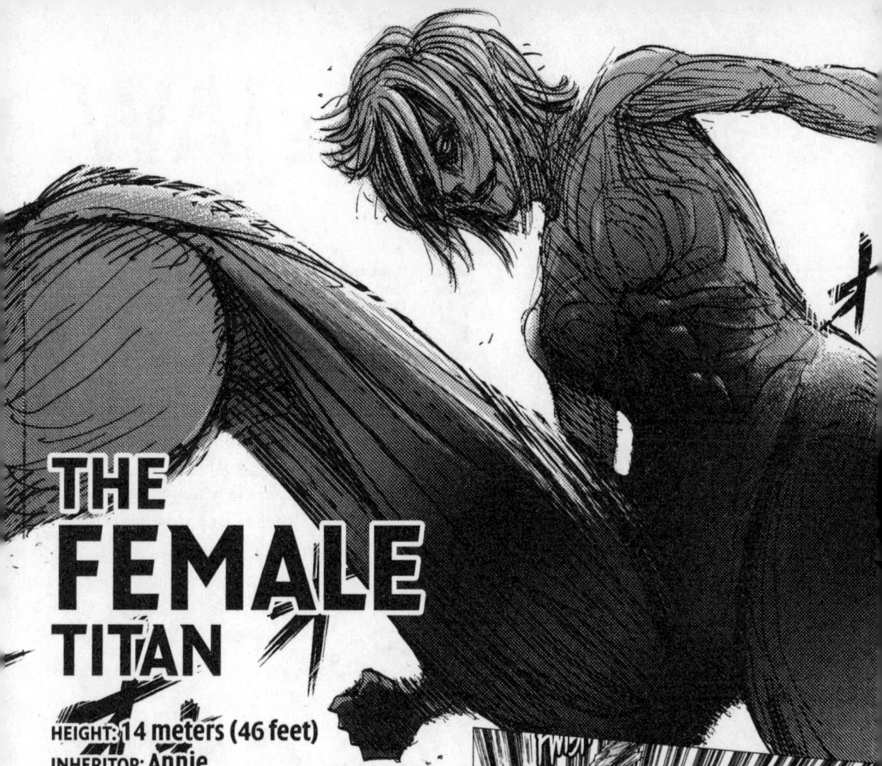

THE FEMALE TITAN

HEIGHT: 14 meters (46 feet)
INHERITOR: Annie

A hand-to-hand fighter that uses hardening abilities

A Titan that excels in any situation thanks to its high mobility and endurance. Its ability to harden specific parts of its body synergizes well with the striking attacks learned by its inheritor, Annie, allowing it to unleash incredible destruction. While limited in range, it also has the ability to attract Pure Titans with its scream.

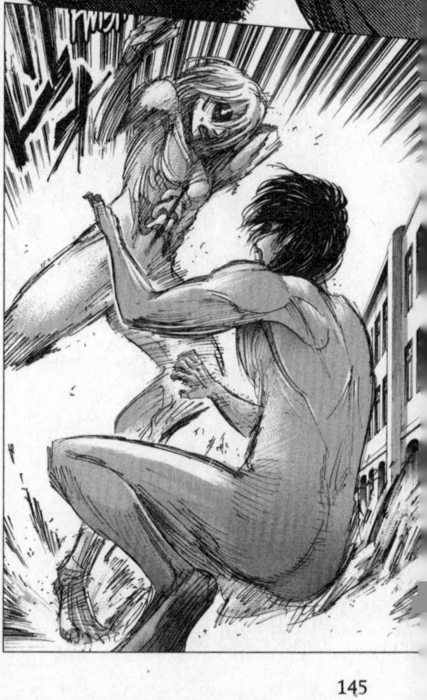

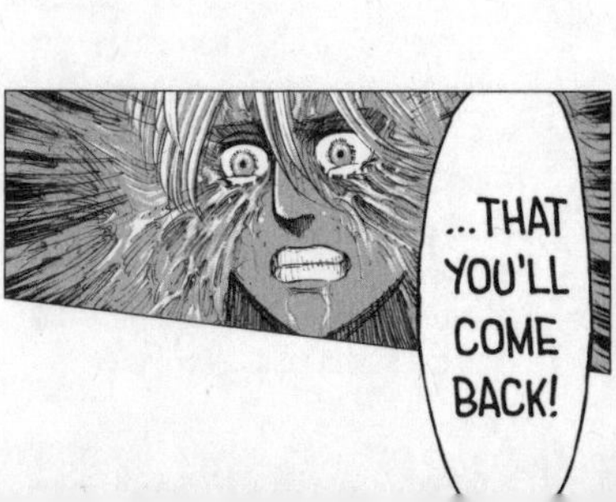
...THAT YOU'LL COME BACK!

THE JAW TITAN

HEIGHT: 5 meters (16 feet)
INHERITOR: Marcel → Ymir → Porco

A Titan stolen from Marley by Ymir

An assault Titan able to move quickly thanks to its small frame, the Jaw Titan uses its powerful nails and jaw to crush its prey. After being turned into a Pure Titan, Ymir ate Marcel, the inheritor of the Jaw Titan's powers, resulting in it then residing inside of her. It has now returned to Marley's hands and has been inherited by Porco.

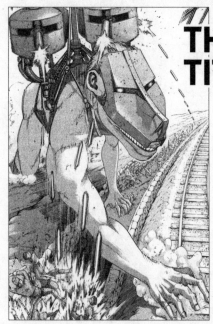

THE CART TITAN

HEIGHT: 4 meters (13 feet)
INHERITOR: Pieck

A quadruped Titan that defeats its enemies with a battery of guns

A Titan that is able to take long-term missions by making use of its exceptional endurance. The Cart Titan can take on various kinds of armaments depending on what is needed on a mission, playing an important role in providing more options for strategic plans. It participated in the decisive battle in Shiganshina District, where it saved Zeke from a close call during his battle with Levi.

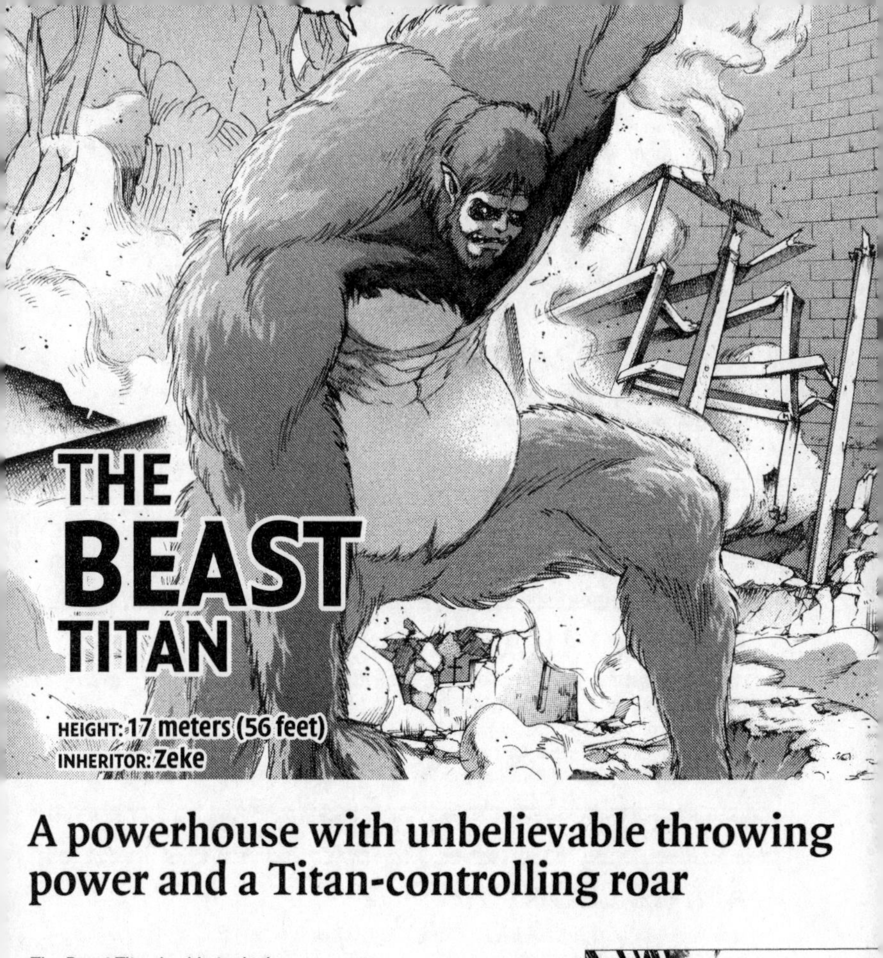

THE BEAST TITAN

HEIGHT: 17 meters (56 feet)
INHERITOR: Zeke

A powerhouse with unbelievable throwing power and a Titan-controlling roar

The Beast Titan is able to deal massive damage to its enemies from far distances by crushing rocks and throwing them like a shotgun blast. Furthermore, because Zeke inherited the Beast Titan, those who were administered Zeke's spinal fluid were turned into Titans, and Zeke controlled them with his roar, making it possible for these Titans to be active at night. This is why the Titans were able to attack the ruins of Utgard Castle while it was dark.

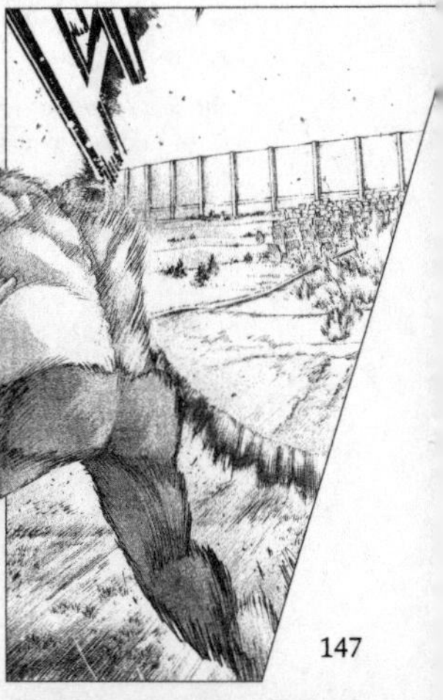

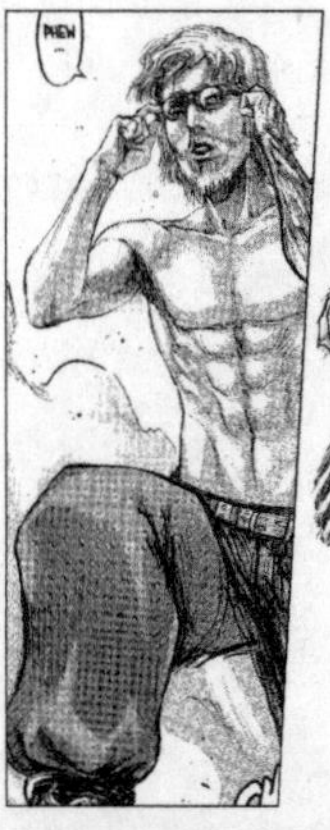

HAJIME ISAYAMA Reveals

How His CHARACTERS WERE BORN: Part 5

REINER BRAUN

I created Reiner by combining the eyes and eyebrows of former soccer player David Beckham with some of the defining traits of Matt Damon in *Saving Private Ryan*, as well as one of my friends from my hometown. At first glance, he's a bit muscular and seems scary, but he's a kind person who's athletic and has a pretty outstanding personality, too. That's the kind of vibe I was going for—where you know this character's destined for big things.

BERTOLT HOOVER

I started off with the visuals for the Colossus Titan and came up with Bertolt by thinking, "What kind of character would I get if the somehow weakly and docile Colossus Titan was turned into a person?" Bertolt is actually the only character I created after creating a Titan first.

ANNIE LEONHART

I designed Annie as a small but conceited character. I based her hairstyle on a photo taken of Avril Lavigne by the paparazzi.

The Japanese word for "older brother" is *ani*, and so I wanted to make people think of that word even though she's a woman. I also liked the nickname "Ani" that is used in the film *Kisarazu Cat's Eye*. I combined this first name with the family name Leonhart, which shows internal strength. It sounded like the kind of cool name that a middle schooler would come up with.

From ZEKE'S Birth in MARLEY to His Attempt to Once Again RETAKE the Founder

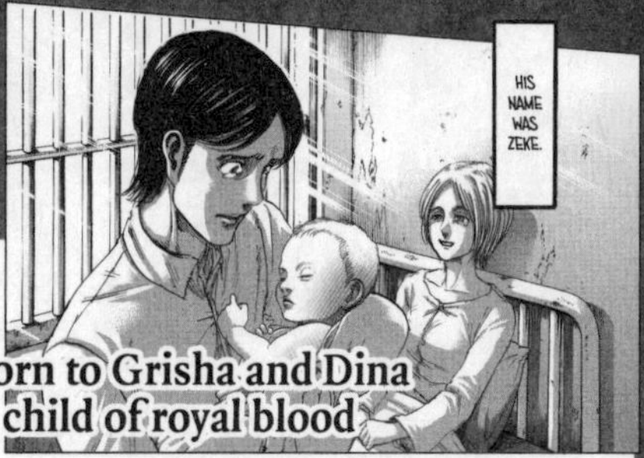
HIS NAME WAS ZEKE.

Around 820 onward	• **Zeke is born to Grisha and Dina Fritz as a child of royal blood** • Grisha and Dina indoctrinate Zeke from a young age so that he can assist the Eldian Restoration • **Around the time that Zeke is 7, he exposes his parents to the Marley Government to protect his grandparents and himself**
845 The Fall of Shiganshina District	• **Zeke awaits in Marley?**
850	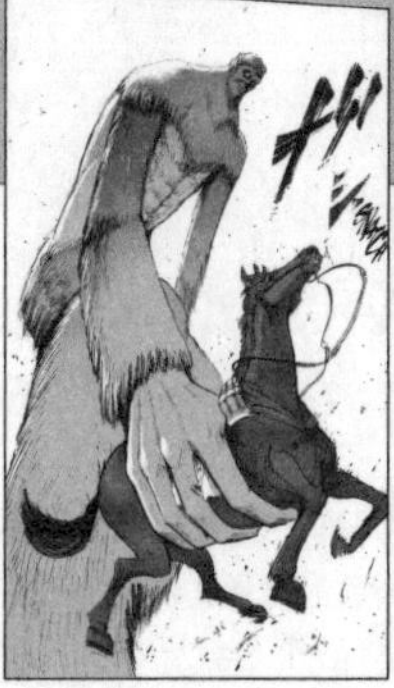 • Zeke appears inside Wall Rose and uses the power of the Beast to turn humans into Titans • Zeke meets with Reiner and the others as they are carrying out the plan to retake the Founding Titan • Zeke forces Reiner to submit when he insists on saving Annie • **Zeke faces off against Levi in the decisive battle in Shiganshina District and is forced to flee**
854:	• **Zeke participates in the war between Marley and the Mid-East Allied Forces, leading Marley to victory** • **With his last year as the Beast approaching, Zeke suggests carrying out the plan to retake the Founding Titan once more** 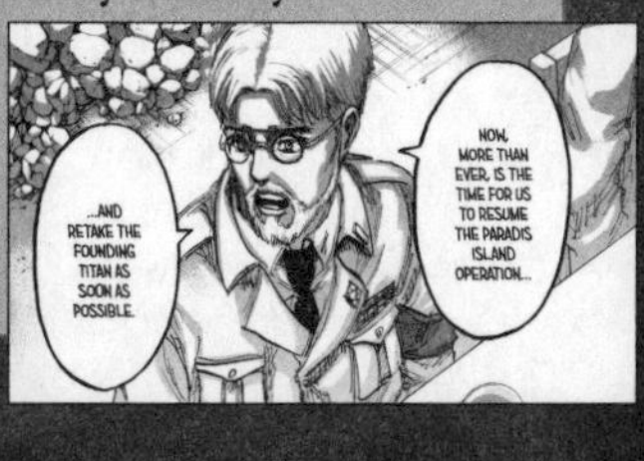 NOW, MORE THAN EVER, IS THE TIME FOR US TO RESUME THE PARADIS ISLAND OPERATION... ...AND RETAKE THE FOUNDING TITAN AS SOON AS POSSIBLE.

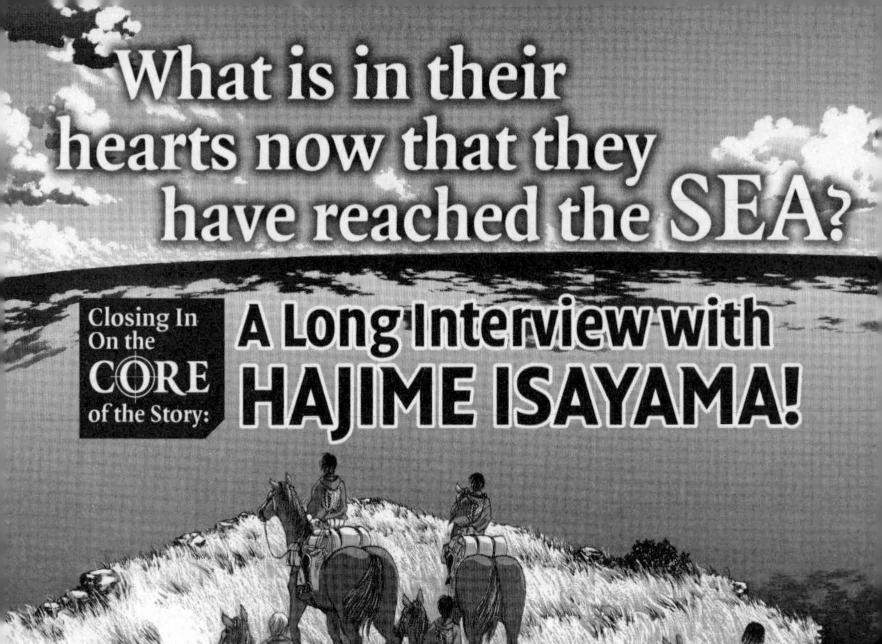

What is in their hearts now that they have reached the SEA?

Closing In On the CORE of the Story:

A Long Interview with HAJIME ISAYAMA!

Eren and the others see the sea—will this be the moment when Eren and Armin's paths diverge?!

Q: As we see on the cover of Volume 22, the day has finally come when Eren and his friends reach the sea! How do you feel when you look back on everything that's happened until this point?

HAJIME ISAYAMA: The idea of "seeing the sea" that the story revolved around was a short way of saying that if humanity was in a position where it could reach the sea, there must not be any Titans left beyond the Walls. It was like a reward or a trophy given to Eren and the others for eliminating the Titans. So I'm relieved that I was able to make it to the point where I could draw them seeing it. At the same time, though, while I was thinking about the way the story would continue on the other side of the sea, I can't deny that I started to feel a sense of loneliness, like "What should I do now?" It feels like leaving a home I'd lived in for the seven years since *Titan*'s serialization started and moving to a new piece of land.

HAJIME ISAYAMA PROFILE

Hajime Isayama's series *Attack on Titan* began serialization in 2009. In 2011, the title received the 35th Kodansha Manga Award in the Shonen category. He is now fully engrossed in creating the title's new "Marley Arc."

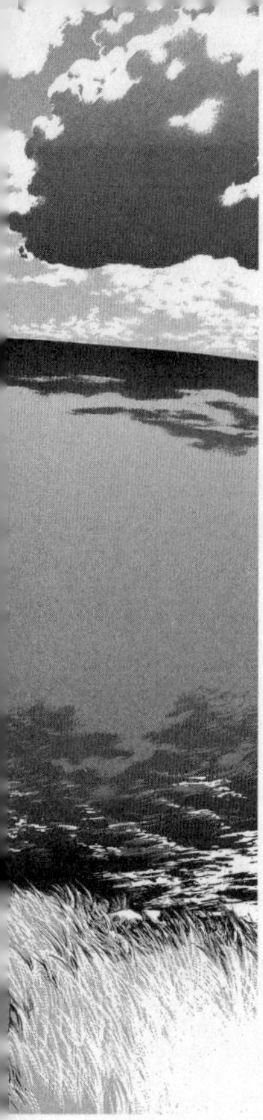

Q: So if the characters have gotten a reward, they must be happy.

ISAYAMA: Hmm. As far as Eren, Mikasa, and Armin go, I think it's more of a feeling of "We can't continue to be children" than a feeling of happiness. From the point of the Survey Corps, the three could still afford to be boys and girls when they still had senior officers like Erwin and their captains. After the death of so many of these people who stood in positions of support, though, it's now their turn to fill those spots. At the same time, it's hard to say that their childhoods have truly ended... If you're curious about this question, you should be looking forward to the chapters to come.

Q: Alright, then! In interviews such as the one in the *Attack on Titan Guidebook*, you've talked about Eren being a character who is forced by the story to move, or as a slave to the story. Do you still feel that way?

ISAYAMA: I feel like Eren being forced to move has become the core of who Eren is as a character.

Mikasa and Armin, too. They've gotten in the habit of thinking about things while basing them around Eren. At first it was just their way of playing favorites, I suppose... If your family was in trouble, you'd lend them a hand, right? But if a stranger came up and asked you why you're helping them, it might be hard to explain exactly why. Eren, Mikasa, and Armin have the same kind of relationship.

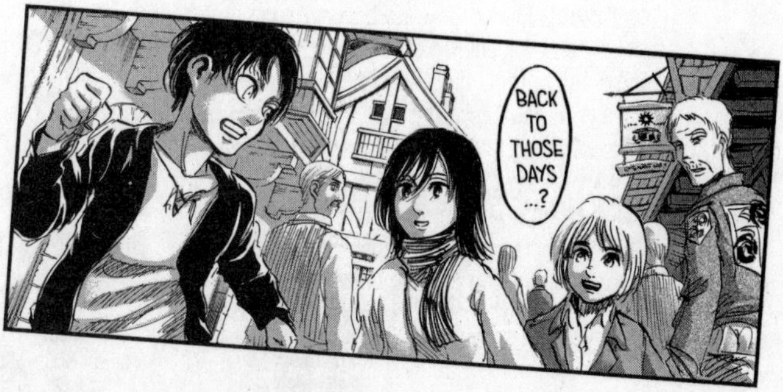
BACK TO THOSE DAYS ...?

Q: While it felt to me like Eren and the others had at last come to a major milestone in their lives, it sounds like things are far from being settled.

ISAYAMA: So, the part of the story where things are gearing up for the decisive battle in Shiganshina District—around Volumes 17 and 18—is actually a refrain that calls back to Volumes 1 and 2. You must have felt that way because those chapters create a sense of the story coming to a climax. For example, in *Saving Private Ryan*, items that show up in the beginning of the story like chewing gum and glasses appear once more right around the climax of the movie, making you feel like the conclusion is approaching. That was the kind of effect I was going for with the way the manga is drawn around the decisive battle in Shiganshina District. Eren and the others are eating with their friends before they go off to battle, and there they get in a fight with Jean before the three leave the mess hall and talk. In Volume 1, that's where Hannes appears.

Q: Oh, the scene in Volume 18 where they talk about seeing the sea together once more!

ISAYAMA: Yes. But while Armin has fought his entire life just to get a glimpse of the sea, in that moment, Eren isn't actually too fixated on it. While Eren and Armin became friends because of the shared dream they had of seeing the world outside the Walls, their dreams were always rooted in slightly different emotions and ideas. Armin's intellectual curiosity drove him to want to see the sea, while Eren was angry that he didn't have the freedom to see it, even though it was right there. It isn't as if he had a specific interest in the sea.

...WE'LL BE FREE?

I guess it's like three friends who had been together for the longest time going their separate ways after graduating school...

Also, the circumstances surrounding Eren have changed in so many ways until now, and he's thinking about the sea less. That scene in Volume 18 is the moment that Armin is shocked for the first time because of the clear way their paths have diverged.

Q: That's what was happening there?!

ISAYAMA: When he faces the sea, Armin takes a seashell, a representation of something that can only be found there, and tells Eren to look at it. But Eren, the all-important character, doesn't even look at it. This seashell that Eren doesn't even glance at as it sits awkwardly in Armin's palms is meant to symbolize their dreams coming to an end, or maybe their childhood coming to an end. I guess it's like three friends who had been together for the longest time going their separate ways after graduating school...

Q: So you're saying that the three characters are going to start walking separate paths?! When you take all of that into consideration, the fact that it's the three characters' backs you're seeing as they look out into the sea on the cover of Volume 22 seems to suggest some kind of turbulence in the future.

ISAYAMA: From the time I first thought of it, I always wanted to give an ominous feeling to the scene where they look out into the sea. I'm hoping that the meaning of that scene changes as the story progresses.

...AT THE MOMENT WE LEARN THE TRUTH ABOUT THIS WORLD.

I HAVE TO BE THERE...

The death of Erwin, a man who lived for his dreams. What will happen to Levi, his friend and his equal...?

Q: The decisive battle in Shiganshina District also had another very shocking moment in the form of Erwin's death.

ISAYAMA: I'd made up my mind that Erwin would die there. I'd always wanted to draw Erwin and Levi as having a relationship where they were on equal footing. Erwin joined the Survey Corps out of an innocent desire to know the truth, paired with his feelings of wanting to atone for setting off the chain of events that led to his father's death. Eventually, he finds himself in a position where he's responsible for leading the entire organization forward, and wavers between himself as a child who follows his dreams and himself as an adult with responsibilities. In an attempt to compromise, Erwin began to trick himself into working under the false pretense of "doing it for humanity's future," and he never stopped believing that.

Q: It was very shocking to see a man who said he was willing to abandon his humanity be unable to fully abandon his own dreams.

ISAYAMA: I'm sure Levi felt the same way. Levi had always seen Erwin's goal of doing things for humanity's future as an unimaginably altruistic act, and made it his life's mission to reach the same heights. That's why he also wanted Erwin to be a man who was loyal to his mission and capable of

That's why those words were exactly what Erwin needed to think about the future and give up on his dreams.

coolheaded decisions. When he learned that Erwin actually had the self-interested goal of fulfilling his own dreams, he must have felt nearly betrayed. But at the same time, he must have also been shocked to learn that a man he saw as untouchable actually had an innocent, childish, dream-chasing side to him.

Q: And when Levi learns that this great man was just as human as himself, he tells Erwin to "Give up on your dreams and die for us." What a cruel decision to make...!

ISAYAMA: I'm trying to remember what it was like when I was drawing that part of the story as we speak, and I remember thinking then, "People show their true selves when they're in a situation where they're going to die no matter what happens." For Erwin, this moment where he shows his true self was during the decisive battle in Shiganshina District, where the Beast Titan has them cornered. The person he showed Levi there was someone who wavered between fulfilling his dream of going to the basement and fulfilling his responsibility to fight the Beast Titan until the very end. When Levi saw that, he picked up on the way that Erwin was asking him to say what he said. That's why those words were exactly what Erwin needed to think about the future and give up on his dreams, growing up in the process to become an adult who values his own mission.

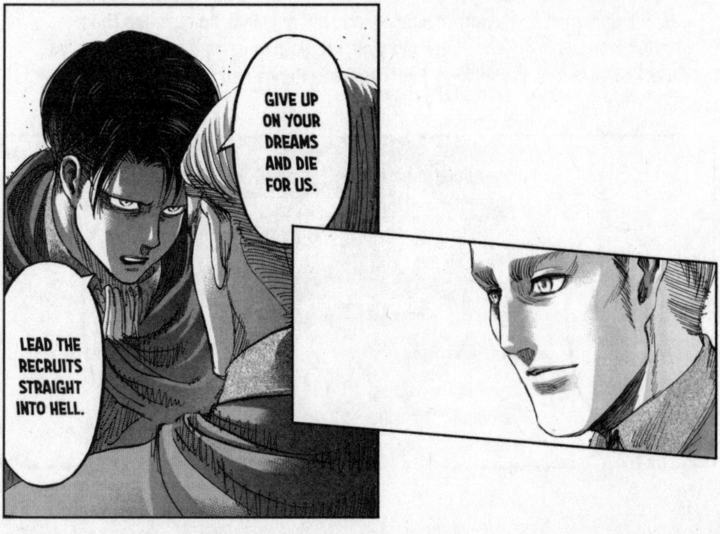
GIVE UP ON YOUR DREAMS AND DIE FOR US.
LEAD THE RECRUITS STRAIGHT INTO HELL.

Levi must have decided to treat Erwin as a human and allowed him to die rather than reviving him.

Q: But in his final moments, Erwin's thoughts turned to the classroom he shared with his father, the spot where his dream began. Was that sight a happy one for him?

ISAYAMA: I wonder about that… I feel like he died before figuring that out for himself. Or maybe Erwin decided to leave that question unanswered. It's hard for me to state decisively that he had no regrets, though…he may have had some. I remember thinking as I wrote those thumbnails, "We're all a slave to something." For Erwin, you could say that something was his dreams. There was no way for him to be freed from his dreams aside from death. Levi giving up on reviving Erwin must have been his way of allowing death to free Erwin from his enslavement.

Q: So Levi understood the way Erwin felt, too?

ISAYAMA: Yes, I'd say that Levi was influenced by his experiences with Kenny during the scene where he was forced to choose whether Erwin lives or dies. He'd experienced parting ways with Kenny when he was a child, and he always carried with him the feeling that "Kenny left because I wasn't able to live up to his expectations." When he was reunited with Kenny, this time as an enemy after the revolution inside the Walls, Levi attempted to do something he'd wanted to do since he was a child. In the end, though, Kenny was injured by the underground cavern collapsing, and not only that, he gave the Titan transformation injection to Levi and died, rather than using it to extend his own life. Levi saw this as shocking, because while Kenny had lived his entire life

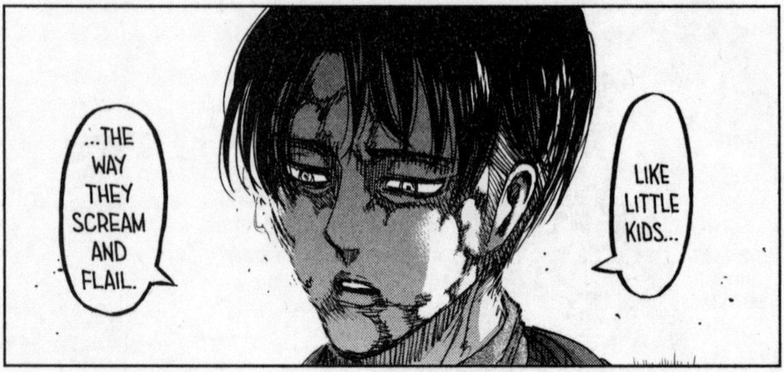
LIKE LITTLE KIDS...
...THE WAY THEY SCREAM AND FLAIL.

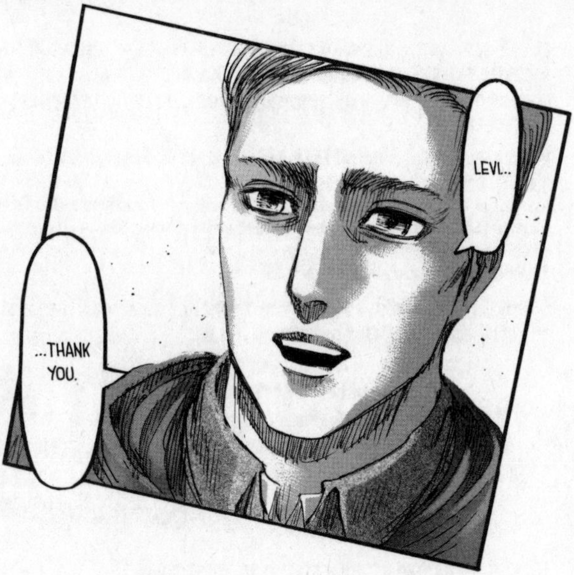
LEVI..
...THANK YOU.

selfishly, he chose to be altruistic in the end. That experience must have been what caused Levi to treat Erwin as a human, allowing him to die rather than reviving him.

I just thought of something, actually. You often hear people say that dreams are better left unfulfilled. As I was drawing Erwin's last moments, I took this to mean that one's life is better lived if they chase their dreams until the very end.

Q: Yes, dreams are dreams precisely because they're something unattainable that you keep chasing after. But as a result of his choice, Levi loses someone irreplaceable to him in Erwin. What is going to drive Levi to fight now?

ISAYAMA: That's still up in the air. Part of me feels like Levi fulfilled his duties by being there for Erwin's last moments. He of course does still have his goal of stopping the Beast Titan, but as far as who it is they're going to expect to fill the hole in the Survey Corps left behind by Erwin, it's probably going to be Armin, right? Ever since the scene in Volume 18 where they search for Reiner as he hides in the Wall, I've tried to draw Erwin and Armin as contrasting characters, the past and the future. Erwin died without fulfilling his dreams. Meanwhile, Armin does fulfill his dreams and is forced to face reality as a result.

Q: We have some questions from members of the "Mingeki" official fan website.* Our first question is, "The characters of *Attack on Titan* are constantly fighting in extreme situations, but when or where can they feel most relaxed?"

ISAYAMA: Members of the Survey Corps are constantly moving from one room to the next, and they can't own many possessions, either. So I guess they would feel most relaxed when they're together with their fellow soldiers in familiar locations. For example, there's a scene in Volume 1 where they're servicing the wall-mounted artillery. While they're able to pause for a moment when they're in unique situations like that, those kinds of opportunities are rare. After all, as soldiers, they shouldn't be wasting resources.

Q: I see. You're right, even if they might not be at war, they'd still be expected to act like soldiers. Our next question is...

We ask ISAYAMA your FAN QUESTIONS!

"Please tell us how a soldier spends an average day."

ISAYAMA: When the Survey Corps isn't on an expedition, they train and practice for the next Expedition, perform maintenance on their weapons, and so on. Depending on a soldier's position, they may have multiple meetings they need to go to. After training, they might even have time when they're allowed to return home.

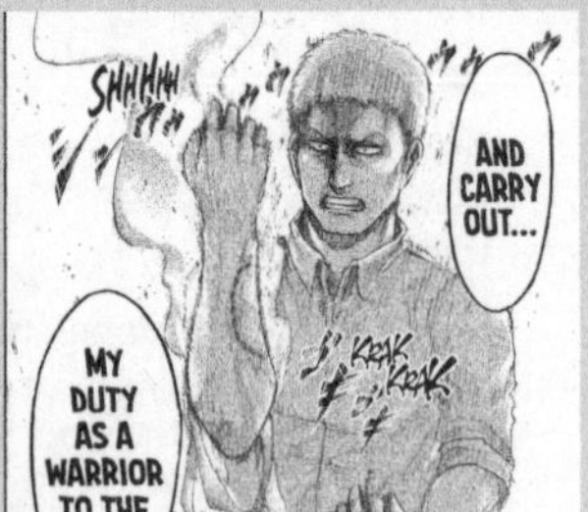
SHHHH
AND CARRY OUT...
KRAK KRAK
MY DUTY AS A WARRIOR TO THE END.

Q: So, like you mentioned earlier, even brief periods spent with fellow soldiers are a way to relax when you're forced to be on alert at every moment. Alright, here's our final question. "Do the characters have a favorite strength training exercise or routine?"

ISAYAMA: I'd have to say *kaatsu* occlusion training. While bodyweight exercises are good, too, they would probably focus on anaerobic exercises because of their ability to build muscle in a short amount of time. While Reiner had a large body from the time he was in the Training Corps, this is thanks to his parents, not any kind of training. Reiner's father appears in Volume 23, and we see there that he has a large build. While mixed martial artist Fedor Emelianenko has a solid, strong body, I understand that his build isn't the result of strength training. Reiner is kind of the same way. His body was always going to turn out that way, kind of like hammer thrower Koji Murofushi or Hulk, the Brazilian soccer player. Speaking of which, the Marley arc takes place in a world four years after the decisive battle in Shiganshina District, and Reiner has grown taller. Could you please update his character profile?

Q: Alright! So, if the 104th had an arm wrestling contest, who would win?

ISAYAMA: Mikasa would have to win. She's almost unfairly strong. Second would be Reiner. Eren and Jean would probably trade wins and losses. While the two are always fighting, there's almost a kind of constant balance between the two of them. It's to the point where they essentially have started to be physically comfortable with each other.

*Mingeki: short for *Minna no Shingeki* or "Everybody's Attack." Kodansha's official fan website in Japan for *Shingeki no Kyojin (Attack on Titan)*.

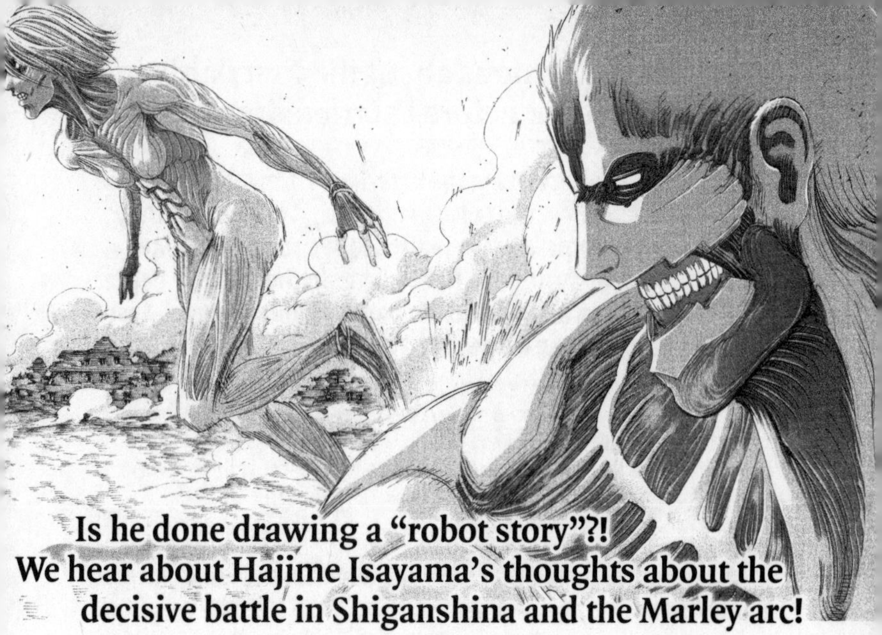

Is he done drawing a "robot story"?! We hear about Hajime Isayama's thoughts about the decisive battle in Shiganshina and the Marley arc!

Q: When we look back at the decisive battle in Shiganshina District like this, it's a very substantial moment in the series where all kinds of dramatic threads intertwine!

ISAYAMA: It feels like I released everything that had been building up to that point. I'd always wanted to draw that scene where the Beast Titan throws a bunch of rocks. There's a kind of anti-personnel tank round called the "canister shot" with a wide spread, kind of like a shotgun. I wanted to try doing something similar with the Beast Titan. I'd also always planned to have the final battle with the Colossus Titan take place during the decisive battle in Shiganshina District, which meant that was another scene that I'd wanted to draw for a long time. While I didn't have everything set in stone when I was designing the Colossus Titan during the early stages of putting the story together, at some point along the way, I decided that Eren would have to finish him off while in human form. If there's anything I regret not being able to do, I guess I would have wanted to dig deeper into the relationship between Eren, Reiner, and Bertolt before that battle. I wanted to show more scenes of Eren giving an intense amount of respect to Reiner, depicting him as someone that Eren saw as insurmountable.

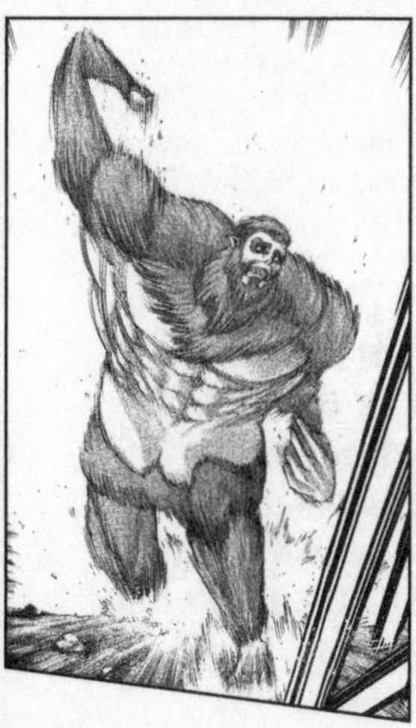

I was just so anxious about the first battle in the Marley arc, even before I started drawing it.

Q: During an interview in the *Attack on Titan Guidebook*, you said that you drew the Colossus Titan and others as if they were giant robots, and we really did see something like robots appear during the fight scenes in the decisive battle in Shiganshina District and the battle against the Mid-East Allied Forces in the Marley arc. They had my heart racing!

ISAYAMA: Actually, drawing those left me thinking that I didn't really need to draw any more robot stories. While human faces are soft, expressive, and endlessly changeable, creatures and objects that are made of hard materials require you to draw them the same way over and over from every different angle. It's a lot of work.

Q: I never imagined that we'd see a mecha appear in *Attack on Titan*!

ISAYAMA: I don't think you're alone. That's why I was just so anxious about the first battle in the Marley arc, even before I started drawing it. I still can't fully shake that feeling, either. For example, drawing the armored train in the first chapter of the Marley arc (Volume 23, Episode 91) was incredibly difficult. I was looking at a number of different possible designs beforehand, and some of them were more complex than what I drew. But when I considered that I would actually have to draw them, I decided to use a simpler design. Even so, I just barely finished drawing my manuscript in time for my deadline. There's also the fact that the setting changed from the fantasy world we had seen until then, to one that's similar to the real world about a hundred years ago, which meant putting a lot of work into gathering reference materials.

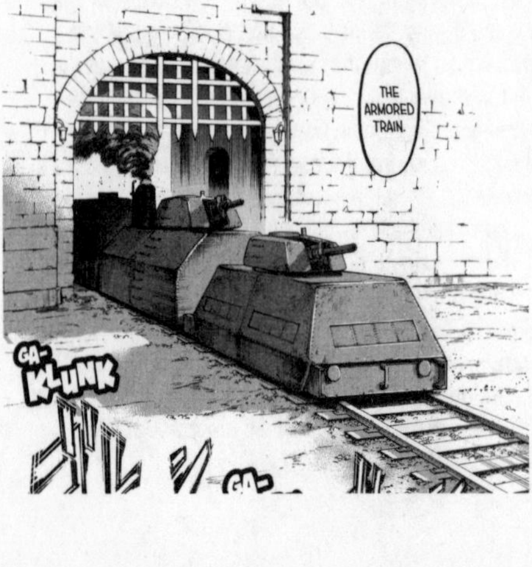
THE ARMORED TRAIN.
GA-KLUNK
GA-

Q: I was also surprised to see the Cart Titan appear with different equipment from when we saw it in Shiganshina!

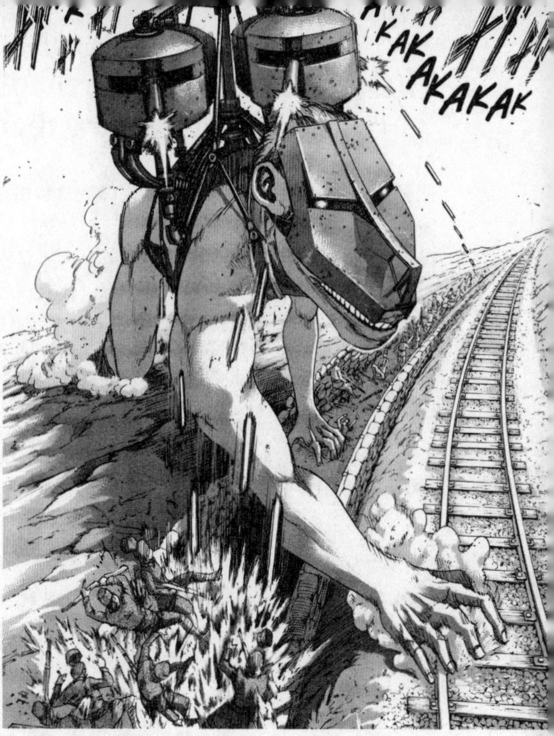
KAKAKAKAKAK

ISAYAMA: Those armaments are influenced by the love I used to have for *ZOIDS.* To tell you the truth, that scene in Episode 92 where an entire page is used to show the appearance of the Cart Titan was completely blank until the day of my deadline. The design of the mask that it wears was taken from a sketch I did in high school and so it was fairly easy to draw, but the equipment on its back was so much work… I had to think about how it carried the load, then I had to create the supports that fixed everything in place using wires in each direction, and then I designed the four-manned machine gun units hanging from those wires. I will say that drawing the page was fun, though.

Q: The Marley arc not only takes place in a new location, we also see a new cast of characters. It seems like a pretty courageous decision to make for a story-driven manga...

ISAYAMA: When I was drawing the first chapter of Volume 23, I was thinking about how it was an essential story to tell when looking at the overall structure of the story, but I was also unsure of whether or not the readers would accept it. It made me feel very uneasy. At the same time, it was a different kind of anxiety from what I felt when I was first starting *Attack on Titan* as a series. I think I was feeling much more anxious back then. I didn't even know if my monthly serialization would be collected into volumes, or if I'd be able to make a living as a manga artist. At the time, I thought there was a higher chance of *Titan* getting immediately canceled than not… But while I say I was feeling anxious, I was also enjoying the feeling of getting to try something completely new, rather than a pure continuation of what had come before.

The scene where the Cart Titan appears was actually blank right up until the manuscript's deadline.

There are a lot of scenes that I want to depict, and I want to show them to you as manga!

Q: Is it because you can now draw a world unlike the one we've been seeing?

ISAYAMA: First of all, it was so fun getting to draw the new characters. Though almost all of the major characters are new, I wanted to draw them more as characters who you feel like you've seen somewhere before. Like when you finally get to see what was on the other side of the sea, it turns out to be a world inhabited by people similar to the ones inside the Walls. That's why I made the decision to not put Reiner at the center of the first chapter of the Marley arc (Volume 23, Episode 91), even though it's about Gabi as seen through his eyes. Since it was the first episode of the Marley arc, I wanted everyone in it to be a character that had never been seen before.

Q: I was also shocked when you revealed in Episode 95 that each of the Titans has their own role, like the Armored Titan and Jaw Titan acting as a shield and as an assault unit, respectively. I'm looking forward to seeing where this new side of the Titans goes...!

ISAYAMA: I'd always wanted to show what kind of kids Reiner and the others were, as well as how the military used them, who they were fighting, and what they were fighting for. But I have to say, drawing the strategic Titan battles is pretty hard.

CAN'T YOU TELL...? IT'S SO THEY CAN FIGURE IT OUT.
WHICH ONE OF US WILL BE...

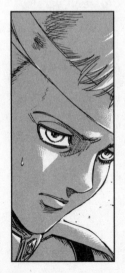

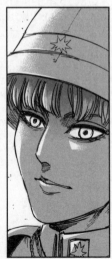

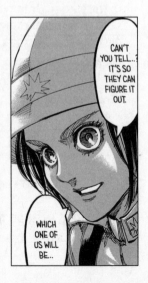

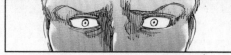

Q: I see! Even so, I think all of the readers are just as excited to see what's coming next. If you don't mind, I'd like to ask what you want to draw from here...?

ISAYAMA: If I get the opportunity, I should be showing you what happens next to Armin. While by nature he's the character who hates fighting the most, he's now been put in a situation where, in part due to the way the system is set up, he has to stand on the front lines—and with the power of the Colossus Titan at that. He'd been able to soldier on because of his dream of seeing the sea, but now he's going to need to face reality and deal with it. There are a lot of scenes that I want to depict, but that would spoil what's coming up next... I guess I just want to show them to you as manga!

(This interview took place on July 7, 2017.)

INDEX

A new series from Yoshitoki Oima, creator of The New York Times bestselling manga and Eisner Award nominee *A Silent Voice*!

An intimate, emotional drama and an epic story spanning time and space...

TO YOUR ETERNITY

An orb was cast unto the earth. After metamorphosing into a wolf, It joins a boy on his bleak journey to find his tribe. Ever learning, It transcends death, even when those around It cannot…

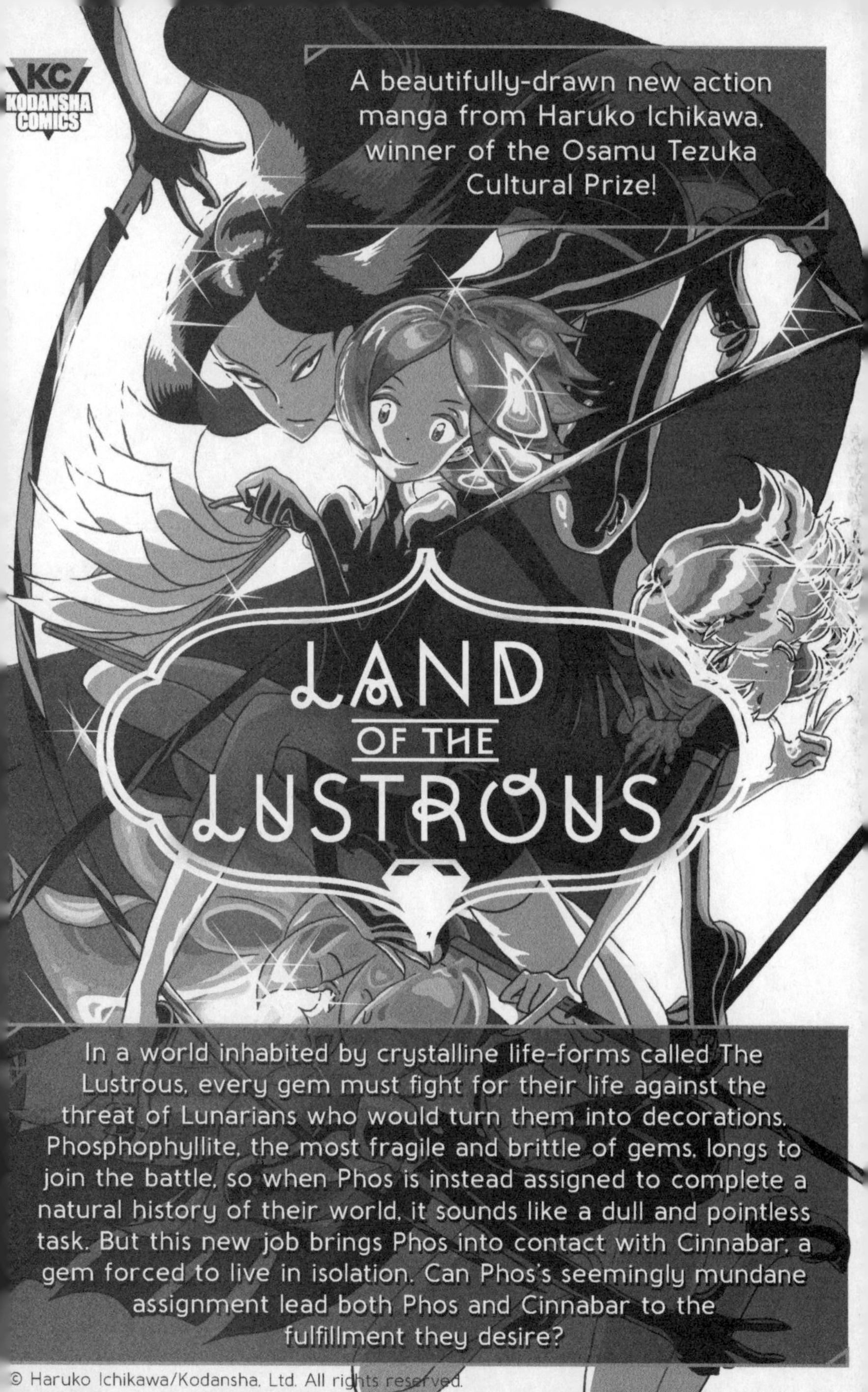
KC KODANSHA COMICS
A beautifully-drawn new action manga from Haruko Ichikawa, winner of the Osamu Tezuka Cultural Prize!
LAND OF THE LUSTROUS
In a world inhabited by crystalline life-forms called The Lustrous, every gem must fight for their life against the threat of Lunarians who would turn them into decorations. Phosphophyllite, the most fragile and brittle of gems, longs to join the battle, so when Phos is instead assigned to complete a natural history of their world, it sounds like a dull and pointless task. But this new job brings Phos into contact with Cinnabar, a gem forced to live in isolation. Can Phos's seemingly mundane assignment lead both Phos and Cinnabar to the fulfillment they desire?

KC
KODANSHA
COMICS

A new series from the creator of *Soul Eater*, the megahit manga and anime seen on Toonami!

"Fun and lively... a great start!"
-Adventures in Poor Taste

FIRE FORCE

By Atsushi Ohkubo

The city of Tokyo is plagued by a deadly phenomenon: spontaneous human combustion! Luckily, a special team is there to quench the inferno: The Fire Force! The fire soldiers at Special Fire Cathedral 8 are about to get a unique addition. Enter Shinra, a boy who possesses the power to run at the speed of a rocket, leaving behind the famous "devil's footprints" (and destroying his shoes in the process). Can Shinra and his colleagues discover the source of this strange epidemic before the city burns to ashes?

Mikami's middle age hasn't gone as he planned: He never found a girlfriend, he got stuck in a dead-end job, and he was abruptly stabbed to death in the street at 37. So when he wakes up in a new world straight out of a fantasy RPG, he's disappointed, but not exactly surprised to find that he's facing down a dragon, not as a knight or a wizard, but as a blind slime monster. But there are chances for even a slime to become a hero...

KC/ KODANSHA COMICS

THAT TIME I GOT REINCARNATED AS A
SLIME

DELUXE EDITION

BATTLE ANGEL ALITA

After more than a decade out of print, the original cyberpunk action classic returns in glorious 400-page hardcover deluxe editions, featuring an all-new translation, color pages, and new cover designs!

KC
KODANSHA COMICS

Far beneath the shimmering space-city of Zalem lie the trash-heaps of The Scrapyard... Here, cyber-doctor and bounty hunter Daisuke Ido finds the head and torso of an amnesiac cyborg girl. He names her Alita and vows to fill her life with beauty, but in a moment of desperation, a fragment of Alita's mysterious past awakens in her. She discovers that she possesses uncanny prowess in the legendary martial art known as panzerkunst. With her newfound skills, Alita decides to become a hunter-warrior - tracking down and taking out those who prey on the weak. But can she hold onto her humanity in the dark and gritty world of The Scrapyard?

OTOMO 大友克洋
A GLOBAL TRIBUTE TO
THE MIND BEHIND AKIRA

A celebration of manga legend Katsuhiro Otomo from more than 80
world-renowned fine artists and comics legends
With contributions from:
- Stan Sakai
- Tomer and Asaf Hanuka
- Sara Pichelli
- Range Murata
- Aleksi Briclot
And more!
168 pages of stunning, full-color art

KC
KODANSHA
COMICS

A Kodansha Comics Trade Paperback Original
Attack on Titan Character Encyclopedia copyright © 2017 Hajime Isayama
English translation copyright © 2018 Hajime Isayama

Published in the United States by Kodansha Comics, an imprint of
Kodansha USA Publishing, LLC, New York.

Publication rights for this English edition arranged through
Kodansha Ltd, Tokyo.

First published in Japan in 2017 by Kodansha Ltd., Tokyo
as *Shingeki no Kyojin Character Meikan*

ISBN 978-1-63236-709-9

Planning and text:
Ryosuke Sakuma
Munehiko Inagaki

Design:
Takashi Shimoyama (Red Rooster)
Saya Takagi (Red Rooster)
Yukino Onuma (Red Rooster)

Production: plus beta

Original cover design by Takashi Shimoyama/Saya Takagi (Red Rooster)

Printed in the United States of America.

www.kodanshacomics.com

9 8 7 6 5 4 3

Translation: Ko Ransom
Lettering: AndWorld Design
Editing: Haruko Hashimoto
Kodansha Comics edition cover design by Phil Balsman